OUT OF THE BOX

OUT OF THE BOX

✈   ✈   ✈

THE HIGHS AND LOWS OF A
CHAMPION SMUGGLER

JULIE MCSORLEY AND MARCUS MCSORLEY

ROARING FORTIES
PRESS

Roaring Forties Press
1053 Santa Fe Avenue
Berkeley, CA 94706

www.roaringfortiespress.com

Cover design by Anna Morrison; interior design by Nigel Quinney.

Library of Congress Cataloging-in-Publication Data is available.

I978-1-938901-32-4 (print)
978-1-938901-33-1 (PDF)
978-1-938901-34-8 (ePub)
978-1-938901-35-5 (Kindle)

For the late, great Bille Brown, who insisted that
"there was room for mad bastards,"
and set us on our path

"I've seen so much and lived it all. I wanted to bite the earth and taste it. It is both bitter and sweet, and if I had my time to live over again, I wouldn't change a damn thing."

— *Reg Spiers*

Contents

FOREWORD

BY LYNN DAVIES CBE

Chatting with friends about the "box story" recently, I joked that perhaps male throwers are the "wild men of athletics." The jury is still out on that one. There have been few comparative studies on the personality traits of track and field athletes, but the eventful life of one javelin thrower, the aptly named Reg Spiers, may fuel further speculation!

Elite track and field athletes of Reg's era operated in a very different environment than those of today. Most of us were forced to fit our training programs and international competitions around employment commitments. Sponsorship for athletes was scant and access to coaches and mentors often depended on geographical location, the knowledge base of local athletics clubs, and a fair amount of luck. Imagine these conditions against the backdrop of the swinging sixties, and Reg's saga is all the more intriguing.

Most athletes, including myself, are opposed to drugs in any circumstances. Reg is thus somewhat of an enigma, because his misadventures began when he was a talented, high-profile sportsman: Reg won the National Australian Javelin Championships on two occasions and came fifth in the 1962 Commonwealth Games.

The British javelin thrower John McSorley built Reg's infamous box. John broke the United Kingdom and Commonwealth Javelin records in 1962 and was later a Commonwealth Games silver medalist.

Out of the Box is surely one of the most colorful stories to emerge from the sporting world, one that deserves to be told.

Lynn Davies is President of UK Athletics and Vice President of the British Olympic Association. He won gold medals at the 1964 Olympics, the 1966 European Championships, and 1966 and 1970 Commonwealth Games.

PREFACE

When John McSorley took us—his wife and young son—to visit one of his old sporting friends, he would never have believed that a couple of decades later we would write a book that featured that day. It was never going to be an ordinary get-together. Reg Spiers had roamed three continents as a fugitive since John had last seen him, and the two old friends would have their reunion in a jail.

We were more than a little curious; we'd never met Reg, but knew that John had been instrumental in helping him pull off a seriously outrageous stunt back in 1964. The tale of the box and ensuing episodes had gained mythical status in our household. Friends regularly sat riveted at our dinner table, some suspecting it was just a good yarn, others looking for reasons why it couldn't possibly be true.

The impression we were left with, after Reg wandered freely into the prison car park to bid us farewell, was that normal rules didn't apply in his world. The gregarious, resilient character that John had described was still in evidence. Our fascination with Reg's story survived the twenty-some intervening years before we came to write it.

A definitive biography of Reg's life would fill several volumes, each the size of *War and Peace*. And a chronology of facts could never convey the drama, pathos, and love story that define his nomadic years. For these reasons, we have created a narrative to tell the story that Reg told us over many hours of conversation when he stayed at our homes in Queensland and southern Spain, and during a late-night drinking session at a hotel in London. Every episode we describe in this book actually happened, but we have sometimes compressed the chain of events, created composite characters, or modified the setting to capture the essence of the story. And, of course, we have had to imagine much of the conversation between the characters—but the voice of Reg rings clear and true throughout, as anyone who knows him will attest.

Mindful of the rights and privacy of the real people who played their parts in this colorful but true story, we have changed the names and characteristics of some individuals. This is not a history book; it is a story of a man who made his own kind of history. We have told that story as faithfully as possible.

This same desire to be faithful to the story and to Reg's voice has led us to stick with Australian terms, slang, and colloquialisms. Reg and his friends thus park in "car parks" rather than "parking lots," lounge around in "lounges" rather than "living rooms," and "flog" rather than "sell" whatever they can when they are "skint," or "broke." For the benefit of American readers (British readers probably won't need the help), there's a glossary at the back of the book showing Australian terms and their American equivalents.

JULIE MCSORLEY AND MARCUS MCSORLEY

ACKNOWLEDGMENTS

To John McSorley and Lucia McSorley, for keeping the faith; for Lucia's brilliant attention to detail and proofreading; and for Johnny Mac's re-creation of his box to help us get in situ.

To Deirdre Greene and Nigel Quinney at Roaring Forties Press, for sharing our commitment to the story.

To best-selling author and former barrister John Gordon Davis, for editing early drafts of the manuscript and advising us on courtroom procedure.

To our dear nephew and cousin, Charlie Candlin, for his great powers of reason and literary insight.

To Raz and Freda Shafi, for cheering us over the starting line.

To all our friends who read early drafts, listened to our readings, and encouraged us along the way. You know who you are.

Thank you.

OUT OF THE BOX

Prologue

Adelaide, Late 1980s

"The eyes, wait till you see the eyes."

Greg Denton rushed into the editor's office at the Adelaide *Inquirer*, brandishing his evidence.

"The Frenchman calls himself Patrick Albert Claude Ledoux." The two journalists studied the photograph of a bearded, fair-haired man flashing a confident smile for the camera. Denton placed another photo alongside the first. "Last one I took of him before he disappeared. Check out the nose and hair. A few years younger of course, but it's him. I'd put money on it."

"Not sure," Davies, the editor, said. "So long since I've seen him."

Denton shaped a viewfinder with his hands, moving it between the two pictures.

"I'd recognize those blue eyes anywhere."

Davies nodded slowly. The eyes convinced him as well. "Okay, run with it." He picked up his phone. "Mary, get Denton on the next flight to Colombo."

"You won't regret it, boss." Denton hurried out, delighted. "Got the headline: 'Top Javelin Thrower Hurled onto Death Row!'"

Denton had planned to sleep during the long flight to Sri Lanka, but he had too much on his mind. Every so often a story came along that made his job worthwhile. If his hunch proved right, this was one of them. After the dinner trays were cleared, he ordered another beer and settled down under his reading light to review his notes, to collate every bit of information he had on the suspect, and to establish a timeline.

When Denton was a rookie journalist with the *Express*, the editor had sent him to interview the athlete several times. "Think yourself lucky you're getting such an easy lead," his old boss told him. "You won't have to ask questions; this bloke does all the talking."

Every journalist in town loved interviewing the high-spirited javelin thrower. Denton recalled that sweltering day he visited the track to photograph him training, stripped down to the essentials: underpants and spikes. "But he couldn't half make that javelin fly," thought Denton.

The last record Denton had of him competing was in the national championships shortly before he skipped bail. Since then, there'd been a few reported sightings but nothing concrete, and he'd been on the run from the feds for years.

"Until now," Denton hoped.

Colombo was sweltering when Denton arrived the following day. He took a cab straight to Mahara Prison. The entrance was barred by a heavy iron gate, attached to a rectangular concrete hut, both topped by a tangle of barbed wire that ran the length of the towering perimeter walls.

"I'm here to see Monsieur Ledoux," he told the gatekeeper through a small window of the hut.

The guard waved him on, and the gate was opened from the inside. Denton strode confidently through the entrance of the compound but was quickly stopped by two officers in khaki uniforms. Denton noticed the guns in their holsters. They ushered him into a small, prefabricated shed and signaled for him to open his briefcase. One guard rifled through the contents while his colleague gave Denton a frisking. Denton removed his spectacles and kept his mouth shut. When they released him, he walked in the direction of the arrow for visitors, down a terraced walkway clinging to an imposing, old stone building. He passed inmates tending vegetable plots who seemed more interested in the tall Westerner with an expensive briefcase than in their gardens. He was nervous, excited at being on the verge of the biggest story of his career—or his biggest mistake.

The path ended at a second checkpoint, a dingy office crammed with people and flies; the whirling blades of a rusty ceiling fan sliced the hot, stale air. Denton loosened his tie and waited in line to speak to the guard who was issuing orders to two other men in uniform. When it was his turn at the counter, Denton lowered his voice, telling the head guard that he would be grateful if he could spend some time with the French prisoner. The room turned quiet when he said, "Patrick Ledoux." Then the head guard turned to his colleague with a smirk, and Denton thought they might share his suspicion that Ledoux was an impostor.

"I'm the superintendent." The stocky head guard lifted his hat to wipe greasy straggles of black hair from his forehead. "He's a popular man, your Mr. Ledoux. This way please." He came around the side of the counter, taking the keys from his belt and unlocking a heavy, wrought-iron gate. Denton's pulse raced as they walked into the inner compound. Denton heard the clank of the gate shutting behind them and felt like a detective closing in on a suspect, albeit one who was already in jail.

He hurried to keep up with the brisk march of the superintendent, down a labyrinth of ancient, musty corridors layered with crumbling plaster. The occasional bare bulb hung from the ceiling, barely lighting the perpetual night that inhabited the warren of windowless passageways. As they passed a distant hum of movement and shouting, the superintendent pointed out a door and told him it led to the largest cellblock in the prison. Denton wondered if Ledoux had ever been held there. A man's cry echoed after them. It was a penetrating holler that made Denton shudder.

He heard a couple of men laughing as he focused on the shiny black heels of the superintendent's shoes as they clicked smartly on the flagstone floor ahead, and then he heard a door slam twice. Somewhere between laughter and clicking and slamming, Denton recognized the faint strains of a voice, the kind of voice he'd heard every day of his life. A voice with a familiar Australian twang.

As they turned the corner, the prisoner Denton had come to see stopped laughing and stood motionless in the corridor, looking him square in the face. In that moment, the eyes of the man known as Patrick Ledoux betrayed him.

"Mr. Patrick, you have a visitor," the superintendent announced.

Ledoux composed himself. "Great to see you again, good of you to come."

As they shook hands, Denton looked into the face he'd spent so much time thinking about. It was older and more relaxed than the one he remembered, framed by a beard and shaggy, fair hair that made his sparkling eyes seem even bluer. Denton thought he detected a look of relief at finally being found.

The other guards were disappointed that they had to go; one took a packet of cigarettes from his pocket and gave it to Ledoux. "See you tonight Sudda. You sing your Bruce Springsteen again tonight, yes?"

"Yeah, sure," the prisoner answered. He turned to the bemused journalist. "Come."

Denton followed the imposing figure in his flowing white kaftan down the passageway, aware that the superintendent was behind them. They came to the entrance of a dismal little space containing a solitary table and a couple of chairs.

"I'll be outside. How long do you want?" the superintendent asked.

"Would two hours be all right?" Denton lowered his voice, wondering if the guard expected an incentive.

"No longer," the superintendent shook his head.

The superintendent straightened the lapels of his well-worn jacket and plonked his round frame onto a spindly wooden seat by the door. He seemed disappointed when the prisoner escorted his visitor into the room and closed the door behind them.

When they were alone, Ledoux shot Denton a knowing smile. "You got me," he said with a peaceful kind of resignation.

"So, Greg," he continued, "will you be here for my big day in court?"

"Sure will. Last place I saw you was the Adelaide Athletics Club. Sounds like you've been bloody busy since then."

"Too much to tell, buddy. Way too much to tell."

"I've got all afternoon, and you don't look like you're going anywhere. How the hell did you end up in this godforsaken place?"

The prisoner leaned back and sighed, shaking his head as if asking himself the same question.

PART ONE
EARLY 1980S

Chapter 1

Adelaide, 1980

"That plane that went down at Sydney Airport last month," Annie peered at the newspaper on the kitchen table, "had only just taken off."

"Don't talk about it." Cheryl shook her head and collected two mugs from the draining board.

Reg sat at the head of the table with his beer and notebook. This was going to be an important meeting, and he didn't want plane crash stories putting a damper on his proposal. He swept his fair hair out of his eyes and scribbled a couple of dates onto a clean page. This evening he needed a final confirmation of who was in, and if anybody was out. "Christ," he thought, "please don't let anyone be out." Looking for a replacement at this late stage would be a nightmare.

"Lara phoned, she'll be a bit late," said Annie as she dried her newly washed hair.

Annie was glad everyone would be at the meeting. She'd talked to Cheryl the previous night, and they'd both agreed the itinerary sounded easy, although Reg still had to explain the procedure in more detail. Cheryl had pointed out that Reg had a tendency to be optimistic about most things, so Annie was interested to hear what Ted and Niko had to say about his game plan. She was sure of one thing: she and Reg needed more income if they were going to be able to keep paying their rent.

Cheryl poured two coffees and handed one to Annie, then rifled through a cupboard for a package of chocolate biscuits. She soon found a packet of her favorite indulgence: Tim Tams. Annie watched her ceremoniously empty them into a bowl and wondered how dear, sweet-toothed Cheryl had managed to keep her figure.

Cheryl devoured half a biscuit with one bite and placed the crumbling remainder on the table. She took a clasp from the pocket of her skirt and secured her unruly blond mane at the side of her forehead. Her eyes darted, full of intrigue. Reg's scheme sounded really hopeful. It couldn't have come at a better time. Since she and Ted had left Nottingham, she had stuck with teaching, but this new idea sounded like a much easier way to earn money.

Niko tucked his baggy, gray T-shirt into the waistband of his jeans and joined the other three at the table. His dark eyes greeted Annie's as he swigged his beer. She watched him as he joked with Reg and thought how relaxed he looked.

Niko was relaxed. Reg had done more traveling than the rest of them put together, so he had to know what he was talking about. They went back a long way, he and Reg, and there was nobody he trusted more. This new ploy could be highly lucrative. It might be the only chance he and Lara would ever get to make some decent cash. They sure as hell weren't going to do it on what their dad paid them for waiting tables.

"Hurry up, Ted," Cheryl called.

Ted sauntered into the kitchen, mildly irritated that he'd had to turn off Pink Floyd's *The Wall*. It was the second time he'd listened to their latest album that day, and he thought the bass guitar was absolutely brilliant. His tall, angular frame stooped over the sink as he hummed and rinsed his mug. He gave Cheryl's shoulder an affectionate squeeze, grinning through the long hair that covered his eyes as he slid onto the chair beside her. She had been more like her old self since Reg had run his idea past them a few days ago.

The scheme sounded feasible, but Ted wanted to see if the others had any reservations. Cheryl deserved some time off; she worked damn hard at that school. He hadn't mentioned it, but he was seriously thinking about going back to university to finish his degree. With the sort of income Reg was talking about, he might have the funds to do it. His old man was going to be thrilled.

Annie had left the front door ajar for Lara. When Reg heard it close, he checked his notes. "We all need to concentrate tonight," he looked around the table. "So we're really clear on what's involved and how this thing will work."

"Sorry I'm late," Lara interrupted him as she bustled into the kitchen. She could have passed for a schoolgirl in her baggy checked shirt and jeans. She flopped onto the only empty chair. "Did I miss anything important?" She smiled at the circle of serious faces, breathless as she tightened her ponytail, her black wavy hair identical to her brother's.

"Just confirming everything for next month," Reg put his bottle of beer on the table. "My contact reckons it's better to travel in mixed pairs, and I can see why. Looks like a couple on a nice romantic trip. So the routine is, number one couple board in Bombay."

"That would have to be you." Niko attempted to lighten the mood. "You know Bombay better than the rest of us . . . seen it from a different perspective and all that."

Reg smirked. "God, Niko," he said when the others laughed. "You've done that one to death, mate!"

Lara wasn't laughing. She stood and helped herself to lemonade from the fridge.

"I'm still uneasy about this, Reggie," she blurted as she sat down. "I just don't know how I'm going to keep Geoff in the dark. I told him I was seeing a girlfriend tonight." She plonked her glass on the table. "If he knew where I was, he'd go bloody bananas."

"For God sake, sis, you're letting him control you. Why d'you do that?" Niko groaned.

"You sure you want to do this?" Annie asked when she saw Lara's worried face. "Reg could find someone else, couldn't you Reggie?"

"Yeah, I could." Reg was praying he wouldn't have to. "But nobody I'd trust as much."

"And it's only going to be for a few months, Lara," said Cheryl. "We're going to save enough for a deposit on a house and then go traveling, aren't we, Ted? Like Reg was saying the other day, in and out, make some serious cash, then quit while we're ahead."

"That's the plan," agreed Ted, not looking convinced.

Annie said, "I think we're all a bit nervous," and gave Lara a reassuring little smile. "I never thought I'd consider doing anything like this."

The room fell silent.

Niko cleared his throat and turned to Reg. "Perhaps you should get someone else," he said. He'd always looked out for his sister. Not just because she was younger. She'd always seemed so fragile, easily upset.

"I don't want to be left out," Lara insisted. "We've always done everything together."

Reg looked relieved. "If you're sure, Lara, but just give me some warning if you want to bail."

He felt like a weight had been lifted. The enterprise was going to depend on controlling who knew what. Although they'd become distant lately, they were still a tightly knit group. He had other mates, but not like these; he'd trust this lot with his life.

"Great stuff," he said. "The first time will probably be a bit hairy, but we'll soon have it down pat. The riskiest bit is the last lap into Oz, so first trip it'll be me and Annie doing the home stretch."

Annie's and Cheryl's eyes connected. Annie twirled a strand of hair above her ear, as she did when she felt uneasy. Cheryl thought that perhaps Annie felt the same way she did—in too deep to pull out now.

"There'll be three legs between Bombay and Australia," Reg continued. "Bombay Australia, Australia New Zealand, and then New Zealand back into Australia."

"Hang on, I'm still not getting this," Cheryl said, scratching her head. "Did I miss something?"

"No, that's what we were talking about last night," Ted reminded her. "That's the bit that makes it foolproof. Go on, Reg."

"Nothing's foolproof, mate, get complacent and we're fucked." Reg's tone turned sober. "It's about no deviations, acting normal, enjoying everything, young Aussies doing a bit of traveling." He reeled it off as though reading a list.

Ted shifted uncomfortably.

"So where were we?" Reg continued. "Oh yeah, when number one couple disembark in Melbourne or Sydney, they leave the boombox in the overhead locker of the plane. No risk there; nothing for customs to find. Then number two couple board the same plane, now bound for New Zealand. They have the same seat numbers as the first couple. When they land they take the hand luggage from the locker. They have to go through security, but here's the thing . . ." Reg drained his beer, savoring the best bit of his plan. "As far as the bloody Kiwis are concerned, it's a flight from Oz. Number two hand over to the third couple at the airport and they do the last leg home. And the Aussie customs blokes won't be looking for anything, because it's a flight from New Zealand."

He looked pleased with himself as he waited for a reaction.

"Penny's dropped now," said Cheryl. "The New Zealand people won't be suspicious because that flight's come from Oz." She smiled triumphantly at the sisterhood. "Gotta admit, it's pretty clever!"

"Like pass the parcel," Niko mused as he leaned back on his chair.

"Sure is," said Reg. "And by the way it has to be British Airways, they go via Melbourne to Auckland."

"So what's this thingy going to weigh? D'you mean something like Ted's boombox?" asked Cheryl.

"Bigger than mine, hey Reg?" said Ted.

"Has to be," Reg agreed. "We're talking resin here, not grass, so it's compressed. It'll be bloody heavy, but we need a good bit, at least seven kilos. Plus the weight of the machine once the guts are taken out."

Cheryl turned to Ted with accusing eyes. "You knew about this all the time!"

"Yeah, obviously, secret men's business," Annie agreed, peeved that Reg had already discussed the details with Ted and Niko.

"We don't have to buy one of those blasters every time we do a run, do we?" Lara asked, worried that here was something else she'd have to lie to Geoff about.

"Won't be a problem," Reg reassured her. "Number one couple in Bombay will have the machine at the hotel and we'll recycle it every run. By the way, I'll be the only one dealing with our contact here, none of you need get involved with any of that. It's cleaner that way. I'll be getting the loot, organizing shifts, everything. So think of yourselves as shift workers."

"Always wanted well-paid, part-time work," joked Cheryl, warming to the whole idea.

"Me too," said Reg, relieved his proposition was going down so well.

"Now, for every run, each couple will have a different shift number: Number one will already be in place in Bombay; number two will get on in Oz; number three will be ready for the home run from New Zealand."

His eyes floated around the group. "Any questions?"

Heads shook; the modus operandi didn't appear to have any flaws.

"Sounds simple enough, doesn't it?" Lara broke the silence, looking Niko's way for approval.

"I agree with Cheryl, though," said Annie, "that we should see this as a short-term thing to make some readies. I think it could work, but let's just make what we can and get out."

"We're all agreed on that one," said Niko. "I don't want to be doing this for long. I like the thought of being able to get ahead, though."

"Yeah, but we'd better make stacks of money." Cheryl's schoolteacher eyes narrowed. "Ted and I are the only ones quitting jobs here, so it's gotta be worth it."

"Lara and I will keep up appearances at the restaurant, but if it all gets too much, we might pack up as well," said Niko.

"You're kidding!" Lara's voice rose. "Mum and Dad would cotton onto something in no time if we left."

"She's right," Reg added. "I'd already thought of that. Anyway, let's make a pact." His intense blue eyes flitted around the table. "A sort of all for one and one for all." He drew his hands up, collecting Annie's on his left and Cheryl's on his right.

Mouths widened into warm smiles as Niko held Annie's other hand, then Lara's; Lara took Ted's, and Ted finally took Cheryl's. And they were looking at six pairs of clasped hands on the tabletop.

"We're family," said Reg. "We stick together like we've always done. Keep our mouths shut and our ears to the ground, and we'll be in clover before we know it."

"Now, who's rolling that joint?"

CHAPTER 2

If it hadn't been for an advert in the local paper for evening classes at Marryatville High School, Reg's and Annie's paths might never have crossed. He'd read something about how athletes should exercise their minds as well as their bodies, and he enrolled in a class on Australian literature. The curriculum included a section on poetry.

"Poetry?" Niko had scoffed. "You going soft, mate?"

At the end of the first session, the young teacher had tried to spark a debate.

"'Though his crimes they were many no lives did he spare, we still see our hero when we picture him there.' So who agrees with Spencer—do you think as a nation we have idealized Ned Kelly?"

The sandy red mane of the girl fidgeting in front of him was close enough to touch. She sighed impatiently at the teacher's question, leaning so far back in her chair that her wispy tresses swept the back of his desk.

"Annie, am I right to surmise that the question has kindled a bit of passion? Give us your thoughts," the teacher encouraged.

Reg listened intently as the mystery redhead made her case.

"Yes, you're right about the passion, and no, I don't think we've idealized Ned Kelly. For starters, Kelly was a victim of the times, and who knows what any of us would do in his situation. All around him he could see wealthy people who had everything, and I think he was a champion of the poor. How's he different from someone like Nelson Mandela? He deserves to be a hero, I suppose you'd call him an antihero really, but I don't think he's been idealized."

Her hair! Reg loved long hair, but he'd never seen it like this.

This was redder than strawberry blond but not ginger, more of a sandy kind of red. Faded. Like bleached saffron in some exotic bazaar. Definitely not out of a bottle. You couldn't bottle that!

She didn't seem to be in a hurry at the end of the class, so as the other students filed out, he hung back to talk to her.

"You held your own there, Annie."

She was surprised to find someone was still in the room. He would always remember the first time he saw her face. Those almond-shaped eyes, and pale, sea green irises that he would later learn flashed with anger or softened into pools. Her milky, freckled skin, and that cute little tip at the end of her nose. They were all parts of the sum, and the sum of the parts was Annie Hayes.

The morning after the housemates' meeting at Ford Avenue, Reg and Annie slept until ten. They'd all talked late into the night, apart from Lara, who'd had to rush home to cook her boyfriend's dinner. Reg had purposefully organized the discussion for a Friday so that nobody had to worry about work the next day.

Lifting his weight onto his elbow to get a better look at his sleepy girl, he gazed at the sandy red swath of hair. Annie. He wondered what she'd be doing if they had never met. God! She might have married one of those toffee-nosed executives from her office.

He swept a wispy lock from her freckled cheek and thought about how upset she'd been when she was "let go" from her secretarial job the previous week. He hadn't said anything, but suspected that someone had tipped off her employers about the goings-on in the house where she lived. She'd received a letter stating that "the opinions she was frequently heard voicing in the office were at odds with the ethos of the company."

"That's so fucking unfair!" Cheryl had commiserated. "What is the ethos of the company? I bet nobody knows. I don't think my school even has a bloody ethos—if it does, I'm definitely at odds with it. God, I wish I could get fired. Then Ted and I could trek around India or something."

Cheryl's outburst had got Reg thinking about his own predicament. Something in the house had changed; everyone was starting to "do their own thing." The banter had dwindled and the place was getting an apathetic vibe. He'd mentioned this to Niko, who'd brushed it off with a joke about everyone having early midlife crises.

They'd even stopped going to the beach—that patch of sand near the lifeguard lookout that had been their weekend hangout for so long. Where they'd surf and Ted would strum his old guitar. Where they ate chips and drank beer until way after sunset. Lazing around the living room watching late-night movies together was a thing of the past. Nowadays the kitchen was piled high with unwashed dishes, the drawer in the living room was full of unpaid bills, and nobody felt like going to work. Their warm, chaotic household was falling apart. Not their friendship, but the structure that bound it.

Reg's other, more-pressing concern was the way his advertising gigs were drying up. Although he'd placed third in the National Javelin Championships in 1979, it had now been over fourteen years since he'd been the Australian champion, famous for his exploits both in the sporting arena and outside it. Until a few years ago, he still got magazine covers every month, television, radio, the lot. Nowadays, he'd be lucky to hear from his agent once in a blue moon. At this rate he'd be hard-pressed to find next month's rent, and if his latest plan didn't come off, he might even have to go back to a full-time sales job.

Cheryl had awoken early that morning, excited at the prospect of giving her notice at work. She'd been having second thoughts about her job since Annie had moved in with them. She longed to be more free-spirited and independent, like Annie, who had ditched her teaching plans when she'd moved in with Reg and taken a job as a secretary across town. Unbeknownst to Reg, Annie knew Cheryl from Teacher's College, and when she joined his notorious hippie household on Ford Avenue, she and Cheryl quickly became the best of friends.

Cheryl and Ted had been in Adelaide for six years; he was a university dropout and she was a teacher at the local primary school. She loved living in their faded, old, blue weatherboard beach house in

Adelaide. They all did. It was in a continual state of disarray, but what the heck? Most of their friends' places were just as disorganized.

It was the routine of teaching that was driving her crazy. The certainty that every Monday morning her third graders would line up at her desk to have their diaries marked. Every Friday afternoon she'd supervise cleaning up after their art lesson, and a hundred other mundane chores in between. She'd become fed up with the predictability of it all. Now she saw a real opportunity to turn her life around, and Reg's brainwave was going to make everything a whole lot better.

She had persuaded Ted that their good fortune warranted a celebration breakfast down at the beach. A couple of young women in shiny, Lycra-shoulder-padded jackets and big hairdos strutted past their table. It was a cool morning, and the shoreline was almost deserted. A dog walker threw a stick into the water, and his retriever chased it into the surf. Three young boys wedged a body board into the sand for a wicket. The bowler yelled, "Howzat!" when his ball knocked it flat.

Cheryl gazed contentedly across the Southern Ocean, savoring her new situation.

"This will turn our lives around," she told Ted for the nth time that morning.

Ted sipped his espresso. "We'll give it a go, but if it doesn't work out we'll have to find jobs again quick bloody smart."

"It's okay for you, you like your job," Cheryl reminded him, "but those kids are taking it out of me."

It was true—Ted did like his job at the local music store, but he didn't see it as a permanent career. His dad had been furious when he'd packed up his engineering degree and left England. They were lucky to have such good friends, and he loved living near the beach, even though the rent had gone up since Lara had moved out.

"Let's face it, we've got into a bit of a rut lately," said Cheryl.

Ted drained his coffee, reminded of an Arnold Bennett quote about the advantage of being in a rut.

"When one is in a rut, one knows exactly where one is."

✈ ✈ ✈

Niko and his younger sister Lara had grown up on the same street as Reg, who'd protected them from the local bullies who called them "wogs." Nowadays, the siblings worked shifts in their parents' restaurant, and the communal fridge was always stocked with Greek dishes like taramasalata and moussaka.

The evening after Reg's meeting was the first Saturday that Niko hadn't had to work at the restaurant for some time. Cheryl wandered into the kitchen, where the others had congregated. "D'you think Lara always cooks for her new man?" she asked as she emptied two containers of minted meatballs into a saucepan.

"Probably," Ted said. "Older blokes expect that."

"Reckon he's got her doing bloody everything," grumbled Niko. "She'll be back," he insisted. "When she realizes what a dead loss Geoff Devlin is, how much she misses us all, she'll be back."

"There's something about him that gives me the creeps," he confided to Reg later.

"Give him a chance, mate, it's early days."

"Only one chance," Niko warned as he bunched his dark curls in a knot at the back of his head. "He gets only one chance with my sister."

✈ ✈ ✈

Within weeks, Reg's courier syndicate had executed the first run. Each couple was in place well before its rostered leg of the journey, with Reg and Annie escorting the contraband on the last flight into Australia. After the initial run, Reg changed the order of each couple's leg of the journey. Pair number one would be given instructions for a different collection point in Bombay. This would usually be a room number in a hotel, sometimes the same hotel where they were staying. Only the men would collect the neatly wrapped one-kilo slabs of cannabis resin. The door would slowly open, just enough for them to take the bag. They never got to see the face of the man behind it, only his yellow-skinned hand.

Each run became a finely tuned feat of coordination. The first courier couple would take the contraband to their room, pack it carefully into the hollowed-out boombox, and board a plane at

Bombay Airport with the machine in a carry-on bag. They would deposit the illicit hand luggage in the overhead locker of their seats at the rear of the cabin and fly to Tullamarine Airport, Melbourne, or to Sydney. The bag would be left in the locker when they disembarked, and the second pair would board the same plane for its leg of the journey. These two would have the same seat numbers as the first pair. When the plane touched down in New Zealand, they would collect the bag and discreetly pass it to the third couple in the terminal of Auckland Airport.

"You'd think the cabin crew would check the lockers when people left the plane, wouldn't you?" Cheryl asked Annie one evening when they were cooking spaghetti.

"Why would they, though?" Annie pointed out as she strained the pasta into a colander. "Think about it, they always check that the lockers are closed before takeoff, but they couldn't care less if you've left something behind."

As Reg had predicted, the detour to New Zealand was proving to be the perfect smoke screen for their smuggling operation. The Australian border authorities for incoming flights from New Zealand showed little interest in passengers' hand luggage. Every five or six weeks, the third couple breezed through Melbourne or Sydney passport control. They would meet a regular contact in the car park and hand over the bagged boombox before catching a domestic flight home to Adelaide. Reg always took care of things after that.

Because everything was running smoothly, nobody asked questions; the less you knew, the less you could be implicated. Cheryl calculated that, even after paying for airfares, two runs netted more than she'd earned as a teacher for the whole year. Not bad for part-time shift work. This was more like it: the land of plenty, and now they were all getting a big slice of the cake. All the house bills were paid, and Annie found a woman to do a couple of hours' cleaning every week.

Ted bought himself a guitar, and Niko put down a deposit on a new Ford Corsair. Annie treated herself to Chanel perfume and chose a swanky new watch for Reg. He planned to place an order for a new javelin, even though his training schedule had suffered lately. Shopping for clothes in trendy little designer boutiques became one of Cheryl's and Annie's favorite pastimes; the bar-gain basements of Adelaide were a thing of the past.

The only person who wasn't enjoying their newfound wealth was Lara; how could she explain spending money Geoff thought she didn't have? Everyone had agreed they would never discuss business on the phone, so one afternoon she called Reg to say she urgently needed to talk to him and to ask him to meet her in a cafe nearby.

"And Reggie," she added before she hung up, "don't say any-thing to Niko about this, I'll talk to him later."

"Thanks for coming." Lara sounded nervous when Reg arrived at the cafe. "I wasn't sure what to do."

"What to do about what?" Reg asked, though he anticipated that Geoff would figure as her problem.

"You know, finding reasons to give Geoff for my being away for days at a time. I don't think he's going to buy it next time. Anyway, I wanted to ask if I could leave it for a while . . . nothing perma-nent."

Reg studied the face of the small, frail girl he'd known for so long. He thought of Lara like a sister. She was pale and tired, no lipstick, with dark circles under her eyes. Her usually shiny black hair looked unkempt. He felt for her. Perhaps it had been a mis-take to get her mixed up in all this. Lara had always been a worrier, unsure of herself.

"Sure, Lara." He hugged her. "Don't you worry about a thing, Niko can go it alone for a while. Leave it to me to sort out."

It was the first time Reg had felt uneasy about the syndicate since it had started operating. Soon Lara was feeling better; she'd bought herself a few weeks' peace of mind. When they left the cafe twenty minutes later, Reg kissed her good-bye next to his green Holden before she hurried into the bakery a few doors away. He got into the driver's seat and switched on the ignition, but as he started to move into the road, he saw the shadowy face of a man in his rearview mirror, a man staring intently at him from the win-dow of the launderette.

Reg recognized who it was immediately. He was sure Geoff Devlin had been spying on him for some time.

CHAPTER 3

Geoff Devlin suspected that his girlfriend was cheating on him. When she'd first moved into his flat, Lara would rarely go out alone, apart from doing her waitressing shifts and shopping for groceries. Lately it seemed she was never home, and she often stayed away for days at a time. If she thought he believed her story about spending nights with a friend to help her look after her sick mother, she was naive. He'd suspected she was up to something that morning when she left to run a few errands. That's why he'd followed her to the cafe entrance and taken up a position in the launderette next door. He'd had a hunch it was Reg she was carrying on with, and now that he'd seen their tête-à-tête, his fears had been confirmed.

His initial sadness and pain dissipated within minutes. By the time he got back to his flat, those emotions had been replaced by a huge sense of injustice. He slammed the front door and stormed into the bedroom he shared with the girl he had planned to marry. This was his flat. He'd supported her, done everything to make this relationship work, and here she was screwing around behind his back. The bitch would pay!

He threw open the closet, pulled her largest suitcase down onto the bed, and started venting his fury on Lara's belongings, emptying drawerfuls at a time. He despised the fancy blouses and dresses hanging in the wardrobe—the thought of her wearing them for lover boy sickened him as he ripped them off their hangers. He'd show her; he'd have everything she owned sitting on the doorstep by the time she got back. God, he loved her in those little black heels, but who cared? There were stacks of women in Adelaide with good legs.

The case bulged, the awkward zipper making him angrier as it whizzed the last few inches with a squeak of finality. He commandeered a couple of pillowcases and a big string bag because he still had her stupid trinket boxes and books to sort out. Then there were the photos; albums of memories. He randomly opened one and gazed at a picture. Him with Lara at the beach last year, Lara in that great little bikini he'd bought her, laughing as she straddled his broad, tattooed shoulders. Two fucking years wasted, he thought, tossing the album across the room.

He chucked *Crochet for Beginners* into the string bag. Then the next book caught his eye. He couldn't remember seeing it before. The square diary had a thick linen cover, decorated with butterflies. He saddened momentarily, thinking about how she loved butterflies. He ran his finger over the patterned wings, and then turned his attention to the central strap with a tiny metal keyhole. As he suspected, it was locked. Where the fuck was the key? He rampaged through every drawer and cupboard looking for it. He tried wrenching the strap apart but it refused to budge, so he resorted to sawing it apart with a bread knife fetched from the kitchen.

Worn out, he fell back onto the bed to discover whether his effort had been worthwhile. He held the journal above his face, flicking through pages of calendars, public holidays, and assorted useless information. The first months were blank; then he found pages where Lara had written "number one," "two," "three," or just "me." Some days had "Reg & Annie," "Niko & me," or "Ted & Cheryl" next to the numbers. At first he thought it might be a tally of points for some weird game, until he found several names, addresses, and room numbers of hotels with Indian-sounding names. Every page had flight details for routes between Bombay, New Zealand, and Australia, and even seat numbers. Geoff was baffled. What the hell did it all mean?

Then he spotted a stranded little note scrawled across the bottom of a page. It was difficult to decipher because Lara sloped her writing when she was in a hurry. He mouthed the words, "Nearly forgot to leave the bag!"

Got it, thought Geoff. It all made sense. Lara and that idiot of a brother of hers and all the other idiots in his house were into some sort of smuggling operation from Bombay. They'd deliberately kept him in the dark because she was having an affair with Reg. God knows who else she was screwing—hippies usually slept with everyone. They were probably so stoned all the time they didn't know what the fuck they were doing. But she knew what she was doing: making a fool of him! This wasn't over yet. Not by a bloody long shot.

Geoff seethed with a renewed vigor as he locked the front door, enjoying setting the dead bolt that Lara had no key for. He stepped over the pile of her belongings on the mat, adding a note saying he never wanted to see her again. Then he strode down the street clutching the diary, hell bent on revenge. Nothing else would quell this tight knot in his stomach, or his pounding chest. Nothing.

When he arrived at the police station, he took a deep breath before nodding to an officer he knew at the reception desk. He had to appear calm. He rehearsed how he intended to play his hand as he took the stairs to the third floor. He walked through the swinging doors into the open-plan office and saw his uncle sitting at a desk at the end. The senior sergeant looked surprised when he saw Geoff approaching.

"Geoff, lad! What brings you here?"

"Nothing good, I'm afraid," said Geoff soberly.

"It's not your mum is it?"

"No, it's nothing like that. Look Ron, I've got a bit of a dilemma." Geoff cleared his throat.

He revealed the diary.

"This doesn't sit well, but I have no choice, . . . take a look at this." He slid the book across the desktop.

His uncle pushed his thick glasses closer to his eyes. He spent several minutes carefully fingering the pages, his breathing intensifying.

"It's obvious to me what this is, Geoff," he finally said. "And this is serious stuff. Whose is it and where did you get it?"

"I'm afraid it belongs to Lara."

"Lara. Not your girlfriend Lara? You don't mean her?"

"I do. I found it today when I was cleaning the flat."

"Well I never!"

The sergeant was shocked. He'd met Lara at several family get-togethers, and she hadn't struck him as the type to get involved in anything like this. It was common knowledge between family members that his nephew had a temper, and he wouldn't put it past him to bring the diary in as some kind of payback. His duty now was to pass it on to his colleagues and see what they made of it.

"You did the right thing, lad; looks like this has been going on for a while. These people could go down for some time."

"I know," Geoff mumbled, trying to sound concerned.

By the time he'd caught the elevator to the ground floor and walked out into the street, his mouth was curled into a satisfied smirk. Reg Spiers and his merry little band deserved everything they had coming. And so did Lara.

CHAPTER 4

Lara wasn't in the habit of ringing the bell at the house where she used to live, but these were exceptional circumstances. When she'd moved out, the others had insisted she keep her door key, but she thought it too presumptuous to let herself in with all her possessions. So a drenched Lara waited on the porch, bedraggled and exhausted; she had lugged everything onto the bus, then carried it from the end of Ford Avenue. All in the pouring rain.

"Lara!" Annie was surprised to see her and knew something was wrong when she saw the pile of soggy bags. The tension of Lara's past weeks coupled with the pain of being jilted erupted as she fell into Annie's arms, sobbing.

"It's over, he's kicked me out," she spluttered, as Annie stroked her wet, disheveled hair.

"Did he say why?" Cheryl asked later, as the three women sat in the kitchen. "He owes you that at least."

"Just that I'm never home," said Lara. She was feeling a little better after a shower and hot chocolate. "He doesn't think he can trust me anymore, and we were never that suited anyway. Oh yeah, and he's met someone else. That's what he said in the letter," she sniffed, wiping her swollen eyes with a crumpled tissue.

Cheryl opened a new packet of ginger delights and offered one to Lara. "Just like that, no warning?" she asked.

Lara nibbled her biscuit and shook her head.

"God," Cheryl scoffed. "Men are bastards!"

"Not all of them," said Annie. "I don't think Reg would do that."

"That's because Reg has balls, he'd tell you to your face," said Cheryl.

"Reg would never leave you, Annie," Lara said. "He's crazy about you, everyone can see that." She blew her nose, tears welling again.

Annie gazed out the window, hoping Lara was right.

Late that night, everyone was sprawled on the sofas and bean bags in the lounge room, mellow because they'd smoked a couple of joints of hash. They'd also devoured a heap of moussaka that Niko had brought back from his stint at the restaurant. Weekends were the only time they were likely to spend together; they purposely carried out their illicit dealings between Monday and Friday so that Niko and Lara could continue their weekend shifts at the restaurant. Everything had to appear normal.

Lara was sad, but cheered somewhat by the company of her friends. At least now she wouldn't have to make up stories for Geoff every time she went away.

"You sure it's okay to have my old room back?" she asked the others.

"Dunno about that, sis," winked Niko, delighted Devlin was off the scene.

"You know it is," Reg assured her. He'd been troubled all day since he'd spotted Devlin in the launderette. Surely it wasn't a coincidence that the creep had dumped Lara straight afterward. But Reg wouldn't let on about it, not even to Annie. Not when the syndicate was running so smoothly.

"That Ayers Rock woman is sticking to her story," Annie blew a smoke ring into the air and passed the joint to Cheryl. "Still reckons her baby was nicked by a Dingo."

"No way," said Cheryl. "The dog Benson from next door, maybe, but not a bloody Dingo."

"Nightcap?" Reg asked, passing the tray of smoking paraphernalia to Niko.

"Since I make the best," Niko chuckled.

He pulled a few cigarette papers from the packet, licked them, and carefully stuck them together. Now that they were professional dope importers, Reg always made sure that they had a regular supply for personal use. Prices had risen since a big marijuana bust in New South Wales yielded a massive crop. Smaller, domestic marijuana growing for profit was still in its infancy. Australia's war on drugs, with its increased police powers and penalties for trafficking, had created a drought in the market and taken a number of dealers off the streets. As far as Niko was concerned, Reg was no different from any other shrewd businessman—he'd identified a gap in the market.

"This one, man, pump it up," he called to Ted, who was in charge of the music.

"This one" had been a house favorite since they'd all got sloshed at a crazy nightclub dance party the previous year. Ted leaned over and increased the volume, and Annie and Cheryl leapt to their feet, giggling as they hauled Lara up to dance to "Play That Funky Music."

Reg danced toward the kitchen like the tail end of a conga procession, two steps forward then one back, singing at the top of his voice, "Yeah, they were dancin' and singin' and movin' to the groovin'." Annie dropped to her knees, laughing at Cheryl and Lara, whose movements had degenerated into very goofy dancing. Ted's long body was propped against the wall, hair flopping over his closed eyes as he waved his arms like a conductor. Niko's face was a picture of contentment as he emptied a line of tobacco along the cigarette papers. He was sprinkling in a generous helping of hash when a thunderous hammering on the front door blasted over the music.

Everyone fell silent except Ted, still humming and conducting. Cheryl flicked the music off, and he opened his eyes to her wild stare as she silently shushed him, holding her finger to her lips.

"With you in a tick," Reg called loudly from the kitchen. He raced back into the lounge.

"Right," he hissed. "Dump everything."

"I'm on it," said Cheryl, grabbing the tray from Niko. She emptied it into the bag from the moussaka and swept the coffee table with her forearm.

"I'll do the bedrooms," gasped Annie. She whipped the bag out of Cheryl's hand and bounded up the stairs, two at a time. She scrambled through the bedrooms, seizing packets of marijuana and stuffing them into the bag. Racing back to Niko's room, she grabbed the Moroccan water pipe from his bedside table and shoved it under a pile of shoes in the corner. Then she froze with panicked indecision—should she flush the contents of the bag down the toilet?

"It's the police! If you don't open this door right now, we're coming in!" bellowed an aggressive male voice from downstairs, as Annie imagined dope floating around the toilet bowl after she'd pulled the chain. There was only one thing for it! She squeezed the bag under the waistband of her knickers—it scrunched into her stomach. When she raced downstairs, Reg nodded toward the door to let her know he had no option but to open it.

"Evening, gentlemen. What can I do for you?" he greeted the visitors.

Annie stepped into the hallway as four police officers swooped through the entrance.

"Everyone stay where you are and don't touch anything, we have a warrant to search these premises," said the biggest.

Annie and Reg were escorted into the lounge, Annie desperately trying to hold in her stomach. The others guessed what she'd done by the awkward way she was walking. They avoided looking her way so as not to draw the officers' attention. Reg was certain they'd all be searched. Think, damn it. Think! The front door creaked and he turned back to look at it. Wide open!

"For Christ's sake, who let the bloody cat out?" he yelled. "We're not talking any old cat here!" Reg confronted the officers. "This is a purebred pedigree, a Taiwanese Blue, and it cost me a packet!"

Niko caught on immediately. "Not Bluey?" He sounded worried and peered behind the sofa.

Reg instituted the search party. The officers were most concerned—this animal could be valuable, and they didn't want to be implicated in its demise. Reg led his posse through the hall, flashing his eyes at the kitchen door as he passed Annie, sending the thought: "Get rid of it out there, *quick!*"

As soon as the last officer stepped into the front garden, Annie bolted through the kitchen and out the backdoor, praying for Benson not to bark. She sped down the path, flicked the bolt on the gate, and dashed along the dark lane. Her feet crunched the graveled surface as she darted to the refuse bins, gasping for breath as she retrieved the bag from the waist of her jeans and stuffed it behind an old spin dryer. By the time she'd raced back to the kitchen, the drug squad was still at the front of the house, looking for the imaginary cat. She huddled with the women near the lounge window, stifling giggles as they watched an officer's posterior disappear into the bushes.

As they gave up looking, the police lined up the occupants of the house to search them. Her friends looked on nervously when it was Annie's turn. She kept her arms raised, staring blankly into Lara's frightened eyes while the female officer frisked her. Then the officers turned their attention to the rooms, ordering the housemates to remain seated in the lounge with the policewoman. The officers foraged through both floors of the creaky old house, turning out every drawer and cupboard before conceding defeat. Niko was relieved when no mention was made of his water pipe.

"Sorry about the cat, sir," the chief mumbled as his colleagues trailed out.

"Me too," said Reg, feigning annoyance.

He quickly locked the door and joined the others in the lounge. They all stood, quietly listening. There were sighs of relief when they heard car doors slam.

"If that's the state of the bloody police force, then God help Australia!" scoffed Ted.

Reg rubbed his eyes. "Just be grateful they're so useless."

"Next run is off, though, isn't it?" Niko wanted to know. "They'll be watching us now."

"No, they won't." Reg sounded sure. "We're not talking the feds here, just our local lot, and they're on a purge at the moment. Remember I told you that Dave bloke said they'd done two busts in his street last month? They're just expecting that everyone who smokes a bit of grass at home sells a bit around town. Slap on the wrist kind of stuff, not major gigs, not a bloody clue. No worries. Next month will be fine."

"Hope you're right, Reggie," said Ted, "because whichever way you look at it, we're on their radar somehow."

"Yeah, and I'd like to know how," said Niko, glancing at his sister.

Lara rubbed her eye and said nothing.

CHAPTER 5

Despite the raid, Reg's housemates accepted his assessment that the police had no knowledge of their lucrative business enterprise. The next scheduled operation would go ahead as normal. The possibility that Geoff had betrayed them was playing on Lara's mind. After a couple of days, she put her suspicions down to her own insecure, stressed frame of mind. Geoff had his faults, but surely he wouldn't deliberately land her in trouble? Her life was looking up—she'd stick with her buddies and save enough money to buy a little flat. Who wanted to be a waitress all her life? She and Niko were scheduled to collect the next bag from Ted and Cheryl in New Zealand and do the home run.

Reg and Annie left on Monday, successfully collected the contraband in Bombay, and completed the first leg. The other four left the house Wednesday morning. Later that day, Ted and Cheryl boarded Flight 196 in Melbourne and found their seat numbers in row fourteen. As usual, Ted put his coat in the overhead locker and sighted the bag he would chaperone to New Zealand.

"D'you think we'll still be doing this next year?" Cheryl whispered, squeezing his hand as they descended over Auckland.

Ted looked into his wife's eyes. She looked too young and innocent to be involved in all this. That was a good thing.

"Should have enough for a deposit on a house before then."

The only part of flying Cheryl hated was the landing, and she took deep breaths as the plane dipped before the wheels hit the ground. The aircraft powered down the runway. When it was stationary, passengers blocked the aisle as they collected their hand luggage from the overhead lockers. This part of the procedure always made Cheryl jittery, so she avoided looking at the bag. She would pretend they were on a harmless vacation and that none of the things they talked about at the house were real.

Ted opened the door of the overhead baggage locker and passed a black briefcase to a man with glasses standing expectantly nearby. Then he carefully lifted down the big, heavy, canvas carry-on bag and held it by his side as he lined up behind Cheryl to disembark. They were among the last passengers to leave the plane. As they walked through the tunnel, a woman behind them scolded her toddler. Ted cleared his throat as the child scurried past. Something felt different . . . not right.

The man with spectacles from the plane stood at the end of the passageway. Nothing unusual about that, except now there was no briefcase, his hands were in his pockets, and he was with two other men in dark suits. And to make matters worse, they were staring straight at him. Ted tried to steady his breathing. He glanced at Cheryl's profile beneath her bouncing ponytail as she walked beside him. A lump formed in his throat. Five meters from the ominous trio, Ted started to experience his steps in slow motion. He thought of a song: nowhere to run, nowhere to hide. What would he say? What would his dad say? If he'd done engineering, this wouldn't be happening. Closer, they were getting closer . . .

Ted averted his eyes from the suited men, scarcely breathing as he walked by. While Cheryl displayed their documents at the passport control point, he could still feel himself shaking, and he resisted the urge to look back. He trailed her through to the busy arrivals section of the main terminal, his hot, clammy hand still clutching the big, heavy bag.

Cheryl slowed for a moment, swapped her small leather case to her other hand, and looked anxiously around. "Seen them," she blurted, leading the way to the coffee bar down the hall. They seated themselves at a small table next to the one occupied by Niko and Lara. Ted was still trying to slow his racing heart as he positioned the bulky canvas bag between his feet, like he always did.

Niko pretended not to notice the newcomers. "Hey guys," he whispered, focusing his attention elsewhere. Then he slowly rose. "See you soon," he prepared to leave, and nonchalantly collected the bag from underneath Ted's table. Lara flashed Cheryl a mischievous little grin before heading off with Niko down the hallway.

Cheryl turned to Ted, relieved to have the worst part of their trip behind them. His face was white.

"What is it?" she asked. "What?"

Ted sighed, leaned closer, and looked straight at her. "I can't do this much longer," he said earnestly. "We had our warning when the cops turned up."

"But like Reg said," Cheryl looked both ways to check that they were out of earshot. "That was just routine stuff, they have no idea . . ."

"Listen to me for God's sake. For once, just listen," Ted spluttered. "It's too dangerous. I've got a bad feeling about this." He leaned back in his chair and slowly nodded his head. "Really bad."

Ted's premonition had been right. Although the house raid in Ford Avenue had failed to provide corroborating evidence that Spiers and his friends were importing narcotics, a number of other inquiries had proved most fruitful. Detective Brian Collins from the Adelaide drug squad had interviewed Geoff Devlin and confirmed that his girlfriend had been absent on the dates specified in her diary. Information passed on from airport authorities in Bombay, Auckland, Sydney, and Melbourne placed any two of the six suspects at the various locations on the dates she had specified.

Collins was confident that he had enough evidence to charge the group with conspiring to import cannabis resin into Australia on at least five occasions, and a couple of weeks after the syndicate's last run, he obtained an arrest warrant. Ted was taken into police custody at the music store where he worked, and Cheryl was arrested at the gates of her school. When they arrived at the police station, they met up with their four housemates, who'd been apprehended at home.

✈ ✈ ✈

The following day, the six conspirators sat with their solicitor, grouped around a table in his Adelaide office.

"It was lucky you were able to raise your bail money," Atkins, the solicitor, commented, thinking he had a bloody good idea where it came from.

"So, worst-case scenario?" Reg asked, trying to sound positive. "Worst possible sentence we could get?"

The solicitor looked taken aback by his upbeat manner.

"You'd be better off pleading guilty, obviously. There's too much evidence against you to do anything else. I'm not going to kid you here, you could be looking at anything between ten and twenty years."

"What—all of us?" Ted echoed everyone's shock. He hadn't slept the previous night and had dark circles under his eyes.

"The best we can do is try to get a lighter sentence for the girls, but even that's going to be difficult. They were clearly accomplices, even though they might not have handled anything."

The dark cloud enveloping them in Atkins's office was still hanging over them when they reached home and traipsed over their front doorstep. Annie hadn't said much until now.

"I'll put the kettle on. Come on everyone, we'll get through this . . . we will," she told the others on her way to the kitchen.

"Atkins is talking out of his ass," Reg announced as they commiserated with each other over mugs of tea. "We'll get another solicitor, I don't mind paying because I got us into this mess." He put his face in his hands. "I'm so sorry," he said. "Sorry and angry, because I reckon the cops were tipped off."

Five pairs of eyes studied Reg's face for clues. Everyone had suspicions, but no one wanted to point the finger.

"We all had a free choice about this, Reggie," Annie said. "Everyone knew the risks. We were all in it together."

"I don't bloody understand what went wrong," he groaned. "I was so careful."

"What I want to know is how they had every fucking detail," Ted declared angrily on his way to the sink. "Names, flights, dates, and everything."

"He's right," agreed Niko. "Let's be honest, an outsider look-ing at the facts would probably conclude it had to be one of us that snitched."

"Or someone close to us," muttered Ted.

While her friends swapped theories about what had led to their demise, Lara slipped quietly upstairs to her small bedroom. She rummaged through her familiar possessions, impatiently sweeping the hair from her eyes. A tear meandered toward her mouth. She gave little sniffs of despair as she desperately searched for her diary. She hadn't made an entry for a couple of months, since she'd moved out of Geoff's flat. She emptied the drawer of books from her bedside table and methodically replaced them, one by one. Her beautiful butterflies couldn't have flown away. Somebody must have taken them. She wept uncontrollably, be-cause she knew; she knew exactly who that somebody was.

Chapter 6

Annie raced into the kitchen with a newspaper and spread it on the table.

"Told you it'd be in it—front page as well."

"Read it out," said Reg.

Lara peered over Annie's shoulder. "*Adelaide Inquirer*," she muttered. "Always goes for dramatic headlines."

Annie read aloud:

> REG SPIERS AND FIVE OTHERS ACCUSED OF DRUG TRAFFICKING
>
> *Law Reporter: Greg Denton*
>
> *Reginald James Spiers, the athlete who gained notoriety in the sixties for his escapades en route to Australia from England, was yesterday committed for trial in the Supreme Court. Spiers and five other defendants are charged with importing forty kilos of Cannabis Resin worth $1.2 million into Australia between May and November of last year. The presiding magistrate at the committal proceedings, Mr. T. Rowbottom, granted Spiers bail of $4000 with two cash sureties of $2000. If convicted in the Supreme Court, the accused could face prison sentences of up to twenty years.*

Lara exhaled loudly, folded her arms, and stared at the ceiling. "They just like to be dramatic," said Annie. She continued reading:

> *Spiers' co-accused in the Magistrates Court yesterday includes his partner, Miss Annie Hayes, restaurant staff Niko and Lara Alexopoulos, and Ted Bate and his*

wife Cheryl. Until recently Mrs. Bate taught at a local
primary school, where staff and parents have told the
Inquirer they are shocked by news of her indictment.
The defendants pleaded not guilty and "reserved their
defense for the Supreme Court." The group chatted
cheerfully in the dock, adorned in designer wear and
jewelry that typify their jet-setting lifestyle. Spiers
joked with his friends while his vivacious girlfriend,
Annie Hayes, clung devotedly to his side. He told re-
porters outside the court that the whole episode had
been "a huge mistake." He did not elaborate on whose
mistake. No doubt his defense counsel will be making
that clear in the Supreme Court next month.

"Clung devotedly to his side?" Annie repeated loudly. "Yuck!" She pulled a face. "Makes me sound pathetic."

"I'd settle for 'pathetic.'" Lara rested her elbows on the table, cupping her face in her hands. "'International drug ring' won't go down well."

"It's just sensationalist stuff because Reg is well known . . . the box thing, his athletics, and everything," said Niko. "We wouldn't have warranted a mention otherwise."

"Great! Try telling that to Dad. I'm doing the lunch shift and he will have seen this! He's gonna go nuts."

"Tell him I'll be in to see him later," said Niko. He wondered whether he should go with her.

Reg asked, "Where is Ted, by the way?"

"They went to telephone his folks in England; Cheryl thinks his dad is going to take it really badly," said Lara.

Niko sighed. "He's gonna take it a lot worse when we're all locked up."

The four friends fell silent.

"Don't, Niko!" Lara cried. "Don't say that!" She burst into tears.

Niko slid onto the chair next to her and put his arms around her. She sobbed against his chest. Annie sat on the other side of her and stroked her hand.

"It'll be okay, Lara," she said softly. "The girls won't get long. Out in no time with good behavior . . ."

"We all lost our heads," Niko said.

Reg sighed and massaged his forehead. "Starting with me, mate. Starting with me."

He piled the breakfast dishes into the sink and turned the tap on full, squeezed in extra dishwashing liquid, and watched the bubbles rise. He should have recruited a team from outside, not these people. Not his closest friends.

What the hell had he been thinking?

The papers had made out that none of them gave a damn, but it was all an act. Everyone was worried sick about the Supreme Court trial in a few weeks. Being on bail, having to sign in at the main police station at seven every morning and nine every night was awful. Worse was the thought of jail, getting locked up—perhaps for years.

Later Niko found Reg sitting on one of the old wicker chairs on the back patio, where they often talked. Benson, the Rottweiler next door, barked over the fence.

"There you go, mate." Niko handed Reg a beer before opening his own.

"I'd like to flatten Devlin," hissed Reg.

"It wouldn't achieve anything. Look, we can't prove it, so let's try to move on, for Lara's sake," said Niko. "It's going to be hard for Ted and Cheryl, you and Annie. At least the girls will go to the same prison. I keep telling Lara she'll be with Cheryl and Annie. Thank God—she wouldn't last long on her own."

"Annie won't be there," Reg announced grimly.

"What d'you mean?"

"She won't be there, and neither will I. Look Niko, I'm not telling the others . . . but Annie and I aren't prepared to go down. We're just not."

"Shit!" Niko looked stunned.

"I ran it past her to see what her reaction would be. I was expecting her to try to talk me out of it, and, you know what? She was relieved. Said she'd been thinking the same thing for days."

"She's ballsy, Annie. Reckon you've met your match there," said Niko. "But where will you go?"

"Haven't worked that bit out yet, but definitely out of the

country. Mate, keep it to yourself. I'm not even telling Ted, he's got enough on his plate. Don't want to involve him in anything else. I've stuffed everyone up enough already."

"We didn't have to agree. Got too greedy for our own good," said Niko.

"Maybe, but the strange thing is, when my dad asked me why I did it, I told him that, for me, it wasn't just about the money."

"What was it then?" Niko asked.

"Something deep down always says, 'Reggie, this isn't a good idea,' but then I just can't help myself. Dad says I was the same as a kid. It's the excitement, the drama. Sort of thrive on it, I guess."

Lengthening shadows patterned the lawn. A light breeze carried the sweet scent of jasmine and rustled the leaves of the golden wattle as Niko drained his beer.

"Look, don't think it hasn't crossed my mind too." He leaned closer to Reg. "Doing a disappearing act."

Reg sat straight in his chair. He lowered his voice. "Thought I was the only mad bastard who'd consider it."

✈ ✈ ✈

Reg, Annie, and Niko tried to figure out how to lay their hands on false passports. This was made doubly difficult because they couldn't talk about their plans when Ted, Cheryl, and Lara were around. Ted didn't say anything, but sensed something might be afoot when he noticed the three of them were often out of the house at the same time.

"The thing that keeps playing on my mind is Lara," Annie told Reg and Niko. They were huddled in the same little coffee shop where Reg had met Lara that fateful Saturday a few weeks earlier.

"You think she's not on mine?" Niko looked worried. "I'll have to speak to her. I can't just leave her with a letter, no way. Don't worry, she'll keep her mouth shut."

"Course she will," said Reg.

"But what if she wants to come with us?" asked Annie.

"She won't." Niko was sure. "She wouldn't leave Mum and Dad."

Reg had been scribbling ideas on a paper napkin. He reached into his folder and grabbed a set of forms as the smiley waitress served their coffees and doughnuts.

"Reggie, you've got to be careful!" Annie warned when the woman had moved away. "Everyone knows who we are, if they get wind of anything like passport applications, we're stuffed."

"Okay," said Reg, hiding his paperwork. "But this is what I'm thinking. We don't know anyone who could help us get fake passports, right?"

"Right. Keep your voice down," hissed Annie.

"So what we do," said Reg, quietly this time as he leaned over his coffee mug, "is we apply for real passports, with fake names."

"What fake names?" asked Niko. "Don't forget, we have to give a load of information."

"Real names of other people. I've already worked out who I'm going to be," said Reg. "A bloke called Bruce Pennington." He leaned back and enthusiastically chewed his doughnut, his mischievous eyes following Annie and Niko's reactions.

"Who the hell's Bruce Pennington?" Annie demanded.

"Some bloke who used to go to the athletics club and dreamt he could be a pole-vaulter. There's this book there where everyone writes their info, date of birth, and stuff. He left because he wasn't much good. Bit of a wimp our Bruce, and guess what? Terrified of flying, never been out of Australia, and I bet he's never even applied for a passport." Reg smirked. "Until now."

Niko grinned, "D'you think it could work?"

"I reckon it could," said Annie. "Don't have any better ideas. I'm going to have to think about who I'm going to be. Someone who would never fly . . ."

"It wouldn't have to be someone who doesn't want to fly—just has never flown and isn't going to any time soon, is that right?" Niko asked.

"Exactly," said Reg.

"Hey!" Niko turned to him. "Remember that family that lived on our street, the Bramptons? Their son was born on the same day as me and our mums always made us share a party?"

"Yeah, good old James Brampton. Jimmy," said Reg. "Still lives with his mum. I never thought he was the full deck."

"So he's not likely to be jetting off to New York for corporate takeovers any time soon," Annie giggled. "Okay that's you two sorted," she continued, "but who can I be?"

"What about people from the office where you worked? Any girls there you can think of?"

"I've only kept in touch with Sonia."

"What about her then, where has she been?"

"Nowhere," Annie mused. "She was telling me a while ago that is why . . . oh my God! That is why she was looking forward to having a honeymoon in Thailand when she got married in a couple of years!"

"I bet she hasn't applied for a passport yet, if the wedding isn't for a couple of years," Reg said.

"The wedding isn't going to happen . . . ever!" said Annie. "He dumped her for someone else. That's why she wanted to meet me, shoulder to cry on and all that!"

"That's it!" said Reg, so loudly a number of customers turned. "So what's her other name? So I know who I'm going to be traveling with."

"Sonia Priestly," Annie narrowed her eyes. "So that's it then: I'm Sonia Priestly and I'm madly in love with a bloke called Bruce Pennington. Then there's some other bloke we hook up with called James Brampton. What d'you reckon?" She looked at Reg and Niko.

"I've always wanted to meet a bird called Sonia," Reg said, and Annie and Niko giggled into their napkins.

CHAPTER 7

"Look where you're bloody going!" The driver poked his grumpy face out of the window as he passed.

"Phew!" thought Annie, who'd stepped blindly off the curb. "Pull yourself together girl!"

She had been preoccupied with how to extract Sonia Priestly's date of birth. If she wasn't more careful, she wouldn't even make it to the restaurant! There was a myriad of ways to broach the subject of birthdays—she needed only one. She had a plan; she just had to find a suitable break in the conversation to implement it. When she'd phoned Sonia to see if she wanted to get together for lunch, Sonia had sounded pleasantly surprised. They'd arranged to meet in a little Italian place near Sonia's office in the city center.

"It'll be good to get out," Sonia had said. "It's not the same here since you left—everyone's so serious!"

The restaurant was buzzing with midday diners. She spotted Sonia at the back of the room. Sonia was dressed in her usual style: a tent dress she was convinced "hid a multitude of sins."

"Annie!" Sonia's pudgy face beamed. "God, you've lost weight. Got any tips?"

After they'd placed their order with the flustered young waiter, Annie noticed Sonia didn't seem as chatty as she had on the phone. Perhaps she'd heard about the indictment since they'd spoken and now felt compromised. Best not to mention anything about it unless Sonia brought it up.

"Any new men on the horizon?" asked Annie, fishing for information on pending honeymoons abroad.

"Nobody since Dave," said Sonia, who'd finished her main course and was making light work of the bread. "To be honest, I thought we might get back together." Her deep-set eyes saddened as she spread a mound of butter onto the last crust. "But I've just heard he's marrying that girl I told you about. No prizes for guessing where he's taking her for their honeymoon."

"He's horrible!" Annie commiserated. How bloody fantastic. No passport necessary for Sonia. Thanks Dave! "You're not thinking of going anywhere yourself?"

"Saving for a car now, no traveling for a while," said Sonia with her mouth full. She neatened her spoon and fork, and then became transfixed by the waiter's backside.

Annie's eyes skipped nervously around the crowded room. It was only the back of a head at the table near the entrance, but she could have sworn it belonged to Atkins, the solicitor. It was bloody Atkins; that was his young clerk sitting opposite. The last thing she wanted was a conversation with the solicitor in front of Sonia. She wriggled farther into the corner to hide behind Sonia's ample frame.

"Two girls from our shipping department asked me if I wanted to go to Bali with them next month," Sonia continued. "But I won't have the money. Can you believe it? I've never been abroad!"

Annie shrugged. Fancy Sonia coming right out with it!

"You certainly don't look like someone who's lost her job," Sonia said when they were drinking coffee. "Looking good, girl— new blouse?"

"Thanks," Annie smiled, putting her hand to her head and pulling her hair to the side in one luxurious swathe.

"You could be a model, Annie, I always said that," said Sonia sincerely.

This was it.

"That reminds me," Annie rifled through the shoulder bag by her feet, "talking of clothes, I brought something to show you." She pulled out a woman's magazine and flicked the pages.

"Here it is." She slid it across to Sonia, "knew you'd love these, they're so . . . you!"

"Oh, I do!" said Sonia. She leaned over the fashion spread titled *Big and Beautiful,* depicting large women in dresses like the one she had on.

"Mentions the retailers and everything, take it with you if you want."

"Can I? Sure you're finished with it?"

"Except the horoscopes. Can you read Leo for me?"

When Sonia buried her head in the magazine, Annie was left looking directly at Atkins's clerk. Oh Christ, he'd noticed her, and now he was leaning forward to say something to his boss.

Sonia read slowly. "You have arrived at a crossroads and will have a number of important decisions to make. Lucky in love, special day Friday."

"Wonder what's special about Friday?" said Annie. She grabbed the magazine. "Okay, what's yours?"

"Aquarius."

"January?" reeled off Annie, who'd spent most of last night studying horoscope dates. "What date?"

"Twenty-seventh."

Bingo.

Annie read Sonia's horoscope: "Mr. Right could be a phone call away. Romance often blossoms where you least expect it. Watch your finances. Special day Tuesday."

"Wonder what that's about?" Sonia looked excited.

The two men Annie had wanted to avoid rose from their table. Atkins straightened his tie and turned to look at her.

Annie's eyes darted straight back to Sonia. "Sounds like a man is on the cards after all," she said. "And as you've got to watch your finances, lunch is on me."

"I hope you don't mind me mentioning this, Annie," Sonia sounded apologetic when they were saying good-bye on the pavement. "One of the errand boys from the office told me you're in a spot of bother at the moment. All I wanted to say is, if you need someone to talk to or . . . anything, you know?"

"Thanks, Sonia, appreciate that. It's all a mix-up. Solicitor says we'll be fine. See you soon."

Annie hurried off down the road. She wished Sonia wasn't such a sweet girl. It felt uncomfortable stealing the identity of someone she was fond of. She was late for her meeting with Reg and Niko in the coffee bar near their house.

"Get what you needed?" Reg squeezed her hand when she slid in next to him.

"January. Twenty-seventh," Annie said proudly. "I already knew she was the same year as me."

"Good girl," Reg said. "Now I've been thinking, no way should we have photographs looking like ourselves."

"Definitely not," agreed Niko.

"So I've quit shaving," said Reg, stroking one week's growth. "And I'm not cutting my hair again for ages—oh yeah, and I'll probably wear glasses."

"What about me?" Annie looked at Reg, then Niko. "No way I'm cutting my hair."

"Definitely not," Reg said, giving her long mane an affectionate stroke. "Get a wig for the photo and wear it at the airport. Might come in handy later as well."

"I'll just pull mine back, makes me look totally different," Niko said. He demonstrated, flattening his dark, wavy mop with both hands and scrunching it at the back of his head.

"Looks almost intelligent, doesn't he!" Reg joked.

Then he told them about the measures he'd taken in case the passport office phoned to check their identity with a referee. Annie and Niko sat enthralled as Reg explained the ruse he'd set up that morning. He had spent the last couple of days searching the city for a small office space, and had found a room on the third floor of an old commercial block. The building also housed an insurance company and a charity organization for homeless children.

"I'll take it," he had told the owner when he saw six telephone lines around the skirting board. Apparently the previous tenant had operated a small real estate company and fitted multiple lines for his agents before he'd gone bust. Reg had signed a six-month lease and paid a month's rent in advance, then organized new numbers for three of the phone lines.

"Here they are." Reg lowered his voice as he opened his folder and slipped Annie and Niko a note with their personal numbers.

"Hang on, Reggie," said Annie. "Let's get this straight. We put these on our applications, somebody phones up Mr. Smith or Mrs. Jones or whomever we call our referees. So who answers?"

"We do," said Reg. "Niko and I can take shifts because we can be either of the men, but you'll have to be there all the time! We just have to remember which name goes with which number."

Annie and Niko weren't convinced that Reg's ploy was as foolproof as he thought it was. But they didn't have any better ideas, and the court date was looming. Reg drove them into the city and dropped them at the office with the keys. Then he found a parking spot and telephoned the three numbers from a phone box around the corner to check that the lines worked. They established which phone belonged to which person and put stickers on them so they wouldn't get confused.

"When I phoned, it didn't sound like an office," Reg told them when he returned. "It sounded like what it is, an empty room. We want a busy office, and that's what we'll give them." He pulled the small tape recorder he'd just bought out of its box. "Back in a sec," he said on his way out. Annie and Niko were intrigued.

Reg took the stairs three at a time to the floor below, and walked into the Coveright Insurance Company. The girl at reception was in the middle of a phone conversation and gave him an apologetic smile as he passed. He strode confidently into the large office, at least four times the size of the one he was renting upstairs. He counted eight secretaries as he felt around his pocket for the recorder and pressed the button. The women worked on their typewriters, phones rang, and clerks stalked the aisles with piles of documents, calling out instructions. Nobody noticed the only person who didn't work there until the receptionist caught up with him.

"Sorry to keep you waiting, sir, who was it you wanted to see?"

Reg groped in his pocket and turned off the tape recorder, introducing himself as the new tenant from upstairs. She did not ask his name so he didn't give it. He said he wanted to look into taking out insurance for his new company and would come back the following week when he had more time.

"Okay, wait till you hear this," he could barely contain his excitement when he got back to Annie and Niko.

He sunk between them on the floor and pulled out the tape recorder. He smiled, watching their faces as they listened to his recording of the busy office downstairs.

"That'll work," Niko said. "Genius."

Annie grinned. "It sounds so real, I'll be so disappointed if nobody calls!"

Now they were ready to put in their passport applications. They posted the forms and started their roster system the next day. From nine to five, five days a week, they became Mrs. Blake the legal secretary, Mr. Hobbs the architect, and Mr. Burton the encyclopedia salesman. Their schedule revolved around signing in at the police station twice daily and lounging on the floor of their bogus office with three telephones that never rang.

At 4:45 p.m. the following Friday, Annie and Niko were in a sea of empty crisp packets and drink cans on the floor of the office. Annie had just said, "don't think anyone's going to phone," when a shrill ring took them by surprise.

"It's mine," she yelled, grabbing the tape recorder and switching it on.

She placed it by the phone, cleared her throat, and picked up the receiver.

"Good afternoon. Blake Legals, Mrs. Blake here," she said with a condescending tone that forced Niko to look away for fear of laughing.

"Yes, I understand. Oh, he gave you my number, I see," she continued, while Niko paced the floor with his hands over his mouth.

"Yes, I've known Bruce for a long time. That's right, he's worked here in the past. Of course I can vouch for him, a most reliable young man. Yes, my pleasure. You have a good evening as well. Good-bye."

Niko burst into laughter when Annie replaced the receiver.

At five o' clock they locked the office and hurried back to the house to tell Reg someone had called to check him out.

"I reckon the passports will come in the next couple of days," he said, "but we'd better keep the roster going next week just in case anyone else phones."

No one else did phone. And nobody saw Annie padding barefoot to the mailbox one morning a few days later. She retrieved three identical packets and took them upstairs to her bedroom. Later that day she went to the office with Reg and Niko for the last time. They cleared the rubbish and tied the key to a piece of string, locked the door with it, then dangled it back through the letterbox. Annie guarded their new travel documents, storing all three in the zipped compartment of her suitcase in the top of her wardrobe.

They were due in court in ten days, but Bruce Pennington, Sonia Priestly, and James Brampton weren't planning to make an appearance.

CHAPTER 8

The great escape grew closer. Reg, Annie, and Niko arranged one last meeting to synchronize their plan. They met by the children's swings in a park uptown where Reg and Niko had often played as kids. The area was deserted, apart from two boys playing in a sandpit some way off.

"So whereabouts in Singapore?" asked Niko as he pushed the squeaking roundabout.

Reg and Annie jumped aboard, grabbing the bars to steady themselves. "There are two flights to Singapore through Melbourne," Reg announced. "Annie and I will take the morning flight; Annie will go on to Singapore and I'll hang around in Melbourne and take the later connection. You fly straight through on the morning flight the next day. We can't book anywhere to stay. Nothing should be traceable. I've been before, accommodation's never a problem."

"So where?" asked Niko, running with the roundabout as it built up speed.

"I'm not writing this down, Niko, you've got to start storing stuff in your head. When you get there just find somewhere to stay and lay low. And don't bloody forget that they're two and a half hours behind us. We'll meet you on Friday, at midday, main entrance of the Atlantis Hotel. Coleman Street. Don't worry if we're not there, just wait. Now repeat it all back so I know you've got it."

"Atlantis Hotel, Coleman Street," said Niko, breathless as he raced. "Friday at twelve," he added, jumping on beside them.

"So we're going to have to look like our passport photos even when we book our flights?" said Annie.

"Of course," said Reg, "but then we don't become our new selves again until we go."

"Who is writing the letter to the others?" asked Niko as they started to slow down.

Annie looked at Reg. "I think Niko should do it. Lara would appreciate that," she said.

"Niko then. We get our tickets sorted tomorrow at the latest," said Reg. "Then we're off. Think of the alternative—I know which I'd prefer."

Reg had suggested to Annie that they spend time alone with their respective parents. She agreed, but only out of a sense of duty. Her relationship with her mother had always been cold. She definitely wouldn't let on about leaving the country. Reg said he couldn't possibly go without telling his mum and dad he was leaving—he had no qualms about their loyalty, would stake his life on it.

On Sunday morning, Annie walked the path of the neat, detached federation house she'd called home for most of her childhood. She hated the familiar ding-dong of the bell, and when the door opened, she wished she were somewhere else. Mrs. Hayes was a small, frail woman with powdery skin, a thin, lipsticked mouth, and a neat, salt-and-pepper hairdo.

"You'd better come in," she muttered. She cast a nervous eye up the street before shutting it out. "Everybody around here knows you're up in court soon," she complained.

Mrs. Hayes sat primly in the armchair by the mantelpiece with her hands clasped. Annie threw her bag onto the sofa opposite and sank impatiently next to it.

"It's difficult to hold my head up when I go out," her mother continued.

"Here we go again," thought Annie. She fiddled with the hair behind her ear and stared blankly while her mother grumbled about how news of the drug syndicate had spread "like wildfire" through the neighborhood.

"You don't seem to realize how your actions affect me, Annie. You've never learnt . . ."

"Learnt what?"

"Learnt that whatever decisions you make . . . you don't stop to think about the . . . the consequences!" wailed Mrs. Hayes.

The silence was quantified by the ticking of the clock on the mantelpiece.

"You know your trouble, Mum?" Annie said accusingly. "You're too worried about what other people think."

"Someone's got to worry, because you never do!" said her teary mother. "I don't want to fight with you, Annie, but I don't understand what you see in that Spiers fellow. He's got you into all this trouble. You were a good girl before you met him."

"Where did you get that from?" Annie retorted as her mother hurried into the kitchen, "I've never been your good girl!"

Then the familiar sounds: tap run, kettle filled and flicked on, cutlery rattling, then . . . wait for it . . . the big, despairing sigh. And familiar things: photographs on the dresser, dusted every week; the sandy hair and pale green eyes of the cheerful young man in naval uniform next to the grade-eight school photo—all freckles and missing teeth. Droplets of time—photographs were like frozen droplets of time. This room was frozen in time. The net curtains her mother used as camouflage to spy on the neighbors; cushions embroidered with Australian wildflowers; and the large, porcelain spaniel in the center of the coffee table that Annie found hideous.

The kettle rattled as it built up steam. Annie crept quietly upstairs. The door to her old bedroom creaked when she turned the handle. The same checkered bedspread, and the little desk where she never did her homework. A line of stuffed toys: two rabbits, a panda, and a one-eyed, winking kangaroo. They were missing the koala, Oscar, the only one she'd taken with her when she left home. Oscar kindled memories of a faraway day. The day her dad brought it home and nestled it in her arms. His deep, comforting voice: "Koala will look after you."

She peered through the curtains at the lonely street below. Would she ever be able to visit this place without a heavy heart?

"No tea for me, I can't stay," she told her mother in the kitchen. "Don't feel so good."

"There you go again, running away when things get uncomfortable."

"It's not that," Annie snapped. "I'm not well."

"I'm sure you're not; I wouldn't feel well if I had to go to court. I won't be going."

"No surprises there," said Annie. She turned and opened the back door. "I'll be seeing you."

"But not for a very long time," she thought as she closed it.

✈ ✈ ✈

Reg burst through the backdoor of the house where he was raised. It led straight into the kitchen. When he was a boy, he was convinced his mum slept there because she always seemed to be hovering over the sink, the oven, or the table. Always on hand with the Band-Aids when he fell off his bike or got into a scrap with the street boys.

"Reggie, you must have smelt the cake coming out of the oven," Mrs. Spiers beamed as he bustled in and planted a kiss on her cheek.

"Where's the old fellow?"

"Asleep," his mum told him. "Have some tea and cake, and then wake him."

The smell of vanilla and cinnamon permeated the cluttered space. Reg listened to the birds through the open window, smiling as he ate. His mother was a portly woman with a kind smile who had given Reg his blue twinkling eyes. She chatted while she busied herself washing the baking utensils.

"Mum, I've got to go away for a while," Reg said later when he found the right moment.

"D'you think that's a good idea, son?" she asked thoughtfully. "Didn't you say you were going to sort out all your court business soon?"

"I'll see to that when I get back," said Reg, making his way to the front room.

Reg senior, weary from years of working in the factory down the road, nodded off in front of the television most Sunday afternoons. Reg turned the sound down to get his father's attention.

Reg senior, a slim man with a well-worn face and a good head of hair, opened one eye. A smile crept onto his lips.

"I bet that's my boy, Reggie," he muttered with quiet pleasure. "You didn't forget your old dad?"

"Howdy, Pa." Reg patted his shoulder and handed him a bottle. "Your favorite tipple, and I don't mind having one with you."

His dad was a man of few words; he didn't have to talk to enjoy spending time with his boy. Reg stayed silent until they were sipping their second whisky in the fading light.

"I'm going away, Dad." Reg's voice was sad as he looked into his father's eyes. "I haven't hurt anybody, but I have to go. They're running us out of the country, want to put me and Annie in jail."

"How d'you know that lad?"

"Solicitor has said—it will definitely be prison."

"Christ! It must have been bad . . . what you did?"

"Not as bad as they're making out, Dad."

"Think this through carefully, son, no rash decisions. It'll all work out in the end," Mr. Spiers said quietly. "Mum and I will still be here when it does."

CHAPTER 9

On Wednesday night, Niko sprawled across his bed and glanced at the little clock on the side table. Midnight. He was the only one in the house still awake, and disparate thoughts weighed heavily in the silence of his room. Plagued with uncertainty, he tried to piece together a farewell letter. He wanted to say only a few things, but they were so damn elusive. God, this was hard! Lara had cried when he'd told her he was leaving, but she did say she understood why. What about Ted and Cheryl? How could words on a page make things better for them? They were owed more. What would they feel? Betrayed? Abandoned? Perhaps he would never know.

He ripped up his first two attempts. He checked his third draft and couldn't see how to improve it; this was the one he would leave:

> *Dear Ted, Cheryl, and Lara,*
>
> *This isn't easy but it's my job to write it so I'd better get on with it. First, I want to tell you, Lara, that you've always been a fantastic sister. I didn't think what I'm doing was the right thing for you and I knew you'd want to come with me. Don't think you're going to spend much time inside and you'll be out before you know it. This'll blow over in a few years. Please smooth it over with Mum and Dad for me. Don't be angry with me, with any of us. Perhaps I'm being a coward, but you've heard the stories about what happens to "WOG" boys like me in jail.*
>
> *We didn't want to involve you three anymore than you are already. Ted and Cheryl, you've been really*

good mates. We never intended to leave you out of this. Reg and Annie were going on their own, and I found out and wanted to take my chances with them. We know you'll think we're crazy. We probably are. We all send our love and know we'll see you again one day. Just don't know where or when.

Destroy this immediately after you've read it. Take care and good luck with the case. In some ways I wish I were staying instead of facing the unknown.

Love from us all,

Niko, Reggie, and Annie xxx

The next morning, Reg stuck his head into the kitchen to tell Ted, Cheryl, and Lara that he and Annie would make their own way to the police station for bail duty.

"We're going into town straight after," he added casually.

"Niko, come on bro, we're gonna be late!" Lara bellowed up the stairs.

Niko pattered down. "See you soon," his knowing eyes met Reg's as he trailed the others out the front door.

"Time to move, Annie," Reg called ahead as he raced upstairs.

He paced the brightly colored bedroom that they'd had so much fun painting. His gaze wandered along his shelf of athletic trophies, then he opened the top drawer of the dresser below. It was empty, save one bulky envelope containing twelve thousand Australian dollars.

"Where though?" he asked as he handed it to Annie.

Her eyes darted nervously over their luggage—one duffle bag and two backpacks. She quickly retrieved Oscar the koala from the duffle bag, unzipped its back, pulled out her Pink Panther T-shirt, and stuffed the envelope into the bottom of the space where she usually kept pajamas.

"Nice one," smiled Reg, as Annie crammed her T-shirt back into the koala and zipped it up.

She squeezed it into her backpack, alongside her wig and travel documents, and then stood for a moment, staring at the three pieces of luggage. The sum total of everything they were taking into their new life didn't look like much. Suddenly, the enormity of what they were doing dawned on her; she looked for a distraction. She reminded herself that complacency had landed them in this mess, and she asked Reg to help her do a last-minute check for incriminating evidence.

"It's clean," he assured her after he'd looked under the bed. "Now let's get going."

They carted their baggage downstairs and out to the car. Reg piled it into the boot while Annie took her last look at the old house where she'd been so happy. It really was the most beautiful place she'd ever lived in. The soft blue, weather-beaten boards, the quirky windows, the way it nestled between the trees. The memories. She was still picturing the house as they drove down the road to the police headquarters and saw their friends walking down the station steps.

"No, don't," said Reg, as Annie made to get out of the car to greet them. He placed his hand firmly on her knee. "Let's just remember them like this," he choked.

Annie blinked back tears as they watched in silence. Ted took the steps two at a time, looking happier than he had for weeks. The girls straggled behind; wistful little Lara, Cheryl ruffling Niko's hair before he leapt down the steps to his Ford Corsair. He was the only one who'd noticed Reg's green Holden parked along the street. When he chauffeured the others past them, he glanced Reg and Annie's way, and Cheryl's familiar laughter fluttered through their open window.

After they'd signed in with the duty officer, Reg and Annie got on the road. Instead of driving their usual route, they took the motorway and headed for the airport.

"This feels like a dream," muttered Annie, as Reg turned into Sir Donald Bradman Drive.

"No dream. It's real, all right." He kept his eyes on the road, not wanting her to sense his apprehension.

"We're doing the right thing, aren't we, Reggie?" she asked, in a quiet, sober voice.

Reg steered them into an undercover parking space near the

departures terminal. He switched off the ignition, sighed, and turned to her.

"There's never any guarantees in life, ever. It's about choices. This time we're choosing freedom."

Annie pursed her mouth. Reg cupped her face in his hands and softly kissed it. "I wouldn't be able to do that if I was locked up, would I?" he smiled. "Right, Mrs. Sonia, or whatever your name is. Time to get in character."

Annie pulled her backpack onto her knees and reached into one of the compartments. She passed Reg the square dark-rimmed glasses he sported in his passport photo. She helped him comb his wispy collar-length blond hair forward. "Christ," she said when he was done. "Gonna take a while to get used to those specs!"

"Your turn," said Reg. He smirked as he watched her pull on the dark curly wig. She made several attempts to tuck willful strands of her own hair out of sight. The new hairdo seemed ratty and untidy. She studied it in the car mirror and tried to tame it into a more sophisticated look.

"Dark and interesting, but I do prefer my sandy girl," joked Reg. "But I'll have to do without her for a while, she's staying in Adelaide. Sonia and Bruce, Bruce and Sonia. Right?"

"Right," said Sonia.

Bruce opened the boot. When he hauled his duffle bag onto the ground, he remembered it was the same bag he'd brought back from England in the box. He smiled to himself; one hell of a faithful bag!

He slammed the trunk shut and jangled the keys above his head. "What the fuck am I gonna do with these?" He hadn't thought about them until now.

A woman in a headscarf suddenly climbed out of the car next to him. "There's no point in taking them with us, car's not likely to be here when we get back," said Sonia.

The woman looked straight at her, then hurried away.

"Be a pretty expensive parking ticket," Reg mused, throwing the keys onto the driver's seat and closing the door.

They suddenly dissolved into fits of nervous laughter. "Right,

I'm done," Sonia finally spluttered. "Now lead me to the plane."

They carried their luggage into the departures hall and took turns using the toilet while the other guarded the big duffle bag. "Definitely missing my mysterious redhead," Bruce whispered as they queued to check in.

The clerk glanced a smile their way, attached a ticket to the duffle, and returned their passports. "Thank you, Mr. Pennington."

"Almost there," Bruce whispered after they'd breezed through security and were walking down the long corridor to the passport control section. "I'm ordering a bottle of champagne once we're up," he said.

"Don't Re- . . . I mean Bruce," Sonia had a sudden need to swallow hard. "Nothing to draw attention."

The elderly official at the desk flicked the early pages of Sonia's passport. He turned his head to cough and stamped a clean page, giving her a lazy smile as he handed it back. Bruce's passport was already on the desk.

"G'day," he said warmly.

The official located his photo and shot him a cursory glance.

"G'day, Mr. Pennington." He slid the passport back.

Bruce took Sonia's hand as they walked to the gate. Their flight was already boarding. The young woman at the barrier checked their passes and nodded at their open passports.

"Have a good flight, Mr. Pennington." She flashed Bruce a big smile.

The pair drifted onward in a silent fog and then waited in line to board the plane. Bruce was thinking that nothing would stop them now. Nothing, short of a big burly fed saying, "Excuse me, sir, we have reason to believe that you are not who you say you are."

Bruce and Sonia were among the last passengers to take their seats. It was cool in the cabin. Sonia wished she hadn't let Bruce put her jacket in the overhead locker. The soft whirring of the engines built momentum as the dapper steward started his safety demonstration. The plane taxied down the runway. Then it turned and built up speed.

"Next stop Melbourne, then I'll see you in Singapore baby," Bruce smiled and squeezed her hand.

She wanted to share his relief and didn't object when he ordered a bottle of champagne.

"Just like when we were doing the runs," he assured her. "A young couple on a romantic trip."

Then he listed all the places they would go, and all the things they would see. But as she sipped the bubbles and tried to share his excitement, all she could think about were Cheryl and Ted and Lara. And about Niko, what if he got cold feet? And then her mother's words: *There you go again, running away when things get uncomfortable . . .*

CHAPTER 10

Niko thought Singapore had a smell unlike any city he knew. A sweet mustiness, an essence of durian fruit, spices, and who knows what. Not wafting but hanging, infused with engine fumes and spun into the thick warm air. He sat on his bag near the entrance to the Atlantis Hotel at twenty minutes past noon. The Friday traffic streamed down Coleman Street. Excited voices, beeping horns, and tinkling bells swirled. And cars, taxis, bicycles, and rickety old buses, plastered with the toothpaste smiles of young black-haired Singaporeans.

Niko was intrigued by this vibrant city, the suited Chinese executives and giggling street girls, the toothless smiles of the old rickshaw men. His interest was spoiled by niggling doubts. He'd been waiting for ages, anxiously wondering if his rendezvous would happen. What if Reg and Annie hadn't made it, had been taken into custody? He'd just checked his watch again when a taxi wound out of its lane and pulled into the curb beside him.

"Niko, Niko, get in," Annie yelled from the window.

Niko's face softened with relief. He threw his bag onto the floor of the car and sunk into the passenger seat. "Am I pleased to see you!" he beamed at Reg and Annie.

The driver swerved into the traffic, and the trio laughed as they were thrown back in their seats.

"Not good place to stop. Where now?" The driver's disapproving face appeared in the rearview mirror.

"Back to Changi, where you picked us up," Reg directed.

Half an hour later, they were dropped in the one-street village in the northeastern part of the island. They wandered along the narrow pavement past Singh, the Indian tailor, and Malay and Chinese traders who gossiped over glasses of thick black coffee. They felt conspicuous as they weaved their way through the hawker stalls, children and animals, pungent spices, brightly colored silks and shoes, electronics, and every type of inflatable toy.

"I'm starving," Reg insisted. "We can't let Niko leave Singapore without eating chili crab."

"Yeah, we had it last night as well," said Annie as she squeezed Niko's arm.

They sat at the makeshift roadside stall. Chan and Eng served them a chili crab banquet to remember. The red, spiced claws didn't give up their sweet white meat easily. They dipped crusty bread into the piquant sauce, washing it down with cold beer. It all felt good, lighthearted. Friends having a good time, not India-bound fugitives who didn't know what the hell they were going to do when they got there.

After the meal, they sat cross-legged in a treed area overlooking a moonlit beach. Annie was horrified when Reg told them what he'd brought with him, but she still couldn't resist smoking it. She took a long puff and watched her smoke rings fragment into the still dark night.

"We could wait a couple of years, then slip quietly back into Oz on our new passports," she said later.

"We're probably on that international police list by now. What's it called?" Niko asked.

"Interpol," said Reg. "But the thing is, they don't know who they're looking for yet. They will once they check all the departing-passenger lists."

"How'll they do that?" asked Niko.

"Get the lists from the airline," said Reg. He passed the smoke back to Annie.

"They might contact the family of everyone who left Adelaide first," Annie suggested. "Then Sydney, Melbourne, and Brisbane, probably. It's not gonna take them long to find we've skipped on dud passports."

Later they sat in silence, consumed by their own thoughts and the lazy rhythm of the sea.

Annie said, "Niko, what's up? You're so quiet."

Niko lay back with his hands behind his head. "I just can't stop thinking about what sentences the others got today," he admitted. "And how Lara is coping."

"And Cheryl and Ted. Shit! I feel terrible. I've been so tied up in our own plans that I'd totally forgotten," said Annie. Her eyes misted over.

"Me too," said Reg. "We're gonna miss 'em, but tomorrow we're getting on that plane and then we find somewhere to lay low. I mean really low. We'll find you at the airport on the agreed day, Niko. Then we look for somewhere to stay. Just remember—we're three friends on an adventure."

"Yeah, but we've got to watch ourselves," Annie said. "I still can't get it into my head that we're Bruce, Sonia, and James."

"You two could pass for a Bruce and a Sonia, but how d'you think I feel, a Greek boy called James?" Niko smirked.

"Presumably we're just going to bed down here?" said Annie. She pulled out a jumper and made a pillow on the sand. "It's going to be a long day tomorrow."

✈ ✈ ✈

In the morning, they washed in a grubby toilet at the back of a cafe in the village, then took a cab to the airport and implemented their plan to throw the authorities off their trail. Reg and Annie left Niko at the airport, slipped easily through passport control, and flew to Madras, where they spent the night in a local hotel. The next day they boarded a plane to Mysore, disembarked, and immediately purchased a ticket for a night flight to Trivandrum. When they landed in Bombay three days later, Reg warned Annie to be on her guard while they killed time at the airport.

He went to change some Australian cash into rupees. Annie found a *Sydney Morning Herald* in the airport shop and scoured it for a mention of the trial in Adelaide. A face pictured on page two grabbed her attention. Shock and fear pulsed through her.

It was Reg's face, and beneath it was a big, bold headline: "TOP ATHLETE SKIPS BAIL ON DRUG CHARGES."

There followed the details of the criminal syndicate and the date of Reg and Annie's last check-in at the police station in Adelaide. Spiers had absconded with two accomplices from the syndicate, Niko Alexopoulos and Annie Hayes. The three accused had failed to appear in the Supreme Court on October 21, and bench warrants had been issued for their arrest. The article also outlined the trial. Supreme Court Judge Donald DeWinter had sentenced Cheryl Bate to six years in jail. The case against Lara Alexopoulos was withdrawn. Annie thanked God for that small mercy. Then her mouth turned dry as she tried to take in the last paragraph:

> *Mr. Ted Bate looked pale as he stood for sentencing. His solicitor and court officials had to assist him when he became unsteady or4n his feet, as Judge DeWinter sentenced him to fourteen years in prison. The convicted man's father, Mr. Albert Bate, had travelled all the way from England for the case. After his son was sentenced, Mr. Bate refused to talk to reporters and was clearly distressed. Several family members of those convicted were in tears and . . .*

Annie hastily closed the paper and looked around feverishly to see if anyone was watching her. By the time she caught up with Reg, she'd resolved not to say anything for the moment. She couldn't stop thinking about Ted.

Reg told her Niko's plane had already landed, and they made their way back to the arrivals lounge. They stood at the back of the crowd, planning to follow Niko to the exit. He was among the first passengers to disembark. He stepped up to the immigration desk and handed his open passport to the uniformed official. The officer's alert eyes darted between the photo and Niko's face.

"Thank you, sir." The official snapped the passport closed and returned it.

Niko felt almost lighthearted when he collected his bag and walked into the arrivals hall. His relief was short-lived.

"Niko," a voice that didn't belong to Reg or Annie bellowed over the crowd.

He spun around, searching the sea of faces. Then a young man hurried past him into outstretched arms at the barrier. Other men were called Niko, but his face turned white.

✈ ✈ ✈

The three absconders sat at a little cafe in the Muslim quarter off Mohammed Ali Road under a sheet of tarpaulin nailed to the side of a market stall. They'd celebrated safely reaching Bombay with one night in a plush hotel, but now they needed to find somewhere more permanent that wouldn't drain their funds. They hardly noticed their bitter coffee or the rain leaking onto their backpacks—they were too preoccupied with the street life: children and old men with cows, paupers, flower sellers and traders, the humdrum and the spectacle of downtown Bombay.

The rain clouds had cleared, and they took a cab up Maulana Azad Road. Their driver studied an address on a tatty sheet of paper Reg had been given by the cafe proprietor. Car horns honked, and people and animals wound their way along the road ahead as the driver cursed the route.

About twenty minutes later, the driver pulled curbside. "This one," he pointed up a dingy alleyway. "Up there, MS Ali Road, Capricorn Hotel over the market."

"Told you it wouldn't be the Ritz," Reg said when he saw the expression on Annie's face as they lugged their bags up the narrow, uneven lane.

"This is the part we didn't see when we were tourists," Niko muttered as they stepped around a group of giggling children, straight into the path of two squawking chickens.

CHAPTER 11

The fugitives' hideout consisted of two rooms and a bathroom on the first floor of the Capricorn, a run-down budget hotel above a market fronted by a spice trader's shop. The suburb bordered one of the major vice areas of Bombay, Kamathipura, which was rife with crime, drugs, and prostitution. Three generations of the same family lived together in the ramshackle terraces and over-crowded enclaves of the neighborhood.

The Capricorn overlooked a busy thoroughfare. During the hotter months, traffic noise and stench wafted through the open windows. Music wailed in the warm, musty air around the clock—occasionally it was the haunting strings of the sitar, but more often it was the screeching ballad of a jilted lover. It mingled with the barking of mangy dogs and the crying of babies. Reg, Annie, and Niko couldn't interpret the wild, passionate babbling, but they could guess when children were being reprimanded, ar-guments won and lost, hearts broken. They also learned which neighbors were safe to talk to and those best avoided.

The dilapidated spice shop below the hotel was run by Bhag-wat, a frail little bearded man in a white Gandhi cap with gold fillings that glinted behind gray whiskers. Reg was convinced the shop was a front for "other activities." Bhagwat offered a few other necessities besides spice, but they came only in ones: one packet of washing powder, one packet of biscuits, one packet of several kinds of tea. He never seemed to be selling spices, although he had a steady flow of regular customers, and Reg wondered what exactly they were buying.

An old beggar woman everyone called Bethra camped outside the shop. She spent whole days sitting cross-legged in a doorway, rearranging the faded silk draped around her head that revealed only her watchful eyes. Sometimes she wailed at the street kids as they scampered past or at the feral cats that upset her bizarre collection of cups and stones on a tray beside her wizened frame.

"I don't think I've ever seen Bethra stand up," Annie said one day as she peered at the street below. "She's sitting in the same place every night when we go to bed and is still there in the morning. Does she ever sleep?"

"No idea," said Reg. He pondered for a moment. "Perhaps some things are intended to be a mystery."

The entrance to their hotel was located at the side of the market. It was a small hallway with a staircase and a counter on the left where the manager sat. He was a man of few words. His eyes were continually glued to a television screen with a terrible picture and nonstop interference, and he seldom looked up when anyone came or went. The newcomers' accommodation was up one flight of stairs. The only window was in the lounge, and they always left it open because there were no fans. When it was too hot to sleep, they would drag their mattresses underneath it. There was no kitchen, just an old fridge in the corner. The plumbing groaned in the squalid little bathroom. Nobody was game to fill the rusty tin bath. There was rarely hot water, and the toilet needed three flushes before anything went down. They all missed the comfort of their home in Adelaide, but especially Annie.

She hung a butterfly wind chime in the corner of the window. It caught the softest breeze and sounded like distant cowbells. Late afternoon sun fanned shafts of color across the walls, and Niko would often gaze soulfully, caught in the chime's hypnotic sway. Annie always knew when Niko was thinking about his sister, and after a few weeks she worried that he was becoming withdrawn.

"At least Lara's not inside," she tried to cheer him. "It's Ted I worry about."

"Fourteen fucking years," Reg reminded him. "We would've got the same. We did the right thing. We did."

"Probably," said Niko. But he didn't look very sure.

Now a new problem was looming: their money was dwindling.

"We're gonna have to start earning," warned Niko. "At this rate, I'd say we've only got enough left for a couple of months."

Annie hoped that Niko would be happier when they improved their situation. There was nowhere to cook, and they awoke each morning eager to leave their small, noisy rooms. Their days were spent exploring the city. They preferred to take the bus downtown; if none came, they'd take one of the many black and yellow taxis. It was easy to buy hash from the locals who plied their trade in the shadowy alleyways, but Reg was adamant that they couldn't afford to keep getting it. Half their funds had been dissipated by airfares, and their rent and food would soon take care of what was left.

Reg was on the lookout for a large supply of dope he could offload for cash, so they started hanging around bars and cafes frequented by likely looking young foreigners who might be interested in doing business. Reg said he would have no trouble buying, but he needed a good distribution channel. The flatmates were mindful of concealing their true identities when they chatted with other diners and drinkers. They needed to sniff out an opportunity. It didn't take them long to find one; his name was Kurt Danson.

Reg was sitting in a crowded little bar waiting for Annie and Niko when a tall, dark, young, ponytailed hippie with a picture of Che Guevara on his T-shirt sat down at the adjoining table. He struck up a conversation with Reg about other drinking holes he knew and the best places to eat.

He stretched his arm out to shake Reg's hand. "By the way, Kurt Danson," the newcomer spoke in a soft, American accent.

"Bruce." Reg had to check himself. "Bruce Pennington."

Reg was cautious at first—for all he knew, this guy was a cop. He was certainly a lot smoother than the dropouts back home, but by the time Annie and Niko joined them Reg was convinced Kurt Danson was who he said he was: an American student taking time out to travel. Why not invite him back to their place for a smoke? Annie and Niko were always saying how much they missed having friends around.

Kurt was soon a regular visitor at their hotel. Apparently he was studying political science at some obscure university in America. His parents had agreed to finance his travels before he took his comprehensive exams. He was staying in a hotel a few blocks away from the Capricorn. It all sounded feasible.

Kurt never seemed short of cash. Some evenings when he stayed late and they were all stoned, he would insist on buying everyone a curry. The four of them would walk two blocks along poky terraces and alleyways to a little eating house tucked into the side of a smelly tire shop. The cafe was open all hours, selling the best chicken *biryani* on any menu. One evening Reg tried to eke out more information about their new American friend.

"So, Kurt, not doing any work while you're here?"

"Nah, bit like you three—an extended holiday. Only need enough to get by, so I do a bit of tinkering at my Indian friend's boatyard." Kurt straightened his ponytail and swigged the remains of his can. "Help out here and there, saving the hard work for when I get back to Laguna Beach. Mind you . . . ," he shot Reg a knowing look, "I'd put myself out for something really worthwhile."

Annie and Niko were intrigued. Why would Kurt bother with work? He always seemed to have money, and weeks on end at a hotel didn't come cheap. Reg thought this strange as well, but his mind raced ahead. This guy was obviously up for making some decent cash, and what he said about having access to a boatyard was very interesting.

Niko was more cautious. Why didn't the American ever invite them to his hotel? Niko wasn't buying Kurt's story; it just didn't add up. He reckoned they all had a lot in common. Niko was convinced Kurt Danson was on the run.

CHAPTER 12

"What d'you mean, you're not coming with us!" Reg stared at Niko in disbelief.

"It's the crossroads thing," said Niko. "Getting to a point in the road that forks and having to choose."

"We'll still have choices, but we have to make money or we'll bloody starve!"

"Yeah, but not this way, this feels like madness. A mad train I wanna get off before it's too late."

"We'll be fine," insisted Reg. "Just gotta stick a box on the bottom of a boat. It's hardly a big operation."

"Seriously, mate," Niko held Reg's gaze. "We've been here before. Any doubts, call it off."

"It's too good an opportunity, a small job for a big reward."

"Yeah, but. . ." Niko paused. He recognized the resolute look in Reg's eyes and knew that nothing he could say would change his friend's mind.

Niko's voice softened with regret. "I'm sorry mate, I really am," he said. "I just want out."

"But why now?" Reg demanded. "The day we're going!"

"Because . . . because we are going. I only decided definitely last night."

"Is it Kurt? I know you've had your reservations, but this wouldn't work without him. The boatyard and everything."

Niko leaned forward, buried his head in his hands, and rubbed his eyes. He could hear Kurt and Annie in the next room so he sat up and moved his chair closer to Reg.

"What I said in the letter to the others about taking my

chances, that's how I'm feeling now," he said quietly. "The truth is, I don't want to go to Port Cochin. I'll find something. I can do restaurant work anywhere. I'll be all right."

"Mate, if it's Kurt you're worried about I'll just tell him we've changed our minds and we're not going," Reg whispered in desperation. "We could just stay here."

"Look, it's not just him, okay? I didn't want him to move in with us, but that's not the whole reason. I'm really sorry, Reggie, it's just . . . it's just time for me to move on."

Reg exhaled loudly. His eyes filled with disappointment. "That's a big call." He reflected for a moment. "Just do one thing, please." He looked into Niko's eyes. "Don't say anything to Annie until we leave. I'll never get her out of here if she knows you're not coming. She's already having second thoughts."

"You got it," said Niko. "Drop me on the outskirts."

He clenched Reg's palm and shook it.

"Gonna miss you, buddy," whispered Reg, just before Annie bustled in.

"It's all right for some blokes sitting around arm wrestling while their woman does all the packing," she said.

Kurt wandered in behind her. He took a bottle from the old fridge and poured a glass of orange soda. He looked even more like a bloodhound, with his long hair hanging loose.

"Everyone ready to hit the road?" asked Reg. He was still trying to digest Niko's bombshell.

"Yep," said Kurt. He tightened the belt on his jeans and sat on the floor to fasten his sandals.

"Okay, so the checklist of what's already in the car." Reg's voice was businesslike. "Two complete sets of diving gear; attachment brackets; drill; bag of screws—better be the right bloody screws! The torch and the container thing is by the front door."

"Did pretty damn well, didn't I, Brucie?" Kurt drawled, in his lazy Californian accent. "Everything on your list."

Kurt was pleased with how his last few days at the boatyard had panned out. He'd told the boss he'd been invited on a working weekend to help repair a boat. He could borrow whatever he needed as long as it was returned Monday morning. The sealable unit was a one-meter, flat, watertight case normally used for housing marine tools. Kurt had taken it to a garage and had it fitted with brackets. He wouldn't have to explain why at the boatyard because he had no intention of ever going back.

Annie stuffed a cardigan into the duffle.

"I'll carry it, Sonia," Niko volunteered. He hoisted the big bag over his shoulder.

"Thanks," Annie muttered. They traipsed onto the landing, and she closed the door for the last time.

The four conspirators stood stealthily at the top of the stairwell. Annie padded halfway down to check that the hotel manager hadn't started his morning shift. She signaled the others to follow her, relieved that the way was clear because they still owed two weeks' rent. Kurt came down next, lugging his oversized backpack. Although he was over six feet tall, he was slim and wiry and didn't have anything like Reg's solid muscular strength.

Reg carted the bulky metal container with its awkward brackets. When they were at the bottom of the stairs, Annie unlocked the main door, and the four absconders hurried with their luggage along the street. Annie hung back when she saw Bethra's wizened face in the doorway around the corner. On impulse, she softly brushed the worn silk of the old woman's headdress with her hand and thought she detected a glimmer of recognition in her milky eyes. Bethra's hand shook as she offered up a little translucent pink stone she'd been clutching.

"Thank you Bethra. Take care," Annie said, as she stuffed it into the pouch of her backpack. She thought it might be some kind of talisman and hoped it was a good omen. She hurried to catch up with the others.

Their rental car was parked outside the curry house that served the great chicken *biryani*. The tire shop next door was an agent for car rentals. The well-worn car was hardly luxurious, but it was cheap and drivable. Reg hoisted the heavy metal container into the boot and crammed their luggage around it. He made sure Niko's backpack went in last. Kurt was the designated map reader, so he climbed in the front passenger seat next to Reg.

"Port Cochin, here we come," he said as he took a thick rubber band off his wrist and pulled his hair back into a ponytail.

When they neared the outskirts of Bombay, Reg adjusted his rearview mirror so he could track the expression on Niko's face. As they turned onto the major road out of the city, Niko made eye contact and nodded. Reg pulled off the road near a fruit stall and switched off the engine.

"Listen, you two," Reg told Kurt and Annie. "This is as far as James is going."

"What?" burst out Annie.

"Only decided this morning," said Niko. "Know it's sudden."

He felt a strong sense of déjà vu, having to explain reasons for leaving. Feeling guilty that he hadn't said anything earlier. He didn't give a stuff about Kurt, but Reg and Annie were like family.

He squeezed Annie's hand. "Come and help me with my stuff."

"Good luck," was all Kurt said before burying his head back in the map as Niko got out of the car.

Annie confronted Reg and Niko by the back of the car.

"What the hell's going on?" Her green eyes smarted with anger and confusion.

"I was hoping he might change his mind," said Reg.

"But why?" said Annie, crying now.

"Annie, Annie," said Reg, quietly so Kurt wouldn't hear. He put his arm around her. "Don't make it any harder for him."

The trio stood motionless, buffeted by wind and the sound of engines and horns in the morning traffic. Drivers stared at the little group locked together on the side of the road.

"Sorry how this all turned out," Reg said.

"We'll see you back in Oz, won't we, Niko?" Annie tried to be brave.

Niko's black wavy hair blew across his face. "Course you will. Take care, my friends."

He quickly kissed Annie's cheek and patted Reg's arm. He heaved his bag onto his back. As he started walking in the direction of the bus depot, he raised one arm as a final farewell, but he didn't look back.

When they were on the road again, Annie felt miserable on

her own in the back. Reg and Kurt debated their route. Reg took the wrong turn a couple of times and had to backtrack. Annie thought about Niko, Cheryl, Ted, and Lara and the life they'd left behind in Adelaide.

After they stopped for food, Kurt and Annie were lulled to sleep by the drone of the car. Reg was alone with his thoughts on the southbound road to Cochin. It was hot and dusty. The road curled through towns and villages. Sometimes it straightened along desolate stretches where solitary figures and small groups carried vessels on their heads as they walked through the haze.

Reg played and replayed his agenda for the following day. This plan had better work . . . It was obviously the reason Niko had split. Reg wouldn't let Annie know that, lest she try to talk him out of it. It was all right for Niko; he could be a waiter. You didn't need to speak much Indian to be a waiter, but what the hell was he supposed to do? Everything would be fine in a couple of weeks: a steady income and the chance to save some cash.

As the sun sunk behind the horizon, the light played tricks on his eyes. He wound down his window and inhaled a lungful of air to stay awake. When they reached the outskirts of Cochin, he estimated they had driven over six hundred miles. He badly wanted to sleep.

"Right, this'll do," he said wearily as he swerved off the road into the small forecourt of the Lotus Garden Hotel.

"We're going to draw attention to ourselves if one of us has all the gear in his room," he told Kurt and Annie. "I don't want to leave it in the car, so Kurt, you take the diving stuff and tools and we'll take the rest. I'll meet you here tomorrow afternoon, at two."

✈ ✈ ✈

The luxurious hotel room was a welcome change from their hovel in Bombay. Reg slept late the next day, and when Annie told him it was half past twelve, he hurried into the shower and asked her to get them some food. He assured her that money wasn't going to be a problem for much longer.

"We'll soon be loaded," he insisted.

Emboldened by his optimism, she phoned room service and ordered beef curry, spaghetti bolognese, and a bottle of the hotel's best red wine.

Reg knew Annie was nervous about his upcoming venture. Before he left, he told her to keep busy and get her mind off it. "Have some fun while you're here," he encouraged her. "Go for a walk, use the pool, chat with people, but only as Sonia. And order anything you want." He sounded confident. "I'll be back before morning," he grinned and blew her a kiss. "Just make sure you keep this door locked."

Kurt was waiting for him by the car. They drove across the bridge to beautiful, green Willingdon Island in Kerala and investigated the area to get their bearings. Reg was delighted when he found a small yard renting out rowing boats. It was near the bay where the main vessels were docked. His contact had told him the larger ships would be near the warehouses where the freight was stored. Smaller vessels would be on the outskirts of the dock.

They strolled confidently around the busy wharf trying to pass themselves off as boat enthusiasts. Chains clanged as they dangled from big forklift trucks and workers shouted along the dock. Containers and boxes swung and tilted in precarious mid-air movement between concrete and water, putting Reg in mind of other journeys. Then Kurt spotted their target.

"That's her." He nodded casually toward the *Murray*. "That's her, isn't it?"

"That's her all right," said Reg. He was relieved it wasn't a large ship; he estimated its length at around 150 feet. Kurt was surprised at how old it looked, and joked that they would be lucky if it got back to Australia without sinking.

The next stage of their plan was to rent a sturdy small boat and lie low until nightfall. Reg insisted it would have to be a rowing boat—although they would be a fair way from the dock, they couldn't risk drawing attention to a noisy motorboat. On the way back to the rental shed, they stopped at a little shop and bought lemonade and hot samosas. Kurt wanted beer, but Reg was adamant they avoid alcohol until they had something to celebrate.

"Water and alcohol don't mix unless you're on an inflatable raft in a pool. This little escapade might be tricky, so we're better off stone-cold sober."

The young, skinny attendant wasn't doing much business and was delighted to rent them a boat overnight. They chose the best of three, the only one that looked seaworthy. Kurt commented that it looked only marginally safer than the *Murray*. Reg ignored him; he was getting tired of the American's whining. That was probably another reason why Niko had bailed out; Kurt was getting on his nerves.

They pulled the boat along the stony cove a couple hundred feet from where the attendant sat, and then set up camp against the steep bank bordering a small car park. Reg studied the tall ledge of sandy earth behind them.

"If I'm right, we can haul all our gear down here," he told Kurt. "Yes, I am right," he announced when he spotted their vehicle. "The car's almost behind us."

They lay on hotel towels in the late afternoon sun, eating and listening to the chattering of two men casting their rods in the fading light. When the men had gone, a sudden breeze scurried their empty paper bags. Reg grabbed them. One crackled as he crumpled it up and buried it in the sand. He made a funnel at the end of the other and blew it up like a balloon.

Bang! He burst it with a slap. Just for something to do.

Kurt jerked upright. "God, you freaked me!"

Reg saw he was shaken.

"You're a nervous wreck," he said. "You're not losing your nerve, are you?"

"No way I'm taking all this stuff back to Bombay," Kurt said.

Silence cloaked the bay as they waited for nightfall.

Chapter 13

When it was dark, Kurt walked back to the shed to make sure the attendant was gone. Everything was quiet, so he climbed the ramp to the car park. The stony ground at the top crunched under his feet, and a light wind disturbed a pile of rubbish near some bushes. The flurry unsettled him as it rolled a discarded drink can and sent it clattering across the gravel. The other cars had gone. He unlocked the trunk and nervously checked in both directions before unloading the equipment.

"Here we go, Bruce," he called in an urgent whisper.

He lay on his stomach and carefully pushed two bulging bags down the ledge. The large silver metallic unit glistened in the moonlight as he edged it into Reg's hands.

"Gotcha," Reg confirmed.

Kurt clambered down to join him. They stripped off in the darkness and stuffed their clothes and car keys into one of the bags, and then hid it under a bushy ledge. The rubber suits squeaked as they pulled them on; then they stood and zipped themselves into them.

"If the *Murray* had been a bit closer, we could have forgotten about a boat and just swum to her," Reg noted.

"What with the tools and everything? You're joking, right?"

They waded into the water. The rippling tide slapped the dinghy.

"In," Reg ordered.

Kurt pulled down his goggles and clambered awkwardly into the stern. When the water reached Reg's shoulders, he hooked his leg over the gunnel and caught a glimpse of Kurt's anxious eyes, framed by the goggles and his tight black hood. Reg thought he looked absurd and failed to stifle a giggle. He was amused to be floundering in the water with a freaked-out Yank who looked like some weird, aquatic batman.

"Come *on*, man, what's so funny?" Kurt pleaded. "You're going to get us busted."

"I'm okay now." Reg inhaled deeply and climbed into the bows to row.

He had to reposition their kit before he could synchronize the oars. His second stroke sent the boat gliding through the water. Kurt sighed with relief. They could hear distant traffic as the boat glided stealthily along the shore. They cautiously edged around the point of the bay and saw the lights of Port Cochin.

"I'm gonna look for somewhere to tie her up," Reg said.

As they neared the docks, they heard distant voices, and Reg thought it was too dangerous to row any closer. They were near a high concrete jetty, lapped by water a couple of meters from the top.

"Where that pole is sticking up, right of that," Kurt hissed.

"Seen it," said Reg. "Keep your voice down."

He turned the boat toward the pole. Every stroke was getting harder, and he could feel the current in this part of the bay. He breathed deeply as he rowed the last few meters. The boat was bobbing at the foot of the jetty.

"I'll need five minutes," said Reg as he slumped back to rest. "You concentrate on tying us up."

Kurt quickly made a slipknot. He made several attempts at throwing it over the metal pole above his head. The rope finally hooked the target and the boat smacked the wall.

"We're gonna get in and out quickly," Reg whispered. Adrenaline was kicking in. He issued his instructions in a raspy voice. "We'll take the surface until we find her, then I go down to find the spot. Then we both go down and stick this baby on. You take the tools; I'll take the big one. If there's any lights we go down. Right?"

Kurt nodded, his eyes full of fear. Reg's heart pounded as they carefully lowered the metal unit into the water. It bobbed on the surface, buoyant. Reg balanced the bag of tools on top, and then slid over the gunnel next to it. Kurt followed with a splash. Reg led the way, holding the container by the brackets, his legs working like a frog. Kurt clutched the string bag of tools to his chest and swam in a one-armed breaststroke.

Locating the *Murray* didn't prove as easy as Reg had hoped. When they'd walked along the dock earlier he'd noted it was the third boat from the end. Now the third boat from the end looked like a container ship, definitely not the *Murray*. They hovered nervously in the dark sea, gulping air as they trod water and tried to orient themselves. They felt small and vulnerable, peering up the hulls of the mighty vessels amid strange sounds that tricked their senses. Then it dawned on Reg that one of the boats he'd seen at the end of the row had left. He signaled for Kurt to follow him. The current was pulling them in the opposite direction they wanted to swim. They were getting tired. Their limbs ached, and they felt as though they'd been wrestling water for hours. Then their energy returned because there she was, the *Murray*, standing at the end of the line. Reg's eyes lit as he gave Kurt a thumbs up.

They trod water a few minutes more to gain strength for the final assault. Reg was feeling confident again. He pointed at the water to indicate he was going down. Kurt fumbled the torch from the string bag and passed it over, and then took charge of the container. Reg plugged his mouthpiece between his teeth, and then allowed himself to sink slowly down beside the hull.

The murky underwater world teemed with debris and fish, engulfing him in new sensations. A beautiful mermaid with red billowing hair glided silently on her way. Something frightened her; it was Ted, clinging to the bars of some ghastly aquatic prison! His hair swirled, wide eyes glazed with terror. His agonized face morphed into a horrific, zombie-like creature. Then he was gone, and Reg was left with the sound of his own heart thumping.

He had to get a grip of himself—guilt was playing havoc with his imagination. He tried to focus. The scale of the *Murray*'s hull was daunting. He turned toward the stern. His torch beam stretched down the steel hull, illuminating the plates of the vast body of the ship. Then he saw an area he reckoned he could easily find again: slightly darker with a fuzzy texture that looked like rust. He swam to the surface, emerging into the dark night with a gush.

He pulled his mask to the side. "Let's do it!" he spluttered.

"There's things going on up here," Kurt whispered hoarsely. "I've had a problem staying in one place with this fucking current . . ."

Reg ignored him. He clasped the steel case with both arms and prepared to sink down the side of the ship with it. He waited for the pull of gravity, but instead of being taken down, he was being pulled up. Air in the container had made it buoyant. This had been useful for swimming with the tools, but now it was a major bloody obstacle.

Kurt peered helplessly through his goggles. Reg wrestled with the container before bringing it under control. He managed to maneuver so his whole weight was bearing down on it. The two divers used their combined weight to drag the bulky unit down the hull. Then, without warning, their charge broke free. It veered erratically skyward with Reg in hot pursuit.

Kurt followed. He emerged beside Reg, and the pair swiveled, frantically searching for the container.

"There it is," said Reg. The unit's shiny casing was drifting with the tide toward the dock.

Something caught their attention. It was the roar of a motorboat, ripping the water into a huge spray as it powered toward them. Shouts echoed around the huge ships. Kurt panicked and released the bag of tools. A searchlight blinded them as the gleaming steel vessel pinpointed them through the darkness. Three uniformed men towered over them from the side of the motorboat. Their faces shone, gloating in the moonlight.

"Fucking water police!" hissed Reg.

CHAPTER 14

"We bring, you stay," a big, blubber-faced officer called down.

"Nice one, nice fucking one," spat Kurt.

The motorboat drenched them as it revved away. It looped and surged alongside the container, throwing spray up into the night. Reg and Kurt watched the officers grappling over the side as they hauled the big silver unit into their boat. They were playing a weird game. They would throw the unit in the water and laugh raucously as it rode the current, then chase it and haul it back into their boat. They repeated this over and again.

"They taunting us?" Kurt spluttered as he floundered in the water.

The swimmers watched helplessly. Reg was about to suggest they make a quick getaway when the engine of the police boat revved again and the craft steamed back alongside them.

"In," the beefy officer ordered. His big face was wet now and flushed from laughing.

Reg grasped his outstretched hands. The other guards chuckled as he and Kurt clambered into their boat. Reg immediately got a face full of alcohol fumes. Whisky! The bloody guards had been drinking—that explained their stupid games. But were they happy drunks—or happy with their catch?

"Boat, where's your boat?" The big officer smirked, his regimental hat tilted low over his fleshy face.

Reg pointed back toward the cove. He made the effort to smile amiably. These guys were inebriated, and it was a good idea to humor them. Maybe they'd take a bribe, but what the hell with? Surrendering the dope would be a last resort.

The guard who was at the wheel rammed the throttle open and revved the engine, louder this time. "Yahooooo!" he yelled, and his colleagues laughed hysterically when Reg and Kurt anxiously grabbed the gunnel and clung as the vessel careered into a sharp turn.

"What, a joyride?" Kurt whined.

"Obviously love their work," Reg called over the roar of the engine as the boat raced along the dock.

"There!" he shouted to the guards when he saw the old tub bobbing in the shadows.

The motorboat growled and spluttered as it swung alongside the dinghy. The big guard waved his hands as if he was shaking them dry. Reg and Kurt looked at each other in bewilderment. When they realized he was gesturing them onto their own boat they climbed down quickly in case he changed his mind.

"Thanks fellows, very helpful indeed," Reg shouted.

He suspected they were going to steal the container and was stunned when the guffawing trio started hoisting it over the side of their motorboat.

"Big strong men, you guys on drugs?" Reg joked.

Kurt cringed, but the officers chortled appreciatively.

Kurt helped Reg lift the unit into their boat and wedge it into position in the stern.

"No more games!" The beefy guard waved and his colleagues cheered as their boat turned for the last time and disappeared into the night.

Reg and Kurt were left in stunned silence as their little boat jostled against the concrete jetty.

"They thought we were tourists!" Reg gasped in disbelief. They stared at each other and then quickly dissolved into fits of laughter.

"They . . . they thought we were stupid fucking tourists."

Their laughter subsided into sighs of relief.

"Border security, what a fucking joke!" said Kurt incredulously.

"Even if we'd been left alone there's no way it would have worked, not with that current. We need to rethink," Reg said.

Kurt looked astonished. Surely the Australian wasn't suggesting they come back for round two?

"A dose of lady-luck tonight it was," said Reg. "If they'd been stone-cold sober we'd be spending the night behind bars."

When they got back to the Lotus Garden Hotel in the early hours of the morning, Reg said it would be better if they went in separately and gave Kurt the rubber wetsuits to take to his room. Reg tucked his T-shirt into his jeans and swept his hair out of his eyes. He wiped the metal container with a towel and tried to stroll casually as he carried it across the lobby. The concierge didn't notice him; he was thinking about the scruffy man loaded with paraphernalia who'd padded dirty footprints across his shiny tiled floor five minutes earlier.

✈ ✈ ✈

The young hotel cleaner never entered a room on her morning round that had a "Do Not Disturb" sign on the door. Kurt had been so exhausted when he'd got back that he'd forgotten to put his sign out. The girl knocked politely a couple of times. When there was no answer, she thought the occupant had gone to breakfast so she inserted her key. She didn't discover the man until she passed the bathroom. Clothes, papers, cartons, and bottles were strewn across the floor, like remnants of some fearsome struggle. She froze.

The black rubber diving suits had been stacked on top of each other at the foot of the bed. She looked in horror at the contorted corpse and threw her hand to her mouth. Kurt didn't stir. He hadn't bothered to shower before he'd turned in. Neither had he bothered to stem the blood seeping from a cut on his hand. He'd caught it on the metal container when he took the diving gear out of the boot of the car. The white hotel sheets were smeared with sandy soil, but it was the garish bloodstain the girl found most disturbing. In addition, the way the man's hand hung out of the bed. Lifeless!

"Sir, number twenty-nine," blurted the distraught cleaner when she found the concierge.

She tried to describe the disturbing scene she'd witnessed, in particular the bodies, the blood, and the trashed room. The concierge wasted no time in calling the police.

Two plainclothes officers from the Criminal Investigation Department were dispatched immediately. Bhatti, the senior middle-aged officer, was a wiry man with an intense gaze. Chandak was Bhatti's muscle, broad and better equipped for confrontation. They collected Kurt Danson's passport from the concierge and took the lift to the second floor. They could have passed for hotel guests in their white shirts and shiny, dark-gray viscose suits. Nobody would have guessed their jackets were concealing weapons.

The officers were not in the habit of knocking before entering a suspected crime scene, and room twenty-nine would be no exception. They burst in with their guns drawn. Bhatti hollered "Up please" so loudly that Kurt sat bolt upright in bed with a face full of fear at Chandak's imposing frame towering above him. Chandak grabbed Kurt's damp jeans from the floor and slung them on the bed, smugly amused as the disheveled young hippie struggled into them under his sheet.

"I want to know what you're doing here, Mr. Danson, and where you were last night!" Bhatti announced sternly.

Bhatti was a thin, angular man with a well-worn face. Bushy gray brows matched his mustache and swamped his droopy eyelids. Breathing loudly, he directed Kurt to the table by the window and sat opposite him. He lit a cigarette and slammed Kurt's passport on the table like a trump card. "I repeat," he announced in a loud, no-nonsense voice, "what were you doing last night?" He leaned back in his chair and stroked his whiskers, his dark eyes scouring the pages of Kurt's passport.

"I'm taking a year off after university, you know, traveling around." Kurt's voice was shaky. He looked a sorry sight: bare chested, with his matted ponytail plastered down his back. It couldn't be the water police, he reassured himself—if they'd suspected anything, they'd have kept the container. So what the hell could these guys have on him and how much did they know? "I just wanted to do some diving, you know . . . see fish and stuff." He regretted saying this immediately after the words were out.

"Have you ever been in the American Navy, Mr. Danson?" Bhatti asked.

"Never."

"Remember, it's an offense to lie to an officer of the law."

"I'm not lying."

"I'll put it another way. Have you ever been in any of the armed forces, in your own country or any other country?"

"No."

"So your story about last night is that your trip was recreational, is that right?"

"That's right," Kurt said. "Look, can I get a drink or something?"

Chandak glanced at his superior with raised eyebrows and dipped his balding head toward the bar fridge. Bhatti nodded, and Chandak marched to the refrigerator and collected three small bottles of lemonade. Kurt estimated Chandak was at least six feet three inches, easily the size of the bouncers at the clubs back home.

"Drink all you like," thought Kurt. "No way I'm paying the bill."

Bhatti swigged his drink and placed it decisively on the table. "Exactly where were you diving last night?" he asked impatiently.

Kurt took a long drink to buy time; he'd hoped he wasn't going to have to give specifics, and he was cornered already. How much did these guys know? If they'd had some kind of tail on Bruce's car, then he could be done for lying. On the other hand, if they didn't know anything about last night, he could blow the whole fucking plan. It was a risk he'd have to take. He had to tell them somewhere because if they caught him in a lie they might get really heavy, even arrest him.

"Port Cochin." Kurt looked Bhatti in the eye as if it was no big deal.

Bhatti sat up straight and his brow tightened into a deep furrow.

"Port Cochin?" His eyebrows shot up and he shared a snigger with Chandak. "It's hardly the Great Barrier Reef."

"I like diving anywhere. Always loved it." Kurt tried one of his easy smiles.

It didn't appear to be working; Chandak was on the move. He collected a small raffia wastepaper basket from the corner and kneeled on the floor among the garbage. He started dumping everything of no interest into the bin.

"Don't look at him, look at me," Bhatti snapped. "I put it to you, Mr. Danson, that you were on some kind of mission last night. A mission to find out everything you could about Port Cochin."

"Find out what?" Kurt was genuinely baffled.

Chandak rose and stood over Kurt at the table.

"You tell me. You tell me what you've been instructed to find out!" Bhatti insisted.

"Instructed by who? You've got to be kidding." Kurt was getting annoyed. "Are you guys crazy? Are you saying, that I'm some sort of . . . some sort of spy?"

Kurt didn't see it coming when Chandak lunged at him and hauled him to his feet. Neither was he prepared for the heavy blow of Chandak's fist in the pit of his stomach. He doubled up in pain and then dropped to the floor, gasping for air.

"You've failed to give a reasonable explanation," said Bhatti casually, lighting another cigarette.

"Even if I did believe you were just diving, why would you be doing it in the middle of the night?" he added. "I suggest you rethink your position while we complete our search, otherwise what you just experienced will get a whole lot worse."

Kurt's mind went numb, and then raced with what he'd just been told. Chandak's blow had left a searing pain in his abdomen. These men weren't calling his bluff. They were convinced he was a spy, and he had just had a taste of India's methods for extracting information. He was suspected of something far more serious than drug smuggling. There was no way he was going to take the fall for Bruce.

CHAPTER 15

Two hours later, Kurt was still marooned in his hotel room with Bhatti and Chandak. The previous evening's misadventure was catching up with him; he was tired and hungry and his stomach still hurt like hell. The investigating officers were not buying a word of his story, and he was on the brink of being arrested on charges of espionage. Chandak had reduced the clutter on the floor down to a backpack, a pair of underpants, a khaki Che Guevara T-shirt, a giant duffle bag, two damp wetsuits with goggles, and oxygen cylinders.

Bhatti had chain-smoked his way through a pack of cigarettes as the two officers had systematically turned the room upside down. After checking everything in the backpack, Chandak examined every line in Kurt's address book for evidence that he was an agent. Bhatti was fixated on the binoculars and the notes Kurt had scribbled on his map of the West Coast of India. He'd badgered Kurt relentlessly about past employers and places he'd visited. His line of questioning always returned to what Kurt had been doing at Port Cochin the previous evening. By lunchtime, Kurt's interrogators were enjoying a plate of sandwiches they'd had sent up from the kitchen. Chandak took great pleasure in eating his share under Kurt's nose.

"So, Mr. Danson," Bhatti said, "I'm giving you one last chance to tell us what you were doing yesterday evening."

As he leaned back in his chair, he put his hands on his hips, and the side of his jacket fell open to reveal a handgun perched in a holster.

"What's it going to be?" he said, rising to his feet. "Or would you prefer to be left alone with my friend Mr. Chandak?" He pushed the plate away, flicked the crumbs out of his mustache, and stood abruptly, glaring menacingly at the American.

Kurt's spirit was shattered. He was exhausted and bedraggled. On the brink of being prosecuted as a spy. In his worn-out confusion, he grasped at any possibility, especially the idea that he would be in a lot more trouble for espionage than for what he was really up to the night before. He stared at the tabletop.

"Trying to fix a box to the bottom of a boat." His expressionless words hung over the room.

Bhatti straightened with surprise—spies weren't supposed to crack so easily. Chandak's eyes widened as he patted his mouth with his handkerchief.

"Again please, Mr. Danson," said Bhatti.

He opened his notebook.

"Fixing a box on the bottom of a boat," Kurt sounded like a weary schoolboy. He helped himself to the last untidy sandwich. If he was going to come clean they could bloody well feed him.

"A box on the bottom of a boat," Bhatti repeated. "Why?"

"To send it somewhere," said Kurt. Then he thought how ridiculous it sounded.

"Send it where?"

"Australia."

"So it was an Australian boat?"

"Yeah."

"So you've sent a box to Australia?"

"No."

"You're making me angry, Mr. Danson!" shouted Bhatti. "You won't like me when I'm angry. When I'm angry, Chandak gets angry."

I don't fucking like you now, Kurt thought, but he dearly wanted to avoid an angry Chandak. "We didn't send it because we couldn't attach it to the boat. It was because of the current." There, it was done now. They knew he wasn't alone, but why should he have to shoulder all this shit on his own. It was Bruce's idea anyway. He'd just gone along for the ride.

Bhatti leaned across the table and fiddled with his pen. "And where is this box now?" he asked.

"I'm not really sure," said Kurt. The other thing he wasn't sure about was how much to tell them.

"I am sure, Mr. Danson," said Bhatti in an accusing voice. "I am sure that if you were going to the trouble of connecting a box to a boat, which I imagine would be rather difficult, then it would contain something special. I am also sure of what that something special could be. And the other thing I'm sure about," Bhatti continued, on a roll now, "is that you will need to defer your studies for a few years more."

Kurt felt like throwing up. "Even if we didn't do it?" he asked.

He glanced at Chandak who looked comfortably settled in for the afternoon, leaning back in his chair with his arms folded over his wide girth.

"Mr. Danson, you've already made things difficult for yourself, so I suggest you start to cooperate," Bhatti said.

"I thought I was cooperating!"

"Put it this way," Bhatti continued in a more reasonable manner, "you are clearly not the ringleader in last night's activity because you don't have the box. If you give me the information I need to locate the ringleader and the box, then you'll be helping yourself. Understand?"

"Uh-huh," said Kurt. "I just need to think for a while. You know, jog my memory."

"Think quickly. My offer's good only while I smoke this cigarette," replied Bhatti.

Kurt was telling him how to spell "Pennington" before he'd finished it.

✈ ✈ ✈

Twenty minutes after Kurt made his confession, he was bundled out of the hotel into a waiting police car. Five minutes after that, his interrogators barged unannounced into Reg and Annie's room. Reg's eyes shot open as the key turned in the lock. When Bhatti and Chandak tramped noisily into his bedroom, they found him naked at the side of his bed.

"What the fuck?" cursed Reg. His modesty stopped them

in their tracks. He turned toward the bed and met Annie's frightened eyes peering over the top of the sheet. "Be upset," he mouthed while he pretended to look for something under the covers, giving the officers a view of his backside.

"Put your pants on, Mr. Pennington!" Bhatti yelled.

"Easy, buddy." Reg tried to calm him, then prolonged the officer's indignation by putting on his T-shirt first.

"Up, madam," Chandak ordered Annie.

She slid out of bed, pulling her striped Pink Panther T-shirt down to her knees before her feet touched the floor. Cascades of sandy hair swamped her face. Reg thought she looked like a young lion.

"You are definitely the most beautiful woman I have ever seen," he announced dramatically. If he was sinking, he might as well go down having fun. "Don't you think my green-eyed girl is the most beautiful woman ever?" he asked the detectives conversationally.

"For God sake, Reg, not now!" Annie pleaded.

Chandak looked confused. Bhatti knew Reg was toying with them and became more aggressive.

"You, sir," he rasped at Reg, "sit on the bed. And you, madam, cover your legs!"

"Can't she do that in the bathroom?" Reg asked, when he saw how uncomfortable Annie was climbing into her jeans under their leering gaze.

"You don't ask anything. We ask the questions!" Bhatti exploded. "Right now, we want you to sit on the bed!"

Chandak slipped out of the room and came back with two uniformed officers. He spoke to them in Hindi, and they stood watch over Reg and Annie while he and Bhatti began to search the room. First they hauled the big duffle bag into the center of the room. They held one end apiece and tipped it onto the floor. The pile of clothes hit the mat, but loose toiletries and Annie's hairbrush spun across the tiles. Bhatti felt expectantly around the lining of the bag and looked disappointed when it appeared normal.

Then they started on the backpacks. They emptied those as

well, then retrieved all the travel documents, passports, and paperwork and lined them up on a table by the window. Chandak was amused by the stuffed koala and wore a contemptuous little smile as he chucked it in the clothes pile.

"Up!" Bhatti yelled. He ordered his officers to strip the bed.

Reg and Annie were grim-faced as the mattress was upended.

"Why aren't they questioning us?" Annie whispered to Reg.

"Don't need to," Reg sounded resigned. "They already know what they're looking for."

After the uniformed men had searched under the bed, they started on the bathroom and bagged everything that didn't belong to the hotel. Bhatti's tension mounted—what if Danson had made the whole thing up? His angry eyes darted before fixing on a timber cupboard near the entrance. His mouth set into a satisfied smirk as he crossed the room. Reg and Annie stood like soldiers as he blustered past, beyond the bathroom, to the cupboard.

Annie knew what was coming and just wanted it to be over. Reg was thinking about what he'd like to do if he ever got his hands on that bastard Danson. The cupboard revealed its contents: the spare pillows on the top shelf with a rail of swinging coat hangers underneath. Bhatti spied the metal container gleaming at him from the floor. He heaved it out. Chandak hovered behind him like an expectant child, and the two men carted it back to the bedroom and laid it on the tabletop. Reg resisted the urge to make a joke about their strength. He thought it was pathetic—he'd always carried the unit on his own.

"It's a flotation device," he followed them to the table.

"Where you were!" Bhatti hollered, and one of the uniformed men drew a gun and signaled for Reg to go back to the doorway beside Annie.

The other guard cracked the sealed unit open in seconds. Bhatti's and Chandak's eyes lit up as they feasted on their haul.

"Lucky for us it does float, Mr. Pennington," said Bhatti, "because if it sunk we'd have missed the pleasure of seeing it today. Take them now," he ordered the uniformed officers.

"Just be cooperative," Reg mumbled to Annie after they'd been searched, allowed to use the toilet, and then handcuffed.

The lift doors opened onto the ground floor, and they were marched across the reception lobby, where a small group of staff and guests had gathered. News of the drama surrounding rooms twenty-nine and thirty-five had quickly circulated. Even the head chef was among the inquisitive bunch of whispering onlookers. The press was lying in wait outside the entrance; Reg turned his head when a camera flashed. The guards held both prisoners' handcuffed wrists from behind, shoving them through the line of prying eyes. Reg thought this was a good time to not understand what anyone was saying. Annie didn't care what the crowd was saying—she just felt humiliated in her Pink Panther T-shirt.

They were shoved into the back of a police wagon and driven to the local station. The fifteen-minute drive seemed like an eternity. They were ordered not to speak and sat on opposite sides, each next to a guard. Reg held Annie's gaze and mouthed messages of reassurance. "It'll be okay," he told her, trying to calm her frightened eyes.

When they arrived at the station, the duty officer waved the driver through the security checkpoint into the car park.

"Any chance of losing these?" Reg asked as he and Annie tried to maneuver themselves down the steps with their arms wrenched behind their backs.

"Ask the chief," the guard smirked, as if he knew something they didn't. He pushed them down a long, gloomy corridor and knocked on the door at the end.

"Come," answered a male voice.

It was a large square office. Reg and Annie were deposited in front of a central desk, piled with papers fluttering to the rhythm of the overhead fan.

"Sit down, Mr. Pennington and Miss Priestly," the man behind the desk ordered. He nodded to the guard to bring chairs and told him to remove their handcuffs.

The couple rotated their aching shoulders. Annie tried to fight back tears as she rubbed the large welt that had formed on her wrist. The elderly police chief lit a cigarette. Patterns of smoke drifted past his little eyes framed by thick-rimmed spectacles. Reg wondered if smoking was compulsory in the Indian police force. Annie was thinking that jail with Cheryl would have been a better prospect than this.

The chief wiped his graying hair off his forehead with a crumpled handkerchief. Annie shifted and gave a nervous little cough. Reg grabbed her hand and squeezed it. He would think of something—get them out of this.

The chief squinted and blew another smoky trail into the air. "So we have one hashish smuggler and one conspirator, that's your story?"

"No, that's not our story," Reg corrected him.

"It's Mr. Danson's story," the chief cautioned, "and he's signed a statement that says just that. Would you like me to read it to you? It states that you were attempting to smuggle twelve kilos of hashish from Port Cochin to Australia, and twelve kilos is exactly the quantity found in your room. What do you say to that, Mr. Pennington?"

"I say we would like a lawyer," Reg replied, cursing the day he'd laid eyes on Kurt bloody Danson.

"What about the stuff at the hotel, our bags and things?" Annie's scrambled mind clutched at anything that offered security: Oscar, a few photos, and what about her clothes?

The old honcho folded his hands on the desk and leaned forward. "They'll be brought shortly." He raised his eyebrows and peered at the foreigners over the rims of his spectacles. "Although where you're headed," his voice was mocking, "you're not likely to be needing them."

✈ ✈ ✈

Reg was held in a detention center for two weeks. Before he fell asleep each night he would tell himself he was a day closer to freedom. The first week of his incarceration had been the worst, full of worry about Annie. She'd been carted off to a women's facility, and Reg was haunted by the helpless look in her eyes when she was bundled out of the room. He'd tried to get some information about where she might have been taken. He couldn't communicate with most of the local prisoners, but he eventually came across one who spoke English.

"By the central prison, they have women there," the man said clearly, before a guard appeared out of nowhere and whacked him across the head. "Sorry, mate," Reg whispered, cursing silently because he'd caused another man pain.

Then he'd been caged in this hellhole; a dark, dank space that looked like the film set of a horror movie. His roommates were a crowd whose credentials ranged from simpletons to the criminally insane. One evening he counted over forty of them, sandwiched like caged hens in a space no more than twenty by thirty square feet. Their communal room was like a dungeon, a filthy, windowless place at the end of a row of four. The stench of urine and feces oozed from the toilet, a dugout with fly-ridden newspaper, excrement, and squatting men.

These men were unlike any Reg had ever known. The lunatic fringe was the worst: psychotic and dangerous, pressure cookers of violence; ghoulish wild-eyed creatures with bug-ridden, matted hair and tempers that could erupt if they were so much as looked at. The psychos intimidated the weak, who huddled in whimpering groups like frightened children. Reg had experienced what their tormentors were capable of. At the end of his first week, one of them had ruffled his hair. He was used to that; his shaggy blond mop was a novelty. But when a big madman ripped out a clump, Reg had gone berserk. He'd had no trouble overpowering him, but not before suffering deep scratches from the beast's filthy claws and a severe bite on his arm. The guards weren't interested in protecting prisoners; they often dished out beatings of their own. Reg found his best defense was to mimic the screwballs; the crazies always stayed out of his way when they thought he was one of them.

Prisoners moved through their daily routine like robots, thin and ravaged shells of men with haunting, vacant stares. Men who'd lost the thread of being human, forgotten that they were alive. Reg's biggest fear was that he might become forgotten, left to rot, so he became like them. But he couldn't. He had too much to live for. He had Annie.

The thought of losing Annie plagued him the most. That and countless recriminations over what had led to their demise. He'd been desperate when he'd put the Port Cochin plan together, but these were desperate times, and when the money had started to run out, he'd needed a big plan to bail them out.

Their situation was like a festering sore. He'd felt powerful, capable of fixing it, patching up the bloody mess that had become their lives.

Perhaps some things he'd broken could never be fixed. Why did he think he could change something that was spinning out of control with no way of stopping it? Probably because he'd built up this idea that he was invincible, like when he was younger, and anything and everything seemed possible.

PART TWO
1960s

Chapter 16

Newcastle-upon-Tyne, June 1964

The quayside echoed with men's voices and the shuddering shots of rivet machines on a major refit up the dock. The morning tea break siren wailed, and dozens of shipyard workers flooded the wharf, a group of overalled apprentices tussling over sandwiches and cigarettes. Their breath patterned the cold air as they milled around, shouting and skylarking. A big wharfie burst between them.

"I said, gimme a fag!" he yelled, grabbing a worker by the collar.

"Sod off, Dan! Get your own fucking fags!" spluttered the scrawny young man.

Dan flung him sideways with such force that he rotated mid-air and landed in a heap twenty feet along the dock. A crowd instantly gathered, excited workers jostling for a better view of the skirmish. Then they noticed an unfamiliar figure; a stranger to this part of the docks. He pushed through their ranks, conspicuous with his crew-cut hair and brightly colored clothing. He didn't look like one of them. The stranger didn't care; he liked being the new man in town.

"You okay, mate?" He dropped his duffle bag and knelt beside the sprawled apprentice.

"Think so," the youngster groaned and rubbed his head.

"Out the way, pal." The big wharfie barged through the gawking spectators. "This is between me and him. Beat it!"

"Leave him, Dan," one of his mates said. "He's a passenger. Just disembarked, he has."

Dan hesitated. The new bloke didn't look like a tourist, in spite of his tan. "Where you from then?" he asked grudgingly.

"Australia."

"Australia! Here lads, we've got a bloody colonial!" Dan taunted. "Don't think you can come over here and poke your nose into
other people's business. Get back to your fucking kangaroos." He
poked his fingers into the emblem on the man's green and gold
track shirt. The circle of bemused onlookers nudged and whispered. The stranger took his time, muttering encouragement as
he helped the apprentice to his feet. He retrieved his bag, feigned
a look of irritation, and brushed himself off. Then he confronted
Dan.

"Here we go," a voice came from the crowd.

Dan wasn't used to being taken on, and this geezer was bigger than he'd looked kneeling down. Those blue eyes were fixed
on him like the bastard meant business.

The stranger cleared his throat. "I don't think that's a very
nice way to treat a visitor to your shores," he said in a calm voice.
"Taking the piss out of their native animals."

Dan swallowed. "Like I said, this is unfinished business between me and Jim."

"Doesn't seem a fair contest," the Australian pointed out, "the
bloke's half your size."

He stepped forward, his face six inches from Dan's. "If it's a
contest you're after, the reason for this kangaroo," he slapped his
chest, his loud voice satirical as he played to the gallery, "is because I've thrown the javelin for my country. I'm telling you now,
buddy, if you want to make an issue out of this, then prepare to
be hurled into the middle of next week."

The audience was spellbound. "What's a javelin?" someone asked.

"A spear thing that sports blokes chuck," another said.

Dan was in a quandary. His eyes darted sideways, ears turning red.

"Come on, Dan, losing your nerve?" jibed an apprentice.

"Bit desperate are we, Dan?" another added.

The high-pitched siren blared again. Dan's labored breathing slowed.

"Saved by the bell, Danny boy," a man laughed as the crowd
dispersed.

Dan thrust his hands into his pockets. "Javelin thrower, my arse," he muttered as he stomped off.

"Thanks." Jim turned to his rescuer. "Does that to someone nearly every day. Right thug, is Dan. You really a javelin thrower?"

"Sure am, Jimbo, but listen mate, I'm a skint javelin thrower at the moment. Know anyone who needs a razor?"

"What for?"

"Shaving mostly."

"Oh yeah, yeah right," said Jim. "What d'you want to give them your razor for?"

"I don't. I want to sell it. I'm skint, remember?"

"Gotcha! Look, I can't buy it, but the blokes in my dad's shed will still be there. Some of them have money."

"Worth a try," said the new arrival. "Lead the way, Jimbo."

"This bloke's a javelin thrower who wants to sell his razor," Jim said at the entrance to a shed down the dock.

Half a dozen wharfies sat inside. They stopped talking. One continued to pour tea from a thermos flask. Everyone gawped at the six-foot young blond bloke decked out in Bermuda shorts. An older man with a chiseled face narrowed his eyes. He tried to decipher the badge on the youngster's track top.

"Just saved me from Desperate Dan," Jim added when nobody spoke. He turned to a man sitting by the door. "Gonna flatten me he was, because I wouldn't give him a fag."

"Much obliged," the man nodded. He had the same scruffy hair and cautious gray eyes as young Jim. "Let's look at it then."

The newcomer delved into his backpack and produced a small box with a photo of a man shaving round a big white smile. "This top-of-the-range razor has never been used. Electric shaver, still in the box," he announced.

"Why would we want your razor?" asked a little man with a mouthful of pork pie.

"Why?" the youth feigned indignation. "Because it's come all the way from Oz. You won't find anything like this here. Top quality, bargain price. The first to offer me five pounds takes this little beauty home."

"Quit the bullshitting, why d'you need five pounds?" asked the pork pie man.

"Strapped for cash right now." The traveler's face flushed. "Just got off the boat, and I need to buy a train ticket to London. Anyone see their way to helping a young Aussie out?"

"Give us a look at it," said the man by the door.

The young fellow handed him the box as the wharfie ground his cigarette butt under his hobnail boot. He read the leaflet, took the razor out of the box, and held it up to inspect the blade.

"Looks pretty good don't it, Dad?" Jim asked hopefully.

His new friend shot Jim a grateful smile.

"It'll need to be. If it packs up, I ain't bloody taking it back to Australia," said Jim's father. He stood and foraged in his pocket, pulling out two grimy five-pound notes. He peeled them apart and handed one to the relieved young man. "Not because I need a razor," he said. "Because one good turn deserves another."

"Thanks, mate. Appreciate it. Now there's a good chance I'll sleep in a bed tonight."

"Whereabouts?" asked the wharfie.

"Twickenham," said the man. "My mate's house in Twickenham. He's a javelin thrower as well.

✈ ✈ ✈

By six o'clock, John McSorley had finished work and was home in his flat on the second floor of a Victorian terraced house on the Twickenham Road. The suited and booted athlete knelt to stack assorted culinary delights into the kitchen cupboard. Bringing home unwanted samples from his job as a food salesman was a meager perk for trekking a laborious route around the hotels of London's West End.

John was no ordinary salesman. His area manager didn't usually hire such young reps, but the kid had just broken the British javelin record, and the manager felt duty-bound to support the country's sporting youth. Besides, the youngster's baby-blue eyes and athletic build were proving a real hit with the female catering managers. The manager had it on good authority that several of them had only placed orders so they could see young "Johnny boy" again.

Today all John wanted to do was get out of his suit. He'd planned on a couple of hours training at St. Mary's College gym, and was running late because D. J. had dumped an oversupply of beer into his undersized cupboard.

"We're going to be boozing for England with this lot," John told Tom, his Jamaican friend from across the hallway.

"Hope D. J.'s left enough for our rent." Tom's voice was deep, his accent immaculate Queen's English. "Lillian went off her rocker last time it was late. Where is he, by the way?"

"Seeing someone about tomorrow's gig."

"I envy D. J. Wouldn't want to be a disc jockey myself, but at least he gets paid for doing something he loves." A door slammed. "Talk of the devil."

Voices drifted up from the ground-floor hallway, and the old timber staircase creaked.

"Reckon he's got someone with him," Tom murmured.

D. J. threw open the door and bustled into the living room. "Hey Mac, expecting a delivery?" His face was flushed with excitement beneath his shaggy brown hair.

"Hope you haven't bought more beer," said John, irritated because the cupboard door refused to close.

"Nope, unfortunately, they don't deliver booze to the door," D. J. smirked. "Found this instead."

John rose, wide-eyed with disbelief and oblivious to the beer bottles rolling in his wake. He stared at the fellow decked out in garish Bermuda shorts, beaming from ear to ear in the doorway.

"Johnny Mac!" the young man bellowed, hauling his bag into the living room. "Said I'd be over to see you!"

John looked simultaneously thrilled and shocked.

"What the . . . ?" His voice rose. "It's Spiers! I don't believe it! Reggie bloody Spiers!"

The friends embraced, laughing and spluttering as John's mind raced with memories of Reg's wild antics in Perth.

Tom and D. J. looked on, bemused. "Let me get a look at you," John insisted. He held Reg's shoulders at arm's length and studied his face; the trademark roguish grin and mischievous blue eyes. "You haven't changed a bit, Reggie. Not one bit! Fellows," he announced as he turned Reg toward Tom and D. J. "This is the bloke I met at the Commonwealth Games—1962, in Perth—the one who led me astray!"

"Aha!" said D. J. "Your partner in crime."

"You two could pass for brothers, Mac," said Tom. "Except that he's suntanned, and you look like you've spent your life in a basement. God, man! Aren't you cold in those bloody shorts?"

"No, mate." Reg was upbeat. "Women like to see a man's legs, especially when they're this good!"

Everyone laughed. D. J. wished he had half of this bloke's confidence. He imagined himself dressed like the Aussie, surrounded by adoring girls as he put another record on the turntable. Then he had second thoughts and decided he probably lacked the legs or charisma to pull it off.

"Talking of women, Reg," John said, "last thing I heard, you'd got hitched."

"Sure did, buddy," said Reg. "Well and truly spoken for, and a little girl."

Tom smiled politely. He thought John's friend looked way too young to be saddled with a wife and child.

"I had a girlfriend once . . . ," began D. J.

"Only one he's ever had," interrupted John.

D. J. ignored him. "Seriously," he continued, "this girl, she didn't even like me going to the corner shop without her—so your missus must be pretty understanding!"

"No worries there, Marion knows about training and stuff," said Reg. He suddenly looked distracted. "Although she wasn't exactly thrilled about me pissing off to the other side of the world."

John looked thoughtful. "Don't know too many girls who would be."

"Women need reassurance, they're all fickle creatures." Tom's dark eyes glowed. "The art is in the handling."

The others stared at him. D. J. made a mental note to extract more precise details later.

"Well I did promise I'd bring her and the kid over, you know, if things work out," Reg explained.

There was an awkward silence; airfares from the other side of the world required serious money, and nobody wanted to comment on the likelihood of that "working out."

"D. J., get the man a drink." John quickly changed the subject. "You haven't lugged that bag from the station, Reggie?"

"I was chauffeured." Reg smirked at Tom and D. J.

"Very nice," said Tom.

John rolled his eyes; he was all too familiar with Reg's methods of transportation. "I need to warn you blokes," his voice turned serious, "Reggie's favorite lurk is to stand in the middle of the road. Then the next poor soul who drives his way only has two options; kill him or give him a lift!"

"Nice one," D. J. chuckled from the kitchen where he was mopping up beer with newspaper. "Might get some decent birds driving us around!"

Tom slumped across the drab, beige sofa. "Don't think you'd get away with that around here." He sounded cautious.

"Don't worry," John reassured him. "I'll keep an eye on him."

D. J. appeared with Reg's beer. "Just so you know, Reg." He carefully placed a bowl of crisps on the coffee table. "We have to look after this table. Relic from Mac's woodwork class at school, he's carted it around ever since."

"Just as well someone's practical," John quipped. "Kitchen cupboards need fixing, but not tonight." He sunk next to Tom. "Not doing another thing tonight, I'm still trying to get my head around all this, Reggie. If I'd known you were coming I could have collected you from the airport."

Reg perched on the arm of the chair opposite and swigged his beer. "You know me. Always like surprises. Didn't have the cash to fly, came for free on a tanker," he grinned.

"Ha, as you do!" joked D. J. He was starting to warm to this Reggie bloke. John's sporting friends were usually quite conservative, but this one was a real laugh, more of an extrovert, like the guys at his gigs.

"I'll be blowed," John smiled. "So you've already been away for a few weeks, how long you staying?"

"Couple of months. Sure you've got room? I can find somewhere when I get a job."

"Don't be stupid. Brought your training gear?"

"You bet!" Reg said. "All the comps were finished back home. Won't make the Olympics on this year's performance."

"The National Championships are coming up at White City, with your recent performances I'll be able to get you in as a guest. What sort of work you looking for?"

"Anything that pays. Don't know what they'd give me."

"I'll give you something for those shorts," D. J. quipped.

"Sorry mate, not for sale," said Reg. "Present from the wife."

"Seriously, what have you done besides sales?" John looked thoughtful.

"Had a job at Adelaide Airport when I left school."

"I know a bloke at the airport," John said. "From when I was a baggage handler with Air France. Could see if there's anything going there."

"Hey, could you, Mac?" Reg sounded hopeful. "I'm totally skint. If I worked at the airport I might be able to wangle a free ticket back to Oz."

John sensed a problem brewing. Marriage hadn't changed his old friend one bit; he was still chancing his luck with madcap schemes. And he was broke, and he didn't have a bloody return ticket for himself, so bringing his family to London was completely out of the question.

"If you're only staying a couple of months you'll need to find something soon," he told Reg. "Otherwise, how the hell will you get home?"

Chapter 17

Four months later

Reg burst through the door, slamming it against the wall as he stormed across the gym and hurled his backpack to the floor, collapsing beside it on the mat and hanging his head in his hands.

"Last bloody straw!"

The weight bar clanged above John's head. "Reg?" He quickly replaced it and sat straight. "What's the last straw?"

"Today and Waterford."

"What happened?"

"And who's Waterford?" asked D. J.

"Everything's happened, and then I picked up the postcard after work, from Marion. While the cat's away and all that, and I can't do a damn thing about it because my bloody wallet got nicked." Reg was shouting now, his face pale with anguish.

"But who is he?" D. J. asked again.

"A jumped-up, second-rate athlete. Just happens to be a lawyer where she used to work . . . bloody convenient, isn't it!" Reg yelled.

"Reg, Reg, for God's sake, calm down! You'll get us kicked out," said John. "Where was the wallet?"

"Jacket pocket, staff canteen. First time I've left it, and what d'you know?"

"Much in it?" asked Tom.

"Only everything. Everything I'd saved for my airfare, and I really bloody need it now, Mac. If I'm not home soon I reckon Marion will think I've done a runner."

D. J. looked confused. "What's that got to do with Waterboard?"

"Water-ford, Dean fucking Waterford, and by the way I had a dream about him last night and it wasn't much fun, I can tell you."

Tom sprawled next to D. J. on the floor. "It might be . . . you know, platonic," he said.

"C'mon Reggie, it's not anything if it's a dream. You're just tired. We've had way too many late nights and now you've topped it off with a lousy day at the airport. You're worn out, stressed and everything, and it's making you paranoid."

"You don't seem to realize Mac, she's a bloody good-looking woman," Reg went straight back to shouting. "What, you think he'd want to discuss the political implications of the Australian judicial system, do you?"

"You're probably reading too much into it. Tell us exactly what she said," insisted John.

Reg snatched his backpack and groped inside. "Read it yourself!" He spun the card along the floor, and it collided with John's feet. John stooped to retrieve it. He studied the glossy photo-montage for a moment: an aerial view of Adelaide, the banks of the River Torrens, and a Glenelg tram in situ. Then he turned it over and silently read:

> *Dear Reggie*
>
> *I'm hoping you're still staying with your friend John at this address. Everyone's been asking about you, and your Mum phones nearly every week wanting to know when you're coming home. She's convinced you're going to miss your brother's wedding. Megan's well, she's grown so much you won't recognize her. Mum babysat for me last week so I could have a night out with my old workmates. Assuming you'll be back soon!*
>
> *Love*
>
> *Marion xxx*

John sighed and shook his head. "Sounds innocent enough, for God's sake, Reg, there's no mention of this Waterford bloke."

He dropped the postcard in Reg's lap before flopping beside

him on the mat. "What's wrong with seeing old workmates?" he asked.

"Nothing at all, so long as one of them isn't Waterford!" Reg shouted.

"Women like to throw in little teasers, see how we react," said Tom. "Happened to me once, d'you remember, Mac, that girl, Lucinda?"

"What happened with Lucinda?" asked D. J.

"She said if I didn't marry her she was going out with her boss."

"What did you do?" asked D. J.

"Said I wouldn't marry her."

"So what did she do then?"

"Married her boss," said Tom, and Reg let out a huge groan.

"Pull yourself together, Reg," said John. "You're overreacting."

"You don't understand, Mac, this isn't just about Waterford." Reg seemed on a roll. "It's everything. Don't get me wrong, North Devon and everywhere you took me was wonderful, wouldn't have missed them for the world. Shame about my stuffed arm, missing out on the Olympics and everything, I've still had a great time, but . . ."

"But it's time to go."

"It is, Mac," Reg nodded. "And apart from being bloody homesick and missing my family, there's my brother's wedding, my own wedding anniversary—didn't tell you about that one, did I? And at this rate I'm likely to miss my daughter's wedding as well, and she's only two!"

"It's just a setback," said John. "Write and explain that you've been held up."

"Forget letters." Reg was adamant. "My mind's made up; get back quick smart."

"Hang on, Reg. You won't be going anywhere for a while," John said. "You've had your money nicked, remember?"

Reg looked incredulous. "You don't think I'm gonna put a little thing like no money before my marriage, do you?"

Tom looked confused. "I'd say it had to be a consideration," he said as he heaved the weight of his long torso onto his elbows. Reg's frustration hung in an uneasy silence. John sat with bent legs, chin on knees, deep in thought.

"We could all chip in, but you're going to have to work a few more weeks," he said finally.

Reg began a set of sit-ups. "With what I earn, it could take months," he panted. "I'm talking now."

Tom and D. J. used Reg's dilemma as a good excuse to stop exercising. They didn't need to keep up with the javelin throwers.

"You work at the airport, Reg," Tom said. "You'd probably get a discount."

"Chip-ins, discounts, I haven't got time for all that. You're still talking weeks, and while I'm here, Casanova Waterford might be hitting on my bird."

John moved to the weights bench. "We'll think of something," he said as he gripped the rusty bar.

Reg pounded the step-up box. Every beat brought a picture of Marion with a new, red-hot lover: candlelit dinners, barbecues, walks on the beach. Worst of all was the thought of torrid lovemaking. He lunged at the 220-pound barbell and heaved it onto his shoulders. It was weightless beneath his fury. That bastard better not be in his bed. He launched a final power clean to his shoulders. She wouldn't do that. Please God, no!

John heard Reg breathing furiously and hoped he'd be calmer after his workout, rational even. Tom was bound to come up with something. Tom and D. J. were pretending to do sit-ups.

"He'll be okay," John told them quietly as he sunk onto the mat and closed his eyes.

Reg turned back to the box. The box—like the one he used to leap on at school. He would often sneak into the old gym, and could still recall the smell of the worn leather. Perfect for hiding from teachers because it was hollow. Hollow. *Perfect for hiding.*

Instead of lying on the box under the weights, Reg slid it free from underneath the bar. He stood motionless, hands on hips, examining it. He stared for a good minute, lost in thought. He disassembled the top two sections and climbed inside. He sat forward with his head lowered, inspecting the interior.

John heard the box scrape as Reg clambered out. "What the hell are you doing?" he asked, sitting up and hugging his knees. Three sets of intrigued eyes focused on Reg. It was the first time they'd seen him smile that day.

"This is it. My free ride home," he announced with a theatrical sweep of his arm.

"What, you're gonna nick it and sell it?" asked D. J. "Don't think you'd get much."

"Don't be stupid. I'm gonna go in it. Not this one but something like it. I've been thinking about boxes for a few days, watching the loaders move all those crates at the airport."

"What d'you mean, go in it?" asked John.

"Go in it, go home in it," Reg said. "You blokes can stick a label on me and send me as air freight."

D. J. reveled in the diversion. "Get a bird to join you so you don't get bored," he joked, pulling his mat closer to Reg and the box.

"Perhaps Lillian, our lovely landlady?" John said with a straight face.

"Don't forget protection!" D. J. hollered, and the gym echoed with laughter.

Reg felt so much better. "The next woman I will be cozying up to is my lovely wife. And very soon."

The room turned quiet again. The mad bastard sounded serious.

"Think you'd end up paying more as freight than as a bona fide passenger. A novel idea all the same," said Tom, politely.

"You all think I'm joking. I'm bloody serious."

"Don't be daft," said John, "concentrate on doable options."

"This is doable, Mac. I can do it. I can."

"You're not honestly contemplating sticking yourself in a box all the way back to Australia?" John asked.

"You bet I am," said Reg. "Just got to find someone to make it. You know, someone who's a bit of a dab hand at woodwork."

Tom and D. J. swung their gaze to John. Tom looked worried, D. J. like an excited schoolboy. John put his hands up as if to ward off Reg's mad ideas. "No bloody way."

"What about pressure and everything?" asked Tom. "Are all planes pressurized?"

"Don't go there," John's voice was tense. "I know this bloke better than you. Encourage him and he'll bloody well do it!"

"Don't need encouragement. I'm definitely doing it," said Reg. "I'm finding out about pressurization at work tomorrow."

"At the airport?" D. J. chuckled. "God, I love this."

"Come on fellows, ask more questions," Reg said. "You're helping me here . . . you know . . . to work it all out."

"Hang on a minute," John raised his voice. "Let me get this right, Reg. You're saying that you're seriously considering getting in something like this . . . It's an insane idea. Insane."

"Not considering, doing." Reg was adamant.

"Mad." Tom backed John. "You'll never make it."

"Wanna bet? Just watch me!"

John sighed. "Perhaps we all need to calm down."

"It's an interesting idea," Tom said. "Let's just talk it through, even though it's not likely to happen."

"It will happen," Reg said, quieter now.

"Don't think it's ever happened before," said Tom. "Anyone heard of someone being posted abroad?"

The others stared blankly.

"That's because it's so bloody dangerous," said John. "The box, whatever box it is, could end up as your coffin. This is a prank that could go seriously wrong."

"It's not a prank, Mac, I bloody well need to get home," Reg insisted. "You're forgetting I spent weeks on that tanker. Six months, almost, I've been gone."

"Keep it down, else we're gonna get chucked out," warned John. "Okay, let's talk about technicalities. What about things like needing a piss?"

"I'd have a bottle. Two bottles; one for drinking, one for pissing."

"What about cost?" Tom asked. "You know, what I said earlier about freight charges?"

"Hey Tom," chuckled D. J. "You could sort out his insurance. Two pounds should cover it!"

"Tom's right, Reg," said John. "You get done for freight charges and you could end up owing more than the cost of a ticket."

"Dead right," agreed Reg. "Economy fare at the moment is two hundred and twenty-eight quid, and a bit of freight about my size and weight, reckon about three fifty. But I won't be forking out a bean," he looked pleased with himself. "I'll be COD, cash on delivery, and nothing to pay."

He noticed John's worried face. "I've processed some of the forms at work," he reassured him. "Stacks of stuff get paid for at the other end."

"And who exactly will be paying for it at the other end?" asked John.

"That's the point," Reg explained. "There won't be anything to collect. The person who's supposed to be collecting me won't exist, because they'll be invented. By the time the airport people find the empty box, I'll be gone. Long fucking gone."

"Nice one," cooed D. J. "This is bloody brilliant."

"Brilliant . . . but reckless," Tom said.

"Let's say I agreed to make you a box—I'm not agreeing, by the way," said John.

"Not unless he's totally plastered," laughed D. J.

John ignored him. "Even if you get all the paperwork sorted, how do you get out at the other end?"

"I'll break out."

"How?"

"Rubber mallet or something. Yeah, a mallet, because that won't be noisy."

"This is seriously bloody criminal," John groaned.

"You'll be done for illegal entry," said Tom.

"No! I'll have my Aussie passport," Reg reminded him. "You lot can drop me off. I'll have forms on my outsides saying I'm going to be collected. I'll bust out of the airport. Perth, probably. Easier to escape from than Adelaide."

"You're not seeing straight, Reg. You could die! Be killed . . . get crushed . . . suffocate . . ." said John. "Sorry for caring about that!"

"If he gets caught, we'll all be up on charges. Manslaughter or accessory or something," said Tom. His eyes narrowed. "Your athletics career could be over."

"No, if he gets caught we just plead ignorance," D. J. said. "Like we didn't know he was in there."

"Getting a bit carried away aren't you, fellows?" said Reg. "Are you saying it's impossible to not get caught?" he challenged Tom.

"Not totally impossible, fifty-fifty," Tom estimated.

"I'm prepared to back myself," said Reg. He scanned the row of worried faces. "If you blokes don't want any part of it, no hard feelings." He turned to John. "I mean it, Mac."

The door squeaked, and the old caretaker poked his silver-haired head into the room.

"You gentlemen all right?" His eyes darted around. "Bit noisy tonight you are."

"Just on our way now, thanks," said John. He jumped up to help Tom stack the mats against the wall.

"Tell you what," D. J. said when the caretaker had gone, "how about continuing in the pub? Go down better with a pint."

"You get them in," said John. "We'll put the room back, follow you down."

"What d'you reckon, Mac?" Reg asked when they were alone.

"That it's a totally ludicrous, harebrained scheme that I'm mad to be even considering. We need to think this through, Reg. Tom was right. It's bloody reckless. Reckless and dangerous. Needs thought, so I'll sleep on it."

✈ ✈ ✈

John didn't sleep on it. Shortly after they got back from the pub, Lillian, the landlady, hammered on the door and complained about the commotion. He averted his eyes from the stout little woman's curlers and pink dressing gown.

"Sorry, Mrs. Judge." He geared his mind-set to diverting attention from Reg. "Tom's upset." He heard the others cackling behind him. "Girlfriend's left him."

"Psst . . . Reggie," D. J. whispered. "Now's your chance to invite Lillian to join you."

The great debate continued into the early hours of the next morning. Reg found a bottle of whisky behind a stack of tinned soup at the back of the kitchen cupboard. Tom and D. J. helped polish it off before they staggered across the hall.

"He's hell-bent!" spluttered D. J. as they stumbled into their room. "Hope this wife of his is worth it."

"Okay, you crazy lunatic—I'll build your box," a drunken John told an emotional, inebriated Reg.

"Because knowing you, you'll do it anyway. God knows what you'd end up in . . . some agricultural piece of junk that falls apart before liftoff. You don't stand a chance of pulling this off unless someone makes you a half-decent, sturdy container. Looks like that idiot is going to be me."

CHAPTER 18

"If this box is supposed to get you to the other side of the world," John insisted, "it warrants a bit of time on design."

He sat at his kitchen table with a large sheet of graph paper and a couple of pencils that kept breaking. Dissuading Reg from putting his madcap plan into action had proved impossible— Reg had talked about nothing else since he'd hit on the idea at the gym. Then he'd brought a leaflet home from work that clearly stated that all cargo holds on modern planes were pressurized.

"That does it, Mac." He was elated. "Plenty of oxygen up there, so let's bloody get on with it!"

John set about drawing masses of differently shaped boxes. Down the side of the paper, he scrawled a reference list of functions his design had to take into account.

"Breathing, seeing, eating, pissing," he read aloud to Reg. "Room for backpack and duffle bag, food and drink, security."

"Yeah security!" Reg butted in. "I don't want to be falling out when they start moving me about. Christ, can you imagine that?"

"You better start getting the paperwork sorted," said John. "I don't want to begin making the bloody thing, then find out it's not going to happen because of some administrative problem."

They sat in the Crown pub on the Richmond Road and studied the freight lodgment forms that Reg had collected from Smiths the Stationers. It was a three-page booklet, each page with a sheet of red carbon paper to make duplicates.

"Gotta keep a record," Reg joked. "If we're going to make a splash in the export industry, we need records of all our transactions."

"Quite, and we're not likely to fail, because we have such a unique product!"

Reg had to state the name and address of the sender and recipient.

"We can't make the sender either of us," he reminded John. "I'm sure you don't want to face the music after I've gone, and I don't want to be the sender of myself."

They quietly considered their options.

"It's got to be a company of some kind," said Reg. "An ordinary person isn't going to send a bloody great box to Australia. It's got to be sent by a company to another company. A company that makes stuff that needs special stuff to make it."

"Like a shoe company or something," John suggested.

"Spot on, Mac. Let's make it a shoe company. Let's make it what you Poms call a posh shoe company. How about the Supreme Shoe Company?"

"Sounds a bit Chinese."

"Perhaps it is Chinese! Why not? Why can't the Chinese have shoe companies? There's loads of Chinese companies in Australia."

"Keep your voice down," John reminded him. "We don't want to broadcast our plan before we've got it off the ground."

"Okay, what address can we use? An address in London, which could be a big factory."

John remembered an area with unusual buildings around Gloucester Road he'd visited for his monthly sales conventions.

"Let's make it Gloucester Road," he suggested. "But what are we sending?"

"The stuff for the shoes," Reg reminded him.

"Plastic?"

"Emulsion stuff."

"Plastic emulsion."

"What is that, exactly?" asked Reg, in case someone asked him when he lodged the forms.

"Don't know, probably doesn't matter."

After two drinks, they'd worked out that they were going to send a box of plastic emulsion from the Southern Chemical Company at 87 Gloucester Road in London to the Supreme Shoe Company in Perth, Australia. The box would be the largest dimensions allowed on the form, which was five feet by three feet by two feet six inches. They would send it COD, to be collected by a Mr. Graham.

"Cash on delivery," Reg laughed. "Definitely the best way to travel!"

John scraped together just enough pennies to purchase building supplies from Alsford's timber yard. He stored the materials he'd need for the construction under his kitchen table. The heap included twenty-six five-foot-long softwood planks, each six inches wide; eight six-foot lengths of two-by-two-inch timber; a three-foot-square sheet of hardwood, six dozen screws, six dozen nails, and a pot of wood glue. Reg kept tripping over the ends of the timber planks.

Reg was plagued with worry about his family. The box was his only hope of getting back to them, and he was desperate to see one take shape. His brother might never forgive him if he missed his wedding. The clock was ticking; he might be too late.

"So he's definitely going to do it?" Tom asked John when they were alone. "Won't change his mind?"

"Not a chance."

"I know his missus is special and all that, and he wants to see his little girl, but I still think he's crazy."

"That's love, I suppose." John was thoughtful. "Love makes people do crazy things."

✈ ✈ ✈

By Thursday, Reg started to panic. He was hoping to be airfreighted home at the weekend, and he still didn't have a container to go in. John had been unusually inundated with appointments with catering managers in hotels around London, all wanting samples and several placing orders for the company's new line of potato salad. He'd kept his calendar blank for the rest of the week and phoned his boss to say he was coming down with the flu. Lillian the landlady had told him she was going to spend the week with her sister in Bognor. He was free to make as much noise as he liked. He tuned in his transistor to Radio Caroline and set about assembling a very large box.

Meanwhile, Reg was at the freight dispatch department of Heathrow Airport, an open-plan area at the back of the complex.

At the counter, he became unnerved by a couple of warnings displayed on the wall behind the clerk. The posters advised on the serious nature of sending freight, with words like "criminal," "fraudulent," "bogus," and "duplicitous." He didn't know what "duplicitous" meant, but suspected it applied to what he was about to do.

"Right, sir." The bespectacled young clerk relieved him of his paperwork and began to read the forms back to him.

"So your company wants to send a crate of plastic emulsion to Perth. Addresses seem clear. Plastic emulsion, don't think I've heard of that one before," he noted.

"That surprises me," Reg tried to sound casual. "Been around a long time."

"So we have an address for the Supreme Shoe Company in Perth, but Mr. Graham has agreed to pay the freight charges at the other end. Is that right?"

"That's right," said Reg, in a voice he hardly recognized. "We've had so many problems with unpaid international accounts that we have a new policy of cash on delivery."

"Don't blame you. Amazing what people try to get away with these days."

Reg felt hot and decided to hurry things along. "The shoe company needs this immediately, so when would be the earliest I could book it in?"

"Right," said the clerk. "Well, you're booking it in with me today, sir. I'm now going to find the earliest date for you to deliver your consignment. All the regulations for boxed freight are on this sheet," he said, handing the instructions to Reg. "The delivery bay closes at four-thirty every afternoon."

The young man said the earliest date the consignment could be delivered for dispatch to Perth would be the seventeenth, on an Air India Boeing 707 via Paris, Bombay, and Singapore.

"After it's been cleared by customs at the other end, Mr. Graham will be free to settle the account and take it away," said the clerk.

Reg was careful not to sound too grateful. He took his copy and left, surprised at how easy it had been to book his passage home.

Back at John's flat, the building project was underway. He'd constructed two rectangular frames from the two-by-two-inch timber. He'd used these at each end as an inner shell that he clad horizontally with six-by-one-inch timbers, screwed, nailed, and glued to the frames. He'd left a penny-width gap between each timber for ventilation and to enable Reg to see out. By lunchtime, his creation was starting to look like a very big box, but the relentless loud whacking sound vibrated across the floorboards and up the walls to the cornices of the high-ceilinged Victorian room. John realized his blaring music and constant hammering had annoyed someone, who banged impatiently on his door.

"I don't know what you're bloody up to in there," Mr. Jones from the ground-floor flat complained, "but it sounds like you're building the *Titanic*. It better not go on all evening because I've got work in the morning, I can't sleep with that racket going on!"

"I'm really sorry," John apologized. "I'm making a table. Another couple of hours, then you won't hear a peep."

"As long as that'll be the end of it," said Jones, disappointed at missing out on an argument. As he shuffled off, he glanced back to double-check what John was wearing. He wasn't used to a man in athletics shorts in October.

It wasn't illegal to build a box, John reassured himself as he set about making two removable ends. He checked his drawing and continued making lids that would sit flush with the exterior, held in place by an inner lip inside the original frame. He was screwing in eight vertical six-by-one-inch timbers, four at each end, to reinforce the entire structure, when Reg breezed in. He found John lying down hammering the last support, surrounded by sawdust, screws, and cups of cold coffee.

"That's bloody brilliant, Mac, that's what I call a box." Reg was enthralled. "Can I try it for size?"

"Wait until morning, glue's not set. I've still got a few things to do tomorrow: line it with paper so you can't be seen, attach the straps, and make hinges so you can lock yourself in from the inside at both ends."

"Why both ends?"

"In case an exit gets blocked and you get trapped."

By Friday, John was satisfied that everything was ready for delivering Reg to the airport the next day. They walked to the Crown in Twickenham for a last drink, wading through orange and gold leaves in the crisp air of late autumn. Reg felt the promise of an Australian summer beckoning him home.

"Thanks for everything, Mac," he said sincerely.

John gave his arm an affectionate squeeze. "Just let me know when you're home. And look after our box!"

Today was the day. The Twickenham Road buzzed with Saturday morning shoppers, buses, cars, cyclists, and pedestrians. The big timber box sat in the center of the living room, surrounded by drawings, tools, cups, ashtrays, and glue pots.

John had gotten little sleep. His mind had refused to shut down, focusing on various scenarios that all ended in disaster. Reg had slept like a baby, luxuriating in an extra couple of hours because he didn't have to go to work. He whistled in the bathroom, turning up the radio and clutching his toothbrush between his teeth as he danced in a towel. His spirits were dampened when he remembered that he was not allowed to eat breakfast: he'd eaten a meager supper the night before to slow his digestive system down so he wouldn't be faced with midair toilet emergencies. He was hoping to have a major session in the bathroom before he left, because his only option in the box would be a plastic bottle.

Reg spent hours sorting out his luggage. He lined up items to put in his backpack on the living room carpet, starting with a towel rolled around the flashlight John had given him. He had searched secondhand bookshops for a thin book that might be vaguely interesting. The only thing he could find was *The History of British Athletics Coaching: Triumph or Failure?* (As he packed it, he predicted the author's conclusion; the book was very small.) The pee bottle and bottle of fruit juice were identical, and Reg made a mental note not to get them mixed up. He had two large tins of spaghetti bolognese John had gotten from work, one with a tin opener and spoon attached with an elastic band. There was a packet of biscuits, a bar of chocolate, and a tube of fruit gums. He wanted to eat one of the tins of spaghetti for breakfast, but John warned him that he would regret it.

Reg changed into his travel clothes: T-shirt and track pants, and a warm jumper and trainers. His larger bag contained everything else he'd arrived with: one pair of jeans, his Australian track suit, shorts, two T-shirts, underpants, socks, his suit, smart shoes and javelin boots, and table mats he'd bought for his mum because he thought she'd like the pictures of Beefeaters at the Tower of London. He shoved them in the bag along with his passport and other items he wouldn't need en route.

"We'd better get a move on, Reggie!" said John, poking his head out of the box. He was waiting for Reg to zip the bag so he could strap it to the underside of the roof. "You go to the loo and I'll do a checklist."

When he returned from the toilet, Reg gave John a thumbs-up to indicate that his appointment had gone according to plan. They spent another hour checking that everything Reg would need on the plane was in the backpack he would be holding, not the bag strapped to the inside roof. They had finished sticking large labels on the side of the box stating the contents were "Fragile" and should be kept "This Way Up," when Tom and D. J. arrived.

"How's our passenger today?" asked D. J., his voice apprehensive.

Tom looked worried. "Still going through with it, then?" he asked as he lobbed his apple core in the bin.

"Sure am, so if we take my space capsule to the launch pad, I'll be ready for lift off!"

"Right guys, let's get going." John led the way.

Tom and D. J. took the front of the box and Reg carried the back. They slowly angled it out of the flat and down one flight of stairs, taking a chunk of plaster out of the wall before placing it in the hallway.

"Lillian's going to want you to make that up to her," D. J. said before John raced down to open the main double doors. He had just turned the handle when Jones appeared behind him.

"Doesn't look much like a table," he commented dryly as he passed.

"I'll explain later," said John, flustered.

Outside, they placed the box at the top of the steps while D. J. went to open the rear doors of his van. John, Reg, and Tom carted the box down to the pavement. While they were maneuvering it into the vehicle, two old ladies shuffled past, and John saw them make the sign of the cross. He was unnerved when it dawned on him that the women thought they were undertakers, and hoped this wasn't a bad omen.

Nobody spoke as Reg jostled his tall, athletic frame through the vehicle doors and into the box. He checked his watch, and noted that he was getting into his container at 3:17 p.m. on the afternoon of October 17. D. J. and Tom reached in and shook his leg and wished him luck. John leaned in and passed Reg his backpack and clasped his outstretched hand.

"You don't have to go through with this, Reg. It's not too late to change your mind. If you've got any doubts . . ."

"I'm not backing out now." Reg's blue eyes were intense. "I'm too overdue already."

John smiled. "Still think it's reckless."

Reg looked serious. "You know what they say, Mac—that every person's life should include one reckless moment."

"Maybe . . . well, if you do get caught we'll sell the story and pay for the freight charges. Just let me know when you're back. Because I'll be worrying . . ."

"Thanks for everything, Mac." Reg's voice was shaky.

He took a deep breath and tried to swallow the lump in his throat.

John was as nervous as if he'd got into the box himself. He saw the imprint of Reg's smile on the lid after he closed it for the last time.

CHAPTER 19

John checked his watch for the hundredth time. The traffic had been stop-start most of the way from Twickenham, so getting to Heathrow Airport had taken longer than they'd planned. Maybe the delay was for the best; if they missed their deadline, everything would be postponed, and he'd have time to talk the others out of it.

He should have called the whole thing off. If he hadn't been so preoccupied with the practical challenges, he'd have given more thought to all the things that could go wrong. Different scenarios. Things they had no control over. Things they had not even thought about. Possible consequences, such as Reg arriving at his destination dead.

"You've done all you can," D. J. had said. "Too late to be having doubts."

"Come off it," John replied. "Anyone with half a brain would be having doubts."

He knew it was a long shot, but even Tom had agreed it wasn't impossible. He just had to stay calm, focus on where they were going, and forget about why they were going there.

"This is it, follow the sign," he told D. J. as they pulled into the car park. "Don't forget we're on show now. Careful what you say."

D. J. edged his van into a loading bay at the rear of the main terminal. His face was white. Tom leapt out of the passenger side to look for a trolley in the noisy afternoon chaos of the depot. By the time he'd rattled one back to the van, D. J. had the rear doors open and John was squatting inside, deciding on the best way to offload their cargo.

"You're the athlete." D. J. looked nervous as he flicked his bangs out of his eyes. "Slide it our way, then help us lift it down."

John's stomach churned. He stared at the large rectangular timber box and wondered how the hell he'd ever been talked into this. The box occupied most of the space, but he managed to squeeze into a gap behind the front seat, sit with his knees bent, and use his legs to push it through the open doors.

"Stop!" yelled Tom.

John clambered out and D. J. slammed the doors shut.

"Ready?" he looked into John's eyes, then Tom's.

"Probably good that it's so busy," Tom muttered.

The three men hauled their charge onto the warehouse trolley.

"Wouldn't want to be the blokes lifting it on and off the planes," D. J. panted.

"They'll have a forklift for that," Tom said. He leaned toward John and D. J. and whispered, "Doesn't bear thinking about, does it?"

John led the way, senses heightened as he followed the signs for outgoing cargo. The crowded terminal seemed too bright. Women with makeup looked as though they were wearing masks. A man in a hat peered at him with suspicious eyes. Others stared, first at him, then at Tom and D. J., then at the box.

A dark-haired girl with long legs and a short skirt swung past. Tom and D. J. were so distracted that their trolley veered off course and scattered a couple of airport workers.

"Watch where you're going!" John hissed. The least they could do was drop the bloody thing off in one piece.

At the check-in counter, the trio hovered protectively around their box, queuing behind two men with a package half the size of theirs. The one talking to the clerk sounded agitated, and his friend told John they were having problems. John hoped they didn't leave the clerk in a bad mood.

The clerk placed a "Closed" sign on the counter. "Next. Let's be having you," he called.

"Not too late?"

"You're the last."

John's heart raced as he placed his forms on the counter. The clerk ordered him to lift his delivery onto a big set of industrial scales. John nodded at D. J. and Tom to support the far end, and the three men lugged the box onto the platform.

"This is the maximum size allowed," the clerk said when he'd finished his calculations and collected the paperwork.

John's face flushed. He wasn't sure if the man was stating or asking, so he said nothing. "There you are, that's your receipt now. Cash on delivery so there's nothing to pay." The clerk wanted to hurry him along.

"So, we don't have to take it anywhere else?" John asked; surely it couldn't be that easy.

"That's it, we'll do the rest," said the clerk.

John glanced over his box one last time and wondered what would become of it. He gave it a little pat and thanked the man before disappearing with Tom and D. J. into the crowd.

The box sat on the scales for over an hour. The clerk filed paperwork and phoned his wife before mustering four workers to take it into a back room for loading. During the next hour and thirty-five minutes the men jockeyed it around the floor so they could reach smaller crates and packages stacked behind it. Eventually it was placed onto an open truck and driven outside. It swayed around corners as the vehicle sped through the damp air. When the truck neared the storage shed, the driver shouted across the tarmac over the roar of aircraft engines. "This one's a heavy bastard!"

He drove the box to the back of the warehouse and jumped off his truck to consider the best place to store it. The driver scratched his head, his eyes darting between the box and lines of cargo as he searched the crowded columns for a space for his consignment.

"It's big, but it's too late to start moving everything around so we'll just have to get it up there," he said, pointing to the top of a three-meter stack of freight. The forklift positioned itself alongside the rear of the truck and grabbed the box in its jaw. The crate wavered as the pincer hoisted it upward. The supervisor shouted instructions to the driver, who ejected the crate with a thud up in the corner of the shed. The cargo in the warehouse increased throughout the afternoon, but the box remained topmost.

"Let's get rid of this Munich lot so we can all go home," yelled the boss.

The forklift worked through the gloom until the last of the Munich freight had been carted out to the waiting plane. Shouts echoed down the aisles of cargo. The last man wrenched the big metal door shut, and a bolt was padlocked outside. The cargo shed settled into a quiet lull, the stillness magnified by the occasional groan of contracting metal. Silhouettes of crates and containers towered through the shadows. A slight rustling in the left corner of the darkness could have been mistaken for a mouse. Silence. Then a shuffle, before the largest piece of freight sprung to life.

Nobody saw the box as it floated, high in the corner of the warehouse. An illuminated sculpture. A tomb, striped with seams of light shafting over the freight below. Something stirred behind the glowing gaps between the timbers. The whisper of breathing, and a man's eye, peeking out from his lair.

Chapter 20

Five hours later, Reg was hunkered in his box high in the corner of a dark warehouse at Heathrow Airport. The stowaway was cold, cramped, and tired. His flight had been delayed, and he had 13,000 miles to travel. He could stretch his legs out if he sat up, but the five-foot container only allowed him to lie with his legs bent, and he couldn't find a comfortable position to sleep. He hauled himself up and rested his back against the end of the box, his body shaped like an upended Z.

Reg had dispensed with his straps, but the belt to his left had become twisted, and he grappled with it through the darkness. He straightened the padded leather loop that poked his shoulder, and then slowly shifted his weight onto his right hip to relieve the pain down his left side. The stillness of the warehouse magnified every movement as timber creaked under his weight.

He had heard the warehouse door clang shut several hours ago and was confident he was entirely alone. He groped inside his backpack and located the flashlight. When he flicked it on, the rectangular space flooded with a yellowy light, reflected off the lining paper. He focused the beam on the back of his left hand, and fancied he could see blood pulsating through the networked veins. The hand seemed strangely separate, as if it belonged to someone else. He felt queasy as he peered at the translucent skin. He slumped backward, inhaling long, deep breaths.

When the nausea passed, he trailed the torch across the paper, angling his head to find the join. One of the corners of the lining paper had torn away, and he carefully peeled it down and peeked through a tiny gap between the timbers. He estimated he was stacked three to four meters high. When he concentrated, the mountains of freight came into focus, floating in a shadowy void. His gaze wandered along the concrete floor of the closest aisle until it rested on the bottom corner of the warehouse doors, barely visible in the distance.

Something caught his attention. Reg blinked to check he was seeing straight before leaning to take another look. A misty vapor rose eerily from the small gap between the door and its metal frame. He struggled to make sense of what it could be, as the floating tendrils unfurled around the freight and advanced in his direction.

"Christ, it's smoke!" Reg panicked. "I'm trapped in a bloody fire and nobody knows I'm here!"

His heart pounded as thoughts of kicking out the bottom of the box and pummeling on the warehouse door consumed him. Then a flash of logic, as it dawned on him that smoke smells, and he definitely couldn't smell smoke.

He fell back, stroking his head with a deep sigh of relief. There was only the oily smell of the warehouse, like a mechanic's garage, and the fragrance of the newly sawn pinewood of his box.

"It's mist. Mist and fog. The stuff that delays planes!"

He pinned the paper back and turned on his side, pulling his limbs into the fetal position.

He longed for sleep but none came, so he scoured his imagination for a distraction. He had developed techniques in the past that helped him bypass bad situations, but now they didn't work. It was starting to get cold, but he couldn't be bothered releasing his bag from the ceiling of the box. He took the towel from his backpack and wrapped it around his shoulders. He had only two options: sit with straight legs or lie down with them bent. But when he sat and straightened his legs, the wood behind him felt so hard, he was sure he would wake with a stiff back.

Reg was starting to nod off when he realized he needed to use his bottle. He foraged around his backpack, making sure he had the right one. He struggled to find a suitable position to relieve himself. Afterward, he ate two savory biscuits, and then regretted it because the salt made him thirsty. His drink had to be rationed, so he took only a couple of sips. He shaped his backpack into a pillow, buried his face into it, and fell asleep just before dawn.

✈✈✈

"You've just got to follow your training, there's nothing different about this except that the freight's real, and heavy." The man's voice jarred, throwing Reg's world into turmoil. "If you snatch at it, it's not going to behave itself. Got the idea?"

Reg struggled to orient himself: it was morning, he was one of the largest pieces of freight in the warehouse, and because he was at the top of a pile, would probably be one of the first to be moved. He remembered John insisting he do his straps up; that was what he needed to do. The torch and towel were under his head and he tried not to make a sound as he stuffed them into his backpack and secured the strap across his stomach. He looped his arms through the side straps, then grasped as if he were on a swing.

"See how you go with that big one at the top. No one gets it right the first time."

Reg recognized the boss's voice from the day before and surmised he was helping a trainee forklift driver. He was horrified that a youngster was loose in the warehouse—just his bloody luck! He'd gone to all this trouble, only to be flattened by some learner driver before he'd even left England.

The vehicle approached. Reg's limbs tightened at the prospect of being handled by a novice as the squeaking joints of the forklift rotated in his direction. He felt an enormous jolt against the side of his box.

"Slower," the boss yelled, "you're supposed to be picking it up, not knocking it over!"

Reg held his breath as his container was pushed sideways. Then came a whack on the side, and he prayed the novice had him in a secure grip. The box tilted up into midair as shrill voices yelled instructions. Reg was jostled, felt his backside part company with the timber as the box whizzed downward. He landed with a thud on the flatbed of a truck.

"Whatever's fragile in there won't be fragile anymore," the boss bellowed over the vibrating engine. "It'll be fucking broken!"

Reg took long, deep breaths, his heart racing.

"Only those two now, all for the 707," the boss shouted. "Won't be going out for a while in this fog, but let's get them on board."

Reg didn't want to hear about more bloody delays—let's hope the loaders didn't know what the hell they were talking about. The trainee driver was struggling with the remaining freight, and if the idiot dropped it on top of him, his chances of survival would be pretty bloody minimal. Watch what you're doing, you clown.

The drone of the forklift reverberated through Reg's huddled space. He sensed the arm hovering over him for a couple of minutes before it caught the topside of his box and swiped it against something solid. He stifled a cry as his left knee was jabbed against the frame, leaving a stabbing pain. He felt better when he heard the boss telling the novice his shift was over.

It was late afternoon when Reg's truck was driven out of the cargo shed. As it sped across the tarmac, he peeped between the timber slats and saw an army of uniformed airport workers. The high-pitched drone of engines was intense. Men raced around in trucks, refueled the fleet, and waved flags against a backdrop of wailing aircraft. The box was buffeted by a wind that sliced through the gaps and made his eyes water.

He replaced the corner of the paper when he felt the truck reversing and heard the sounds of another forklift approaching.

"Left more," called a voice as his box was propelled forward.

The box shifted to his right, then Reg felt it being shoved into place by several pairs of hands in the mouth of the plane's cargo hold. Someone called, "Let's get this big heavy one to the side. Keep it there, less work for us and the blokes at the other end."

He felt himself being pushed along the floor, glad he was labeled "this side up"—his biggest fear was being turned upside down. Baggage handlers milled around him, just above his head as they jostled him into place—they were close enough to detect the smallest noise. Sweat trickled down the inside of his arms as he grasped his straps and wedged his feet against the end of the box. His body was rigid, his mouth clamped, so the only sound was the breath purring through his nostrils.

Suddenly he wanted to sneeze. He panicked—his arms were trapped, and he wouldn't be able to muffle the noise. He curled his lips inward, thrust his chin on his chest, and stifled the sneeze into a whimper.

"No live animals on this run, are there?" asked one of the loaders.

"Don't think so."

Reg smiled in his dark hideout. He remained stock-still until he heard the voices receding and was sure the last loaders had gone. The sound of vehicles continued outside, and he could hear workers some distance away. He assumed that the cargo doors were still open, so he chanced only the smallest shift of bodyweight. The confinement was becoming unbearable, but he dared not move in case someone was below the doors.

He drifted in and out of consciousness. He imagined Marion begging him, pleading with him not to get in the box. He'd just started to convince her it was a good idea, when he heard a double clunk followed by the suction of the cargo door sealing. He was sure liftoff was imminent and felt like shouting for joy at the thought of being able to stretch his aching limbs. Within minutes, the plane was moving. He held his watch under a small ray of light. It was 7:48 p.m., and he calculated he'd been in the box for twenty-eight hours and thirty-one minutes.

He wanted to believe things were about to get better as his transport taxied him down the runway. He imagined passengers above him, sitting in their neat rows. He pictured some pretty flight attendant standing in the aisle giving the safety demonstration, an oxygen mask around her neck. Then his mind raced with the gathering speed of the plane and exhilaration engulfed him as it lifted him from the ground onto the first leg of his surreal journey.

By the time the plane had reached its cruising height, Reg was ravenous. He knew the first flight would be a short hop to Paris. If he were going to eat something, he'd have to get on with it. He leaned forward and turned the locking dials of the lid. It refused to flatten because something was in the way. He pushed the end panel to the side and maneuvered himself out into a very small space. He emerged into the juddering hold, clutching his backpack in one hand as he steadied himself with the other. The leg that had collided with the side of the box was throbbing. He rolled up his track pants to inspect the damage. His knee looked red and angry.

He hoped that food would take his mind off the pain. First he unscrewed his bottle and gulped as much juice as he dared. Then he lovingly opened one of the cans of spaghetti bolognese, mumbling himself encouragement. Everything looked brighter as he sat on his container and savored each spoonful. He tilted his head and dangled strands of spaghetti into his mouth, until a patch of turbulence spoiled his game. After rapidly consuming half the tin, he took a few more sips from the bottle. His supplies would now be strictly rationed. He was still hungry, so he explored the freight to look for a diversion.

His box was placed near the cargo hold door, with a smaller one in front. Both boxes were tied in. The entire floor was lined with metal rails like a railway track, used for moving and securing the freight. It was cold and clinical, like the cargo shed he had slept in. The frame of the hold curved to meet the metal roof with inset lights that were turned off, and the whole space vibrated in a half-light. He had never imagined it would look and sound like this: bleak and lifeless, almost sinister in the hum of the engines.

He climbed over a large package to get back to his box, and took the plastic bottle from his backpack. His first attempt to urinate into the neck had to be aborted, but he eventually found a position to avoid peeing over things that didn't belong to him. When he'd finished, he got his torch and started looking at labels for something to do. The plane began to descend, but he thought he still had plenty of time so he continued reading the details of his fellow freight. He noticed that a smaller crate than his own purported to contain three hundred umbrellas. That couldn't be right—you'd be hard-pressed to fit a hundred in there, who did they think they were fooling?

He found a few boxes that were going to keep him company all the way to Perth. Realizing that the plane was nearing the end of its descent, he made his way back to his cubbyhole. He bundled his backpack in, and then had difficulty getting inside himself. When he finally succeeded, he turned himself around, lifted in the half-eaten can of spaghetti with the spoon sticking out, and closed the lid.

He was just in time. As he started to tidy the box, he was jolted by a thunderous clank of the undercarriage dropping into place. His mind surged with excitement.

"So far, so good!" he thought. "Please God, no more delays. I've got a girl to see . . ."

The plane was landing when Reg's mood changed. He had a horrible feeling he'd left something sitting on the container opposite.

And it wasn't the spaghetti bolognese.

CHAPTER 21

Reg heard the hissing suction of the cargo doors opening, and his peace was invaded by the commotion of French airport workers. Loud voices clamored as outgoing freight was barged and cajoled across the hold. He felt vulnerable; a blind man trapped on a frantic construction site. He longed for the peace of the clouds again. Heavy boots bumped the side of his container amid the rhythm of men's breathing.

He locked his body and waited patiently amid the confusion, praying that his pee bottle hadn't been found. Whirring sounds from distant runways wafted into his hideaway as other aircraft came and went. Heavy machinery jarred as mechanics thrust massive pipes into thirsty engines. He sucked beads of moisture from his bottom lip. His cheek felt like sandpaper as he stroked it along the inside of his strapped forearm, imagining the luxury of shaving and the bliss of cool water on his face.

It was a struggle to separate his mind from his aching body. Thank God the Frenchmen had stopped shouting. Their babble was a quiet conversation now, floating through the hold door. He tried not to think about how long he'd been stationary, and when he heard the double clunk of the door closing, relief swept over him. His arms throbbed as he pulled them out of the side straps. He released the belt across his stomach, circling his shoulder blades as he arched his stiff back.

The engines gave a low growl as the plane taxied down the runway.

"About bloody time," he muttered.

The plane tilted, and the hold echoed with creaking metal and grumbling rows of freight. Reg groped around the dark corners of his container, relieved to find the warmth of his plastic pee bottle. He prepared to leave the box, and then wondered if he should. Perhaps he should stay put for a while—save something to look forward to through the long hours ahead.

He ate four squares of chocolate and found the fruit gums and flashlight, then fidgeted to find a comfortable position to read the book on athletics coaching in Britain. He stared at the cover and thought about Marion. She liked reading; all sorts of books about interesting people. Waterford had probably read loads of books. He was bound to try to impress her with his incredible knowledge.

Oh God, please don't let her fall for his bullshit credentials!

Reg bunched the towel between his shoulders and head, lay flat with his knees bent, and held the book a few inches above his face to focus the beam on chapter one. The lines of print moved, slowly at first, before they toppled into a jumbled tide of black letters. He couldn't concentrate, and he kept thinking about his meeting with Forbes, the man from the shipping office in Adelaide. If Forbes hadn't offered him a free passage to England, he wouldn't be stuck in this damn box.

When Reg realized he'd read the same paragraph twice, he flicked off the flashlight and rested the open pages on his chest, drifting through the darkness.

✈ ✈ ✈

"Have you got an appointment sir?" the mousy receptionist at the Adelaide shipping office had asked.

"No, but Mr. Brown said I could call to discuss a particular matter any time," Reg lied.

He hoped she thought it possible that Brown had left before she had joined the company. She told him to take a seat until it was his turn to see a Mr. Forbes. While he waited, Reg flipped through magazines with articles like "Cruise into a Different World" and "Fantasy Escapes, Your Dreams Made Real." He liked the sound of them.

"What a beautiful girl," he lied again when he breezed into Forbes's office. "She must be your daughter."

He pointed out a photograph of a pasty, moonfaced schoolgirl with a forced smile.

"Indeed." Forbes didn't sound in the mood for small talk. "Didn't catch your name," said the balding bespectacled man with the same-shaped face as his daughter.

"My apologies: Reg Spiers." Reg leaned over the desk and shook his hand. "Look at that!" He indicated the stuffed fish in an ornate, gold frame on the wall behind Forbes. "That's gotta be a red emperor, biggest I've ever seen, for sure. You catch that beauty yourself?"

The man's demeanor changed. He straightened himself in his chair and puffed out his chest, flicking remnants of his crusty lunch off his trousers as he told a well-worn story of his big catch on Fraser Island in 1959. Reg listened patiently to a stack of useless information on *Lutjanus sebae*.

"Do you fish, Mr. Spiers?"

Reg had been waiting for Forbes to throw him a line.

"Always fancied my chances with fishing, nothing to do with the name or anything! To be honest Mr. Forbes, I'm a javelin thrower. I've seen the way some of those spear fishers go at it and I've always thought, . . . well, I've always thought I'd be bloody good at that."

"That's where I've heard the name—of course you're a javelin thrower, and a good one by all accounts," said Forbes. "I was captain of athletics in my final year at Saint Peter's, you know?"

Reg let him prattle on before laying his cards on the table. Then he explained that he was on the cusp of his career, so close to the throw of his life.

"Call it my red emperor," he told Forbes, who seemed flattered by the analogy. "I'll do anything to work my passage to England. You name it, I can do it. Peel the spuds, clean out toilets, wash the decks . . ."

"Imagine telling your friends what you've done for Australian athletics" had finally clinched the deal.

As he left the office, Reg glanced at the red emperor and thought the fish looked miserable. Reg, ny contrast, felt elated. He had just landed a free passage to England the following week.

✈ ✈ ✈

Reg woke, his mind cluttered with dead fish. He spent the next two hours on his back, gazing through his dark confines and running his fingers along the grainy timber roof. He thought about fishing trips with his mate, Niko, in Adelaide. Mainly he thought about his family, until he couldn't put off having a pee any longer. The urgency set him in motion, shuffling his belongings out of the way, and then rewinding the locking mechanisms at the end of his container. He eased the heavy lid backward. When he'd uncoiled his bulky frame he turned himself around and collected his pee bottle. As he'd suspected, it was almost full.

Now he was in a dilemma. He needed a portable toilet, fast; preferably one that closed. This was the last place to find one, and he wasn't prepared to drink all his juice just so he could urinate in the bottle. There was only one option; finish the spaghetti bolognese. He feverishly shoveled the contents of the tin into his mouth and tried to kid himself he was enjoying it. Even if it had tasted good, the whole experience was ruined by the burning sensation in his abdomen, getting more desperate by the minute. He half-heartedly chewed the cold pasta down to a few mushy strands clinging to the bottom of the can.

He felt more kindly about the tin now that it would serve as a urinal, although the thought of turbulence and the tin's jagged edges made him wince. He steadied himself on a crate and angled it ready for action. He savored the ecstasy of his relief. Shortly after, another problem presented itself. Reg eyed the contents of the can, afloat with tendrils of pasta swimming along the surface in time with the motion of the plane.

The vibration magnified the fiasco he'd created. He felt like an unwilling actor, forced to play the clown in a ridiculous comedy. He needed some kind of lid to prevent the urine spilling; something he could fix with the rubber band that had held the tin opener and spoon. It came to him—the perfect thing. He got to his knees and levered himself far enough into the box to unstrap his duffle bag from the roof.

The bag hit the floor with a loud thud. He hauled it out into a space barely wide enough to accommodate it. Impatient now, he rifled through the contents until he found the set of Beefeater tablemats. He undid the cellophane wrapping and nicked a corner of the sheet with his teeth, tearing it in two. One-half fitted perfectly over the can, so he secured it with the rubber band. He thought the arrangement almost attractive, like frilly pots of homemade jam in his mother's kitchen.

Having solved his toilet problems, he needed to de-stress. A space at the back of the hold was big enough for him to lie face down. He pumped out several sets of pushups, counting every beat. Then he wound through the maze of crates and packages as he exercised. A large flat container in the corner proved the perfect base for sit-ups. He hooked his feet under the ledge of a giant metal safe next to it, clasped his hands behind his head, and then hauled his torso up to his knees one hundred times. Soon his skin glistened with sweat as he puffed and panted his way through vigorous series of squats, lunges, and stretches until he felt weak. He grabbed his towel, stripped off his T-shirt, and wiped his wet limbs. He swigged as much of his drink as he dared and shoved everything back into the box.

He shuffled in, dragging his bag behind him. Lying on his back, he propped the bag on his chest and struggled to strap it to the roof. When he had secured the end of his container, he rummaged through the dark floor space around his hips until he felt his sweater. The tube of fruit sweets fell out of a sleeve. He stuck one in his mouth and sucked noisily in between his deep, labored breathing.

It was so dark that the walls of the box had disappeared. All Reg could see were the dim gaps between the timbers on either side and dashes of light overhead not covered by his bag. The somber, evenly spaced, ruler-straight lines were like the bars of a cage. He saw them first as solid, then as a geometric drawing. He speculated that if the lines continued and his box had no lid, he could be in a never-ending tunnel. The perspective confounded him as he tried to visualize where the lines would reach their vanishing point. Three fruit gums later, he was still staring into the dark abyss. He wanted to eat something solid; exercising always made him hungry.

His food supply consisted of one can of spaghetti bolognese, three salty biscuits, and the remains of the chocolate, flat and gooey beneath him. He thought about the best meals he'd ever eaten, conjuring the smell of a barbecued T-bone steak, medium rare, with a fluffy potato and a fresh green salad. His mouth watered.

He pictured Marion rustling up dinners in the kitchen of their house in Adelaide. The delicate little pastry stars she put on the top of her apple pies. *God!* What if she was baking apple pies for someone else? What if Waterford was a dab hand in the kitchen, and he was cooking fancy dishes for her? Marion and Waterford scenarios: cooking, walking, talking politics. Waterford phoning to ask how she was coping on her own: charming, accommodating, insisting on mowing the lawn, . . . Reg took these thoughts into a troubled sleep.

He was awakened by the hissing sound of the hold door opening a couple of hours later. As the box was swamped with light and heat, he knew he was in Bombay. He could see his straps, and he quickly stuffed his backpack behind his back and gripped the covered can of urine between his thighs before securing his waist and arms. Within seconds, Indian workers clambered into the plane, jostling and pushing his container. When he began to slide in the direction of the door, he assumed he was up for loading onto another aircraft. The rumble of forklift trucks was quickly drowned by the gabble of an army of workers. Their voices soon became distracted, as if signaling a change of plan, and Reg came to a standstill for a good hour.

He heard the groan of a machine approaching and felt sure his wait was over. He prepared to be moved again by tightening his grip on the side straps. The workers laughed and cursed as the bottom of Reg's box scraped along the edge of the doorway. Then he was scooped out of the belly of the plane and drawn skyward through the hot moist air. He took deep breaths through the unfamiliar sounds and smells, praying for a smooth landing.

None came. He hit the ground with a jolt, quickly followed by panicked voices and a violent lurch as the workers upended his crate onto the tarmac to avoid other freight. Now Reg dangled inside a vertical box, strung upside down from the strap ripping into his stomach. His heart pounded so heavily he could feel the pulse in his throat. Every muscle and sinew tightened as he realized that his head was pointing downward!

CHAPTER 22

Reg was upside down in a heap at the bottom of the box. He desperately tightened his grip on the can of liquid between his thighs. He let go of his arm straps and grabbed the can with both hands, his arms still looped at the elbows. Blood rushed to his head, now jutted forward onto his chest and folded torso. His taut arms clasped the tin above his face, pointing it in the same direction as his long legs, which were splayed up the vertical length of the box. What the hell was the point of being labeled "This Way Up" if the loaders couldn't read English? He desperately hoped they wouldn't shove him into the next plane in the same position. He rested the tin on his collarbone and released his arms, then his stomach brace, which felt like it was cutting him in two.

The bag had fallen to a position around his head. He reached backward across his ear and squeezed the can of urine into the corner behind it. His neck was taking most of his weight, and he inched his shoulder blades back one at a time, enabling the back of his head to creep up the side of his container until he had enough room to uncoil his battered body. Mindful of the workers around the perimeter of the box, his every movement was slow and deliberate until his head was uppermost.

When the commotion of men and machines subsided, he was huddled at the bottom of his hideout with no clue as to when he was due to be moved again. The air was hot and thick. He wiped his brow with the back of his hand, and then clawed at the paper lining near his cheek, desperate for ventilation. He angled his watch under a shaft of light. Still going. The glass had cracked when it had been slammed against the side.

It was 4:52 a.m. in England; the second morning since he had left. He'd been stuck in his prison for over thirty-seven hours.

Another baking hour of agony passed before a swerving vehicle squealed to a halt alongside the box. A truckload of workers had arrived. Then he was surrounded by the sound of their boots. There was no time to secure his arm straps before his box was hoisted onto what felt like some kind of metal platform. He glided upward, then sideways as if on a conveyor belt, and he flexed his legs. Hallelujah! They'd turned him around. He was in a horizontal box again and it was on the move.

He remembered that he'd wedged the tin in the corner and reached behind his head to check that it was surviving the ride. It had tilted to almost a right angle but still felt dry, so he pushed it back into place. It was difficult to gauge the distance he was traveling. He was confused when he was laid to rest somewhere quiet. He knew he was still outside. The temperature inside the box was getting unbearable. Then he heard voices closing in again, so he slurped a mouthful of juice before anyone arrived. He prayed he would soon be collected and wouldn't have to face the uncertainty of another delayed flight.

He remained stationary and figured he had been dumped at a lunchtime meeting place for the loading staff. Their relaxed voices mingled with the spicy smell of curry wafting on the humidity. Beads of perspiration patterned his skin, highlighted by tiny shafts of brilliant sunlight that pierced the interior of the box. The sweat trickled down his forehead, forming salty rivulets that mingled around his lips. Reg figured that the only thing to do in a sauna was to get naked, so he started to peel off his clothes. He struggled to pull off his T-shirt. By the time two workers were chatting beside him, he was taking off his underpants.

He was shocked, then indignant when his roof creaked under the weight of being sat on. He pictured two friends on their lunch break. Dehydration and the smell of their pungent food were making him nauseous. His stomach churned. No end . . . The whole situation was getting desperate. A complete fucking emergency! Too ludicrous to be real life, but it *was* real life, and he was the poor blighter who was living it.

How the hell had he ended up naked and trapped in a sweltering bloody box in Bombay?

"You always look on the bright side, Reggie—always come up smelling of roses," his mother used to say.

He didn't smell of roses now, but it wasn't as if someone had made him get into this stupid bloody box! Nobody else would have been nuts enough to think it up, let alone do it. Tom had been right—it was a totally reckless thing to do. He was "cuckoo." If he wasn't cuckoo when he got in to the box, he was feeling pretty bloody loopy now. And if that luncheon party overhead didn't hurry up and leave the table, he was gonna throw up, right under their noses.

Focusing on breathing distracted him from everything else—and everything couldn't have been worse. A vice-like grip took hold of the back of his head, moving upward to his frontal lobes until every nerve throbbed in one spectacular headache. Now the interior of the box was striped with light, which added a buzzing sensation to the pain in his head. When he tried to concentrate on looking at his toenails, the sound was so loud it felt as though his ears were vibrating. He warned himself not to fall asleep. If he was taken unawares by the jaws of another forklift, he could be seriously injured. Christ, now he was seeing quicksand! When he started sinking he groped for his drink bottle and swigged.

It would have been so easy to kick open the bottom of the box and crawl out. To give himself up and let the press have a field day with the mad naked bastard who almost died from dehydration on the tarmac in Bombay. "For what?" everyone would ask. Reg was thinking about his answer when the man sitting on his box gave a loud laugh. Shards of cruel light still infiltrated the box. Reg dozed his way through a semiconscious trail of pain until a new noise emerged from the horrible haze. He opened his eyes and listened, grateful to find the sun had moved and his box was cooling.

A vehicle approached from the distance as he stared through the shadows at his bare thighs. His head had stopped aching, but his thoughts were slow and confused as he swigged his bottle of juice and tried to get himself organized. He was sure the lunch-break men had gone, and he lifted his aching back into a sitting position. He retrieved his underpants, slowly rewinding them up his legs. The engine was getting louder, and he was still looking for his T-shirt when a loading truck parked nearby.

The ground staff banged around the forecourt, carting crates onto their vehicle and drowning the shuffling sounds of a man dressing in the biggest box, which they were leaving until last. Reg stuffed his shoes into his backpack and gazed into the dim recesses above his head. He brushed his fingers across the grainy roof next to his bag, checking that it was secure. He fastened his straps and felt his breathing slow. He was just thinking how much better he felt when there came a loud rumble of thunder, followed by shouts from the workers. Fat globules of rain slapped his box. He grasped his arm straps before his container swayed upward, maneuvered by gabbling men who lifted him onto a sur-face and shoved him against something solid.

He was convinced everything was on track again as the truck whisked him across the runway. The pounding rain drowned the sound of the engine as Reg peeled back a section of lining paper from a corner of the timber roof. He threw his head back and opened his mouth to catch trickles of water, overcome with relief and joy. It had been bad back there, really bad, but never again would he doubt he could complete his journey. It could only be reckless if he didn't stay in control. That was the key—control. He planned to stay in control all the way to Perth.

CHAPTER 23

The monotonous drone of the engines dissipated as Reg imagined himself in a stadium with other athletes. The temperature soared as they paced the field like big cats. A starting gun exploded in the distance as he rallied for his third attempt. When the signal went up, he selected a spear from the pit, carefully grasping the cord to avoid the burning heat of the metal shaft. Now the two markers for checking his strides were in place. He wiped his forehead, standing motionless with the fork-gripped javelin perched on his shoulder, parallel to his upper arm and pointing ahead.

Gently rocking, he glided into his run-up as the crowd clapped at every step. He switched into a fast jog, and his left foot planted on course with the first marker, where he bounded through six long, thumping strides to the second. His left shoulder flexed and he turned as he ran, drawing the javelin down to his side over three paces until he reached a position to muster all his strength. His body arched and his hips straightened.

As he launched the javelin high in the air, Reg's attention was brought back to reality by a violent jolt. Nothing to worry about, he thought, just the usual turbulence around Far Eastern airspace. This had to be a good sign because it meant he was getting closer to Australia. When he got home, he would concentrate on his athletics, spend more time at the club, try to find a better coach . . .

If he got home in one piece, because now the purr he'd found soothing five minutes ago had become a rattling cough, shaking his box. The bag jerked overhead. He felt around the roof, checking that the attachments were still in their washers in case the bag burst out of its strapping and landed on his head. A series of loud bangs erupted, and Reg hoped his container was winched in like it had been until Bombay. Amid the chaos he heard the ring of the seatbelt warning overhead. Then the distant voice of a man he thought was the captain, reassuring the legitimate passengers upstairs that they had nothing to worry about. The plane dipped and shook, buffeted by a tropical storm that made Reg feel very alone.

His container made scuffing sounds, jolting him as it edged around the floor. The noise was soon drowned by the high-pitched clang of metal. Reg felt his body being snatched as the plane lunged, and he desperately wanted to get out of the box. The floor gyrated beneath his hands as they took his weight and he turned onto his knees. He fumbled with the dials, released the last lock, and pushed the top of the lid forward as the plane dropped again, flinging him sideways. Reg scrambled to get out of his juddering container, his heart rate increasing as he emerged into the mayhem. He lost his balance as he tried to pull himself up before deciding to stay on his knees with his arms clasped over the top of a large cardboard box. Now the hold was a frightening shadowed space where every package and crate thrashed and groaned as it pummeled its neighbor. Some parcels had escaped their restraints, hovering between dimly lit piles of larger boxes that grunted in their jangling trusses.

Reg was contemplating whether to stay where he was or get back in his box when a popping sensation in his ears signaled that the plane was descending. The hold was still shaking and plunging—would the pilot land or abort? He felt his way across the top of his support and lowered his head and shoulders back into his shuffling hideout. When he'd locked himself in and maneuvered into a lying position with bent legs, he felt as though he was trapped in a tumble dryer.

The plane would soon be landing—he recognized the change in the engine noise, then the hovering and dipping of the final descent. Reg told himself that the worst was over; this would be his last touchdown before Perth. As he started to secure his straps, he felt the thud of the undercarriage releasing, and he closed his eyes as the engines reached a loud, high-pitched whine. Then his vibrating box was whipped into the most intense frenzy of the flight, and he screwed his eyes as the wheels of the plane thundered onto the tarmac of Singapore.

A screeching hollow from the breaking system gripped the aircraft, and his tension evaporated into long deep breaths as he was hurtled down the runway. Reg thanked God for bringing him down safely. When the plane came to a standstill, he heard clapping from the lawful passengers overhead. Now he had to wait. He knew from his work at the airport that this would only be a fuel stop, and perhaps the offloading of other freight. He pulled a crumpled jumper across the top of his shoulders and wedged his backpack under his head.

Half an hour later, he was still strapped inside the box, exhausted, aching, but too nervous to sleep. When he sneezed, he wondered if he'd caught a chill when he was loaded in Bombay in damp clothes. Then he got frustrated about the delay and tried to imagine what was causing it. Where was everyone? They obviously didn't intend to collect any freight, so why the delay? Muffled sounds floated through the box as he groped inside his backpack, feeling for the spoon and tin opener.

"Fuck," he hissed as he nicked his thumb on the jagged edge of the can.

Perhaps he should go back to being a secret agent in a movie. Pretend stuff, like when he was a kid hanging out with his brother on the beach in Adelaide. God, they had fun. Those never-ending sunny days when nobody cared about anything except what was for tea and copping a whack from Dad for coming home late. Sand in your eyes and everywhere else, and making things, always making things and catching things. He'd caught a fish when he was six with a net he'd made from wire, netting, and a spindly piece of bamboo he'd found behind the shed.

"That's not a fish, Reggie," said Meredith, a big know-all girl with braces who lived on the corner of their street. "That's a baby eel and they're poisonous, and if your Mum cooks that and you eat it, your whole family will die."

So he'd tipped the bucket out under a bush by his front gate.

He would do anything to eat fish now—he was sick of fucking spaghetti, but as the plane finally edged toward takeoff, he spooned a little into his mouth, just for something to do. He wouldn't even bother strapping himself in. What the hell? The smallest action now felt like a momentous chore. By the time he was airborne, every part of him was heavy and tired. This wasn't the luxurious kind of tired—it was a worn-out exhaustion where his mind refused to shut down. Everything about his current state irritated him. What smelled so bad, him or the box? Where did one start and the other finish? The box was like his mind, in total disarray. Wretched. He loathed the feel of creased, dank clothing beneath him. He shoved the spaghetti tin into the corner and sprawled along the floor with bent legs.

Thoughts swirled and then disappeared into the gloom. He rubbed his toes over the rough, splintery timber and followed the veined pattern of the grain. The thin floating lines danced, just for him, then transformed themselves into symmetric shapes, like a butterfly opening its wings. Then a kaleidoscope of landscapes evolved, melting into faces, animals, and words that carried him downstream to an otherworldly place where he didn't have to think and feel. He just was. And then he was asleep.

When he woke, he knew he'd been out only a short while because his foot was still propped up in the corner. Then he wondered what he'd been dreaming about because he had an erection. He swigged the last couple of inches of his juice. God, that was it now; nothing to drink, but at least he had something to pee into. He licked the moisture from his bottom lip and shivered, pulling the woolen jumper over his head and flicking on his torch to try reading again.

He soon abandoned his book and recounted his life story several times. He thought about his little house in the northwestern suburbs of Adelaide, and imagined the look on Marion's face if he ever made it home. Then he resolved to never climb into a box again, because this one was driving him so crazy. He knew he was completely free to stay outside; it wasn't as if somebody might suddenly appear before the plane had landed. He could wander around the hold, but how long could he keep that up for? Every time he lay on the floor, he was plagued with a strange sort of insecurity, so compelling that it drove him back to his wooden sanctuary.

His last hours inside the four timber walls were like a patterned dream of memories and ideas. He recounted childhood scenes long buried in the recesses of his subconscious and wrestled with some of the great philosophical propositions of his time.

"I think, therefore I am" bothered him the most.

No matter where he strayed, he couldn't escape from himself, and in the endless boxed world of shadows, the container played tricks with his imagination. Strange, unearthly noises rippled through the belly of the beast. He longed for any panacea for being adrift in this relentless cosmos, this strange disorientation, feeling his face in the darkness to confirm he was alive.

Reg spent his last hours in the box dozing uncomfortably with the lid open and his lower legs poking outside. He was weary, but most of his harrowing journey was behind him. Every cramped limb longed to break free from this terrible claustrophobia. His drink had run out hours ago. His mouth was dry, swallowing painful—but not long now, almost there, he had to be almost there . . . Just when he started to believe himself, the hold became so dark he could barely see his hands.

As the aircraft descended into Perth, the cargo hold was shaking violently again, but he didn't care. He'd lost track of time, and when he wiped the grime from the face of his watch he calculated it had been sixty-three hours since he first got into the box in Twickenham.

Reg knew his biggest test still lay ahead; the final hurdle where he could come unstuck. He'd traveled 13,000 miles for free, but he still had to get out of the airport. The escape would take every bit of stealth and cunning he could muster, as well as a bucket-load of luck.

CHAPTER 24

Reg had to endure one more forklift truck.

"Geez mate, this one's bloody heavy." The voice of a loader boomed above the commotion as Reg's box was winched onto the concrete floor of a huge holding shed behind a network of runways.

When he felt a rush of cool air with the scent of eucalyptus in its wake, Reg knew he'd arrived in Perth and it was early morning. There was nowhere on earth like Australia. The good old gum trees, bloody kookaburras waking you at dawn, and the best surf in the world. He'd missed it all, but now he was back. He'd made it! Two days at the most and he'd be home with his wife!

His body was wracked; every joint and muscle ached, and his mouth was so dry he could hardly create enough saliva to swallow. Continually grinding his teeth had left his gums sore. He had to get his mind off his thirst; he longed for the feel of cool water washing his tongue and the inside of his cheeks, lubricating his parched throat and flooding every part of him. He detested this worn-out, sordid state. Stale, musty air had long overpowered the sweet smell of newly sawn pinewood. He wanted to be rid of it all. He soon could be, but he had to curb his impatience. It would be so easy to screw up.

He hoped there'd be no more immediate incoming flights for the workers to unload. He sat motionless with his head and arms propped on his knees, willing them to leave. Their jabbering voices echoed over the sound of his breathing as he listened. It felt like a good couple of hours before someone finally said, "Smoko guys." Reg could hardly contain himself as their footsteps filed out, followed by the grating squeak of the shed door closing behind them.

This was his chance! He reached to turn the latches at the end of the box. The lid whacked another crate as it fell away. Reg froze, praying nobody had heard. He quickly released his bag from the strapping on the roof and pushed it out and to the side. This was the moment he'd thought about so often during the past long, lonely hours. He could hardly believe he was climbing out of the box for the last time. His legs felt weak as he crawled. He breathed deeply and tried to temper his enthusiasm.

He rose slowly to his feet, surprised to find himself shaking. He leaned on the end of the box as his pulse quickened and his ears filled with the sound of air rushing through his nostrils. He closed his eyes for a moment and inhaled deeply. The euphoria of this long-awaited moment made him dizzy. The huge warehouse seemed bright, considering there were no windows. He stood motionless, waiting for his senses to return to normal. He arched his back and stretched his limbs. This was it! Back in the real world, the traumas of his bizarre journey behind him. There was one last obstacle to overcome, then freedom.

His exhaustion had been replaced by a new energy; he was alert and focused, pumped with adrenaline. His heart pounded. The workers could return at any minute. He chucked more debris from his in-flight dining through the mouth of the box and crammed his backpack into his duffle bag. He quickly turned his attention to his first obstacle; opening the cargo shed doors. He flitted between the aisles of packages, eyes darting, listening for the workers.

The vast emptiness of the warehouse magnified every sound as Reg wrapped his shaking hand around the levered handle of the heavy metal double doors, pressing it down and pushing in one continuous movement. A column of light sliced the shadowy interior as the doors caught on a waist-high metal chain, padlocked on the outside. Reg's heart sunk as he tentatively pulled the door closed and released the handle. He spun round, scouring every corner of the huge shed as he tried to devise a way to bust the chain without creating a racket.

He raced back down the center aisle of the shed, desperately searching for something strong enough to cut metal. Near the end, he spotted a huge shelf and a long workbench covered in various tools. He'd stumbled on the maintenance area, the one place he might find what he needed. He searched the rows of assorted gadgets, unsure of what some were used for. There were so many tools: hammers, buckets, drills, and spark plugs. Then he spied a sturdy pair of bolt-cutters, nestled between a big tin and a tray of nails. You beauty, he thought as he grabbed them, and sped, rejoicing, back down the aisle.

The door squeaked as Reg dipped the handle and eased it forward again, just enough to study the horizontal chain strung across the opening to the great outdoors. He immediately spotted the edge of the padlock and carefully fed it into the center of the gap. The padlock looked older than the chain, browned with rust, so he opted to concentrate on cutting that. Gripping the handles of the cutters, he applied the big, beak-like blades to the U-shaped arm of the padlock. He feverishly squeezed the unfamiliar handles. They were cold as he fumbled, hands shaking. He felt the pulse in his throat beat for several seconds before the cutters skidded out of his grip. "Shit!"

Reg stooped to retrieve them, quickly repositioning them with both hands, teeth clenched, as he winced with the exertion of one almighty squeeze. A sound like a cracking whip shot through the warehouse as the vicious blades sliced the metal. Reg's heart raced. He quickly dropped the cutters, twisted the arm of the padlock, and freed it from the jangling chain. Then he eased the chain off the outer left door handle and attached the padlock again so it appeared unlocked rather than broken.

The door whined as he pushed it ajar enough to view his surroundings and plan his getaway. He peered cautiously and listened; the coast was clear, nobody in his immediate vicinity. The activity revolved around the only terminal, a long, low building he estimated to be about two hundred yards straight ahead. To his left, more warehouses identical to his own. They extended to an expanse of runways, petering to a row of stationary planes left of the forecourt of the terminal, where a smaller domestic plane was parked. Half a dozen workers clustered around the cargo hatch unloading freight. To his right, an exposed, roughly grassed area fronted a couple of garage-sized sheds. The first shed appeared less than a hundred yards away; he would head for that and take cover. He had to get moving; it wouldn't be long before his handiwork was discovered, and if a break-in was suspected, the whole area would be swarming with cops in no time.

Reg quickly hid the bolt-cutters behind a stack of cardboard and collected his bags. He stopped for a moment to lay his open hand on the box. "Thank you, Johnny Mac," he whispered. Then he took a deep breath and stepped into a bright West Australian morning.

He hurried across the open ground. Each footfall felt heavy, every sound was magnified as he gulped lungfuls of air and strode, his duffle bag over one shoulder. Oh God, he wanted to run! His heart knocked and he dared not look back. Onward he marched, like a power walker, in the direction of two o' clock. He darted around the right side of the shed. His bag made a low thud when he dumped it and crouched, panting. He poked his head around the corrugated iron wall and peered at the terminal. He could almost make out the faces of the loaders, grouped around the hatch of a domestic Ansett plane.

Reg turned his attention back to the big warehouse he'd just come from. Beyond it lay a network of more runways, peppered with trucks and workers, and a vast expanse of nothingness as far as the eye could see. To the right, more warehouses; on the left, maintenance sheds like the one he was leaning against. It was decision time; should he go back and take his chances with the unknown, or head for the terminal? Every muscle ached and he'd never felt so tired and hungry. "Back there" looked a bloody long way. It was too exposed, and a lone figure would be easily spotted. More importantly, he had no idea which direction to take and didn't relish the thought of dodging aircraft. Besides, if he were caught in the terminal, they wouldn't have a clue if he was a worker from the bloody warehouse—not unless they were already on to him. His mind was made up; but if he was going to take the terminal route, he had to get a move on.

He scanned the terminal forecourt. None of the loaders were looking his way so he grabbed his bag and hastened toward an open undercover structure to the right of the terminal building. He bypassed the second shed, marching to the rhythm of his labored breathing and the tread of his training shoes thumping the ground. He reminded himself not to run, striding purposefully with one eye on the airport workers grouped at the rear of the plane. A low groan built momentum as a big jet taxied across a distant runway, and Reg scurried behind a maintenance building at the end of a covered walkway. He leaned against the brick wall, trying to slow his pounding heart. When he'd caught his breath, he ambled casually down the path, totally alone as he neared the side of the terminal.

A straggle of bag-carrying passengers descended the steps of the Ansett plane and drifted across the tarmac to the arrivals entrance. A little girl's hair caught the breeze as she toddled behind her mother. Reg had a flash of his daughter's face, and then his own in 1962 as he proudly walked into the same terminal with the Australian athletics team.

He took a deep breath of courage and walked along the front of the building, trying to adopt a credible, confident stance. He strode in an orderly manner, his bag at his side like a legitimate passenger, hovering at the entrance as a line of people from the Ansett plane filed through. He panicked for a moment; perhaps the terminal wasn't such a good idea, but he still stepped forward and offered the next woman the right of way.

She smiled gratefully, and Reg fell in line behind her, his pulse racing as his shoes squeaked along the shiny linoleum floor. A baby cried as he skirted a group of Japanese tourists handing slips of paper to a petite airhostess in a little peaked cap. A man in a wheelchair passed him down a long, wide corridor that was lined with glossy billboards advertising international airlines and local nature attractions. He avoided a man in a white shirt who looked like airport staff and followed the arrow for Australian citizens, scouring every corner of his route for another way out.

He didn't want to look like he was hanging back, so he caught up with the group ahead. This is it, he thought, shuffling in a line toward the last checkpoint. He threw his bag onto the floor and rummaged for his passport. His mouth felt dry and he was having difficulty swallowing. It was almost his turn; perhaps he *should* go back. Then it was too late. He switched his bag to his left hand and waved his passport. He held his breath, greeting the official at the counter with an amiable smile.

"Have a nice day," the clerk waved him through.

Reg stifled a sigh of relief, his heart still racing as he hurried away.

The excited hum of the brightly lit arrivals section of the main hall hit him like a television had been turned on. The babble of greeters, relatives, and reuniting couples, a stark contrast to the dim, solitary world of recent days. He would like to stay. Wash and shave, drink coffee, lie down, but he couldn't, shouldn't. It wasn't safe yet.

His legs felt weak as he turned out of the main doors, passed a taxi rank, and wished he had the fare to Adelaide. He walked through a car park, picking up his pace down a long, wide road lined with industrial sheds and storage depots on the outskirts of the airport. The buildings to his right soon gave way to bushland and birdsong, interrupted by the occasional growl of a vehicle as it sped by.

The sun was up, and he'd been walking for a good half hour when a new, blaring noise emerged from the road ahead. The wailing siren of a police car was getting louder. Then he saw the flashing lights and his heart clicked into a faster gear. He wasn't taking any chances, and dove into the bush.

The ground was moist and uneven. He dodged trees and saplings, crashed through bushes, tripped on roots, and stumbled over branches. He ran flat out, gulping air as his legs began to fail. He had to put some distance between him and the cop car, so he charged through the undergrowth, his heart pounding and his body weakening. He had no idea where he was going as he breathlessly dodged brambles and thickets, his face burning and arm aching from the weight of his duffle bag. One tree looked the same as another, and he feared he might be retracing his steps.

Disoriented, he came to a standstill, panting to catch his breath. He could still hear the siren as he leaned his outstretched arm against the trunk of a huge gum tree, anxiously looking and listening. The siren stopped ringing, but he thought he heard a crackling noise coming from the direction of the road. They might have parked the car and followed him into the bush. They might have found his box. They might be on to him.

Then he detected the sound of faraway engines between shrill birdcalls, and spotted a vague trail of flattened leaves beyond his tree. He grabbed his duffle bag and raced blindly toward the hum of distant traffic. The bush gave way to a clearing at the base of a steep embankment, and he clambered frantically upward, dragging his bag. He staggered along the grassy knoll and squatted behind shrubbery, gasping for breath as he tried to get his bearings.

His new vantage point overhung a series of buildings. The closest one looked like the rear of a workshop. A loud clang echoed over pop music blaring from a radio, Neil Sedaka singing "Breaking Up Is Hard to Do." Reg spotted a set of legs in greasy overalls protruding from underneath an old car. No more than 150 yards to the right of the mechanics workshop he could see a garage. The same distance beyond the garage he glimpsed sections of freeway. God, it didn't look far!

Then he thought he heard snapping branches and crackling underfoot. If the cops were after him, they'd be upon him in no time! His heart thudded as he crouched low and stalked. *Now!* He skittered awkwardly down the embankment, clutching his duffle bag as he made a dash for the garage. Now it was only one hundred yards ahead, now fifty. He staggered to the side of the building and around the corner. He did not look back.

Reg stumbled into the forecourt of the truck stop. Dozens of vehicles were parked around petrol pumps at the front of a cafeteria. His legs shook as he bypassed big tattooed truck drivers in vests and shorts and headed for the toilets. He burst in, hot and panting. Only one man was standing at the row of urinals. There were two lavatories; he flung open the door of the vacant one and disappeared inside.

The lock on the door was broken, and there was no light. The cubicle smelt of urine and something he didn't want to think about. He leaned his back against the door and took deep, controlled breaths, trying to slow his racing heart. Then he knelt to unzip his bag and foraged for his suit in the dark. He found the trousers and struggled out of his torn track pants. He was about to step into the fresh ones when a couple of men burst into the washroom.

"Hurry up!" One banged on Reg's door.

Reg thanked God; the bloke didn't sound like a cop.

"Piss off!" he yelled. "Can't a guy have a crap in peace?"

He heard some muttering, and then the voices disappeared.

Before he pulled his trousers up, he sunk down onto the lavatory bowl—the seat was broken but he didn't care. He emerged from the toilets feeling a whole lot better, and chucked his duffle bag under the nearest washbasin. The plumbing groaned when he turned the tap on. The pipe hammered, the tap spluttered and then gushed. Reg stooped and gulped long desperate mouthfuls of water, sighing with relief as he straightened.

Then he filled the grubby little sink. He peered at the disheveled young man with tired blue eyes and three days' growth in the mirror. God, he hoped he looked better by the time he saw Marion. The dirty sliver of soap didn't produce much lather, but he hurriedly shaved off every sign of stubble. He wished he still had the posh electric shaver he'd sold on the docks in Newcastle. He splashed his face, enjoying every moment before throwing his head up to meet his reflection.

"You did it. You bloody well did it!" he grinned.

And, by God, he knew how he was going to spend his last five quid. He headed for the cafeteria.

CHAPTER 25

"Breakfast?" inquired the gum-chewing waitress with purple nails and long, skinny legs.

Reg scanned the menu. It included spaghetti bolognese, but he resolved to wait a few weeks before he ate that again.

"Yep, breakfast!" he smiled at the prospect. "The big one, only bigger, with four eggs sunny-side up, double toast, and a mug of coffee. Thanks, darling."

When the sizzling plate of eggs, sausage, bacon, and mushrooms arrived, Reg drew the tantalizing aroma to the back of his nostrils. He folded a bacon rasher into a triangle of toast and dipped it into the golden yoke, cooked just the way he liked it: soft but not runny. He'd almost forgotten how good the combination of rich creamy eggs and smoked bacon tasted, and he relished every mouthful.

He was wiping his plate with the last piece of toast when two official-looking men in suits entered the cafe. One of them was completely bald. They fronted the main counter, three tables from Reg's. His heart sprang into action. The man with hair spoke to the waitress with the purple nails. When she pouted and shook her head, he turned and surveyed the tables, eyes darting among the morning diners. Reg picked up a discarded newspaper from the next seat and pretended to read.

He swigged his coffee and tried to look casual, praying the men weren't detectives. They chatted with the waitress again before they left, and Reg sighed gratefully as he watched through the window as they crossed the forecourt and spoke to the attendant by the pumps. Then they got into a shiny black car and drove off in the direction of the freeway.

He ordered another coffee and slumped back in his chair. It wasn't over yet. He was worn out, and it was difficult to think straight when all he wanted to do was sleep. He'd almost nodded off when he was disturbed by a stocky bearded man holding a plate of food in one hand and a cup of tea in the other.

"Anyone's?"

"It's yours," said Reg.

"Thanks, mate," his new companion nodded. He sat opposite Reg and made himself comfortable. "I'm Dino, by the way."

Reg also introduced himself, and then wondered if he should have invented a new name.

"Where you headed then?" asked Dino, a black ringlet of hair flicking across his sweaty face as he stabbed a sausage.

"Adelaide," said Reg, knowing he was about to be told that Adelaide was a bloody long way.

"Adelaide, bloody long way."

While the truck driver inhaled his food, Reg planned his story. He needed a reason for being in Perth. He resolved to become a lovesick young man who'd been visiting his girlfriend.

"So how you planning to get back to Adelaide," asked Dino. "Train?"

"Nope, spent nearly all my money on my girlfriend. Might try hitching."

"Bad idea," said Dino. "Truckers don't like taking hikers across the Nullarbor. They're always skint, so you end up buying their tucker as well."

"I can buy my own food," said Reg. Then he thought he might as well just come out with it. "If I buy my own food, could you give me a lift some of the way?"

Dino told Reg he could take him as far as Norseman, and he'd be pleased to have someone to chat with to help him stay awake.

Reg yawned as he stepped into the blare of the morning sun, hoping he could live up to Dino's expectations.

"That one." Dino pointed out a large agricultural truck with a blue cab and rusty sides parked to the right of the crammed forecourt.

"Gotta get a load of wheat from Norseman 'n' shift it back to Kalgoorlie, then that's me done for the week," he told Reg.

Reg climbed into the passenger seat, the heavy weight of jet lag bearing down on every part of him. He wouldn't even mind getting back in the box if it meant he could sleep. Dino whistled a shrill version of "Can't Buy Me Love" to the sound of his old wagon chugging down the highway. Reg tried to stay awake by asking questions. Dino jabbered his way through one long straight mile after another. His parents had moved to Australia in the fifties, he was one of seven children, and now he had five of his own. His father had passed the family farm down to him and his brother, but they'd argued and now didn't see eye to eye. He was just about to tell Reg what the argument had been about when he realized it was a one-way conversation.

"How long have I been asleep?" Reg asked later.

"At least three hours I'd say, dead to the world you were. That little Sheila been wearing you out, has she?"

They swapped stories along the Great Eastern Highway toward Norseman, where they pulled into another truck stop that looked remarkably like the last. Reg bought cheese sandwiches and bottles of fizzy orange. Dino slurped the last bubbles through his straw and said he wished Reg were a permanent fixture in his cab.

"Thanks, Dino. Great talking to you," Reg called up to the cab.

"No worries," Dino shouted down over the engine. "Hope you find a lift. Caiguna you want, then Eucla, Nundroo, and Ceduna, then you're almost home. Good luck!" he yelled.

Reg found no luck, though, standing on the corner of the long, hot, dusty road. So far only one truck had been going his way, but the driver had fixed his gaze on the road ahead so he didn't have to look at the hitchhiker. It was so damn hot Reg felt like sleeping again, and he sat down on his bag. He could be waiting in this back-of-beyond goddamn place for a long time. A couple of foraging crows cawed noisily on the scrubland behind. Reg pricked up his ears and shaded his eyes to focus on the source of a new sound; an engine emerging from the haze of the flat, silent landscape. It was heading in the wrong direction, but anything would be better than staying where he was.

He grabbed his bag and darted across the road, standing expectantly until the badly painted utility truck with a cattle dog in the back slowed beside his outstretched arm. A weary, sunbattered face peeked out under a straw cowboy hat, framed by the open window.

"Coming or going?" The driver didn't sound like he cared either way.

"Was going, but not having much luck. Coming now, where you heading?"

"Kalgoorlie," said the man halfheartedly. "You'll have to ride with Scruff, I'm full up here," he thumbed at a pile of bulging sacks next to him.

"Thanks, mate," said Reg.

He threw his bag into the back of the truck and clambered in after it. He was pissed off to be going back to Kalgoorlie when he'd already bypassed it with Dino, but at least Scruff the cattle dog seemed pleased about it, slobbering all over him and wagging his tail.

When he jumped out of the truck in Hannan Street a couple of hours later, Reg was surprised that the driver sped off before he could thank him. The town seemed deserted as he strolled past a convenience store with his bag hooked over his shoulder. He passed two screeching boys playing on the footpath and an old man dragging a shopping cart, eyes fixed on the ground. Then Reg found a little kiosk at the end of the street where he bought a plastic cup of gray tea.

"There you go, love," said the cheery-faced woman at the counter.

"Any idea where the nearest Catholic Church might be?" Reg asked, stirring in two sugars.

"Porter Street. My sister goes to that one. Has to, she married a Catholic," she chuckled.

Reg stood at the gate of the church in Porter Street staring up the path to the entrance, and thought it one of the most handsome buildings he'd ever seen. The red-brick federation facade and arched Gothic windows were a welcome contrast to the madness of the last few days: prisonlike cargo holds, plastic transport cafes, and desolate, barren landscapes. It was late afternoon when he pushed open the heavy double doors. He stepped onto the cool tiles of the vestibule and peered down the long nave.

A lone silver-haired man in robes toiled at the altar. His rustling gowns and clinking chalices magnified the tranquility of the vast hall. He wiped and arranged his gleaming objects as Reg approached him down the half-lit nave.

"Excuse me, Father, can I introduce myself?"

"Who do we have here?" The priest looked startled as he turned to face him.

"Reg. Reg Spiers."

"A new man in town, I'm thinking," said the old man. "Looking for the hand of the Lord on your journey to his kingdom, I'd be thinking."

"Something like that, Father."

Reg didn't have the energy to put on a full performance, but knew he'd have to give a half-decent presentation if he was expecting help from a man of the cloth. He deposited his bag at the corner of the aisle and sat on a pew in the front row with his elbows on his knees and his hands clasped in front, as if he was praying. The priest hovered above him on the altar. This gave Reg the position of subservience he wanted; appropriate for someone seeking some kind of solace.

"I'm new in town but I'm not staying. I need to get home." His tone was humble.

The priest's eyes softened. "Are you in some kind of trouble, son, is it a confession that you're wanting?"

"No, Father, nothing like that," Reg reassured him. "I'm just a bit down on my luck right now. It's a long story."

"God's interested in everyone's story, did you know that, my son?" said the priest. "Come and tell him something of yours."

Reg followed him to the vestry, trying to decide which plight might be more palatable for a Catholic priest. The small room off to the right of the altar had an unusual round window over a wooden table and chairs with upholstered arms that had seen better days. He noticed the sacramental robes hanging on the outside of a cupboard and the ornate crucifix above the chest of drawers next to it; they were reminiscent of his days as an altar boy in Adelaide. The priest came back with a pot of tea in a quilted cozy and two white mugs inscribed with "Sisters of Charity, 1957" in gold swirly writing. Reg had decided he couldn't own up about being a stowaway because of the criminal element. Nor could he use the story he'd given Dino, lest he appear a womanizer.

Father O'Brien was used to helping young people—God knew there had been many troubled young people in Kalgoorlie. He felt sorry for this young man who was clearly trying to help himself. If he had been an altar boy, he must have come from a good Catholic family. It wasn't easy for the young to find work.

"How many babies did you say you have, Reg?" the priest checked some time later.

"Only one, Father, but I've already spent two weeks looking for work and I can't afford another night in a motel. I've tried, Father, I really have. If I don't get back to Adelaide in the next couple of days, my wife will think I've gone for good. And then I have my parents to think about, and they're not getting any younger . . ."

"All right, son," the priest interrupted, not wanting to deal with too many problems.

"I'll tell you what I'm going to do," he continued. "I'm going to let you sleep here tonight. Just tonight, mind. It's not much but you'll make yourself comfortable. Then in the morning I'll get you to the station and buy you a ticket to Adelaide. How does that sound?"

"It sounds wonderful father, you have my eternal gratitude," said Reg, relieved he wouldn't have to stand at the side of the road with his thumb out again.

After Father O'Brien had gone for the night, Reg locked the outside door, as he'd been instructed, and flicked on the small table lamp. The priest had told him to help himself from the fridge. Deciding to show constraint, he assembled a couple of rounds of cheese and Vegemite sandwiches. He couldn't resist washing them down with half a mug of surprisingly acceptable red communion wine. He grouped three old winged chairs into a bed he could access only by sliding under the arms of the middle one. He didn't care—this was his first night free of the box. Just before he sunk into oblivion beneath the dim lamplight, he thought that, in some kind of perverse way, he rather missed it.

Chapter 26

Reg was woken shortly after sunrise by the sound of footsteps on the stone floor outside the vestry.

"Right son, let's be having you." The priest sounded flustered. "We need to be leaving in five minutes if you want that lift to the station."

There was no time to shave. Reg scrubbed his teeth, squeezed into his shoes, and zipped a couple of things into his bag. He scanned the room for a last look at the tranquil little sanctuary. The sacramental robes hanging on the outside of the cupboard and the pile of white, freshly laundered clerical collars. He was still comparing the ordered existence of a priest with the crazy world of Reg Spiers when he set off with Father O'Brien for the station.

When the priest had pulled into the station car park, Reg stood by the open window of the car.

"Godspeed," the old man said, pressing a neat arrangement of crisp pound notes into Reg's palm. He placed his other hand beneath it and held it still for a moment, like he was blessing the money and its new owner.

His weary eyes looked up earnestly at Reg. "Stay at home in the future, son. Whatever difficulties you find yourself in, it's always best to sort them out at home. God will show you the way."

Reg recovered his hand and stuffed the money into his jacket pocket, thanking the priest for his kindness as he waved good-bye and headed for the train station.

He strode into the main lobby of the station building, by-passing the ticket office. The entrance to the platforms was unattended, so he nipped through and quickly found the men's washroom. He was relieved to find it empty, dived into a cubicle, and locked the door. He felt his heart beating as he sat on the toilet seat and gazed at his feet. He'd worried that the priest might have insisted on escorting him to purchase a ticket. He had to make sure he didn't do anything to give the game away, nothing that would draw attention.

He emerged into the washroom and peered at his reflection in the mirror, widening his eyes and combing his hair with his fingers as he focused. The door swung shut behind him as he retraced his route to the ticket office and stood behind a scruffy young man in shorts and flip-flops. When it was his turn at the counter Reg felt suddenly disoriented, patting the sides of his jacket before retrieving the money from his pocket.

"Adelaide, thanks, mate," he said matter-of-factly, placing his banknotes under the nose of the elderly little man behind the office window.

The bespectacled clerk looked confused. This was highly irregular; customers usually waited to be asked for the exact amount of their train fare. He counted the notes and handed Reg his ticket, returning a one-pound note and some new loose change. Reg silently thanked the priest again. Now he would be able to buy sandwiches and drinks on the train.

The platform filled, and Reg located a timetable—only twelve minutes to wait for the Adelaide train. He sat hunched in a corner behind an old newspaper, his bag behind his feet. Reg glanced furtively every time somebody walked past his bench. When a woman announced on the loudspeaker that the Adelaide train was approaching he had to restrain himself from jumping up.

Reg ambled down the platform with his bag. He stood behind the waiting passengers, eyes darting. The train pulled into the station, and he looked down the platform; a guard was chatting with the ticket clerk by the entrance. Reg climbed aboard and made his way along the corridor toward the rear of the train. He chose a compartment with three passengers: a young man and a woman with a small girl. There were two empty adjacent seats. Reg took the window seat and shoved his bag on the overhead rack. He sat behind his newspaper and peered around it onto the platform.

Oh Christ! An official-looking man appeared from behind a big woman, walking right past his window. What if he had a description of some bloke who'd broken out of the airport? The man looked straight into Reg's eyes. Reg jerked his face behind his newspaper. Then he steeled himself and forced a sickly smile before flopping back behind his paper, eyes closed as the train eased out of the station.

Within minutes a bearded man in a uniformed shirt bustled into the compartment. "Excuse me?"

Reg's heart lurched as he jerked his eyes open and stared at him.

"Can I see your ticket, please?" asked the man.

"Ticket?" Reg whispered.

"Ticket, sir. You do *have* a ticket?"

"Oh!" Reg closed his eyes in relief. "Oh, sorry." He clambered shakily to his feet, groped in his pocket for his ticket and handed it to the conductor.

"Nodded off for a moment there." He smiled apologetically at his fellow passengers and sunk gratefully into his seat, closed his eyes again, and told himself to calm down.

This was nothing—compared with the box, it would be a piece of cake. He was just exhausted, and it was making his worry over Marion even worse. In a couple of days he'd be jogging down the street to his lovely little home in northwest Adelaide. He'd be in time for his brother's wedding, and if his calculations were right, he should arrive the day before his own wedding anniversary. Then he remembered he didn't have a key.

He imagined Waterford opening the door. "What did you expect when you piss off for six months?" he asked, just before Reg fell asleep.

✈ ✈ ✈

While Reg's train was lapping the miles between Kalgoorlie and Adelaide, James Coote, sports correspondent for the *Daily Telegraph*, was drinking coffee in his London office and answering his phone.

"John McSorley, good to hear from you. How's that javelin flying?"

"Sorry . . . can you tell me that again?"

"In a box, you've got to be kidding. Don't believe it!"

"Reg Spiers? Well . . . maybe, yes perhaps I can believe it."

"Yeah. Yeah. No, I don't blame you. It's been too long; you should have heard something by now. Jesus Christ, the guy's a maniac!"

"Tell you what I'll do. I've got a contact in Adelaide—Greg Denton—met him in Perth in '62. Too late to phone now, but I'll get onto him tonight and see what I can find out. But I want you here tomorrow to give me your side of the story."

"Okay, John, see you then."

Greg Denton was perched on a kitchen stool with a towel draped around his waist when he got the call from James Coote.

"Cootsie. Bloody hell, mate, this'd better be good."

He listened motionless, his eyes widening.

"That's got to be a winner, love it," he laughed.

"Only Spiers could carry off something like that. Yeah, know him well; he's an Adelaide man. Wait till the airport people find out, there'll be one hell of a bloody raucous. Thanks, mate, I owe you one. And listen, you tell John Mac not to worry. Reggie will be all right. He'll always be all right. He's a survivor."

A few days later, a customs official by the name of Jenkins stood at the entrance of a large cargo shed at Perth Airport, armed with a clipboard. All the major newspapers were following the story of the penniless young javelin thrower who had risked life and limb boxed in the bowels of a jet to reunite with his wife and baby. The airport authorities were at a loss to know how their security could have been so badly breached. The incident was reflecting very poorly on a whole range of airport security procedures.

According to this Spiers fellow, he'd not only traveled 13,000 miles from Heathrow Airport in a box, he'd also managed to break out of the warehouse and breeze out of the airport, calm as you like. And to make matters worse, the sorry tale of this man and his box seemed to be winning the young athlete considerable notoriety. The radio chat shows had been full of callers, all insisting that Spiers deserved his free flight and that the airline should waiver all freight charges. The front pages were already plastered with happy "together again" family portraits, his wife gazing adoringly at him like he was some bloody hero.

Ridiculous, thought Jenkins. He didn't know what the world was coming to. Now he was charged with finding evidence to support the athlete's story before the airport authorities made another statement to the press. If Reg Spiers really had flown all that way in a box, it would still be in the warehouse

"It's probably just a hoax, but I've got to check it out, so let's get on with it," he told the two loaders he'd enlisted to help him.

"What type of box are we looking for?" asked the younger, long-haired worker, thinking this was the most exciting thing that had happened during his time on the job.

"A bloody big one if it carried a bloke all the way from England," said Jenkins, irritated by the smirk on the youngster's face.

The loaders followed Jenkins down the center aisle of the warehouse, studying the assortment of crates and packages. Then they turned left at the end by the workbench and trailed back along the side of the shed, stopping at a couple of larger timber crates to make sure they were unopened.

"Fuck me, I've found it!" the young worker cried, pouncing on the entrance of a large box a couple of feet away.

He crawled halfway inside to prove that it was empty and big enough to hold a man.

"And there's stuff in here," he screeched. "A bottle of something, and tins with bits of moldy food, and they don't half stink."

Jenkins sat on the box to steady his nerves. Heads could roll after this, and he hoped his wouldn't be one of them.

"I ask you," he said, dumbfounded. "What sort of man *does* this?"

"Dunno, sir," the youngster tried to conceal his amusement.

He looked at Jenkins and shook his head.

"Not any sort of man like I know."

PART THREE
1980s

CHAPTER 27

BOMBAY, 1982

The superintendent of the prison was a man called Patmikant, a bespectacled, square-shouldered official, no taller than five feet eight but authoritative-looking all the same. He rarely ventured out of his office to vet new detainees, but he'd had a report about an unusual new prisoner destined for B Block. Apparently this fellow had had an unsettling effect on a number of other prisoners during his two-week stay at the detention center.

The Australian was reputed to be a tall, strongly built man, very vocal, and not easily intimidated. He was prone to wisecracks and joviality, and this sometimes emboldened other prisoners and made them disruptive. Although the man had shown no tendency toward violence, he was reportedly different somehow from the usual crop of Westerners.

Patmikant wasn't partial to difference and thought a few precautionary measures were in order. He would oversee the prisoner's admission himself and at the same time warn the B Block overseers to tread warily until they knew what they were dealing with.

He shuffled his papers into order and stood to attention outside his door.

"Pennington," his shrill voice rang across the foyer.

Reg jerked; "Spiers" had almost ceased to exist.

"Now, Pennington!"

Reg scrambled awkwardly to his feet. He'd lost weight, his hair was long and disheveled, and he was sporting a beard. His collarless shirt was stained, and his baggy pants had seen better days. He'd just regained his balance when a young guard shoved him from behind, toward the superintendent. Reg wasn't about to be manhandled, and he raised his cuffed hands in a mock surrender.

"No need for that, matey," he said, loudly, but not aggressively. "I'm minding my manners here, so let's see some of yours."

A senior officer bustled at the superintendent's side; he was a smaller, runty-looking little officious man with furtive eyes, firing information in their native tongue. Reg was sure this was the man the prisoners called Weasel; the bloke a guard at the detention center had warned him about. Weasel was the most hated officer in this prison. He was the superintendent's sidekick, but far more dangerous, because he snitched on fellow guards and prisoners alike. The superintendent peered sideways at a form on Weasel's clipboard.

"This way now, Mr. Pennington," he said matter-of-factly.

A policeman in a small, pyramid-shaped dark-blue beret with a gold emblem marched past as Reg fell in line behind Patmikant, impressed with the civilized reception he'd been given by him and hoping it would continue. He focused on the heels of the superintendent's shiny black brogues, and the dull, hollow sound of his footsteps, magnified by the bare, high-ceilinged walls. Weasel scurried behind Reg, irritated by the new prisoner's cocky strut and annoyed that he didn't walk with a downtrodden shuffle like the others. Reg's heart felt lighter than it had for weeks. He was relieved to be out of his last place and desperately hoping that he was now closer to Annie.

The big administration foyer hummed with activity as the prison's clerical staff processed dozens of new inmates. Small groups of khaki-clad uniformed guards made way for the superintendent's entourage; some with beret-style caps, others with more senior-looking flattop military hats. Straggles of unhappy prisoners—one here, three there—ranged from smartly dressed Indian gentlemen in shirts and trousers, several in sarongs, to shabby half-wits who looked as if they'd been dragged off the streets.

It was getting dark as Reg followed the superintendent out of the back entranceway of the big admin block and crossed the inner compound of the prison. He could still make out the vastness of the space, dotted with rectangular buildings, all contained within a huge wall. He was led down a maze of pathways, past big barrack blocks with gardens and courtyards separated by tall iron fences. They came to a standstill by two guards behind a big, metal barred gate.

Both men stood to attention as another guard unlocked the gate from the inside. Weasel stayed talking to him while the other, a lanky, twenty-something youngster topped by an oversized hat, chaperoned Reg and the superintendent to a tall, rectangular building identical to others that Reg had seen along the way.

The guard's keys jangled at his hip as he led his party up a stairwell. The landing housed two huge iron gates on opposite walls. Reg peered through the nearest one, praying that he wasn't destined to join the bevy of downtrodden-looking locals sprawled haphazardly across the floor. The guard removed the keys from his belt, hurriedly unlocked the other door, and stood aside for the superintendent to pass.

Reg followed Patmikant into the big, crowded room, immediately aware of several pairs of eyes on him.

"Gotta be the Aussie," shouted a large, tattooed Welshman, propped against the wall on the right. "It's bloody Ned Kelly!" spluttered the grinning Irishman beside him, and the block erupted with laughter.

"That's right, fellas," Reg quipped, delighted at the thought of being expected. "Ned's here."

"That's enough, Mr. Pennington!" bellowed Patmikant, "or you'll find yourself next door!"

He beckoned to Chopra, one of the two overseers at the end of the room. The tubby little man jumped to his feet and hurried to the superintendent's side. The two men conferred quietly while Reg took stock of his new surroundings. The cellblock was a long, wide room crammed with a sea of bodies squeezed next to one another, head-to-toe on adjoining mats. The men were sitting, lying, sleeping, and talking; Reg did a quick headcount and reckoned that there were well over one hundred of them.

He turned to the line of Westerners splayed along the right-hand wall. A couple of them gave him a welcoming grin.

"You have a guest, Mr. Edvardsen," Patmikant announced loudly to one.

A young man looked up from his book and eyed Reg suspiciously through square spectacles. His straight, fair hair reminded Reg of Ted, although this guy was small and frail and looked more boyish.

"We are hoping Mr. Pennington will become quiet and co-operative like you. Any nonsense," the superintendent glared at Reg, "and you'll be joining our less-hospitable guests next door. Jitesh will keep me informed." He nodded at the guard who had escorted him with Reg into the block. Jitesh beamed, displaying a gap between his white buck teeth before he removed Reg's handcuffs.

After the superintendent left, Jitesh relocked the door from the outside, and Chopra grudgingly fetched Reg a mat.

Reg wrestled it into a space by the wall next to Edvardsen. "Howdy," Reg greeted him loudly. "Bruce Pennington, and it's bloody good to be here. It's fucking luxury after the cop shop." The young man peered over his glasses and awkwardly shook Reg's hand. "Jan Edvardsen," he said, in a heavy European accent.

"Paddy," said the Irishman on Reg's other side, as he volunteered his hand. "Ned," laughed Reg, heartily shaking it. "Good to meet ya, Oz," Paddy chuckled.

There were smiles all round, and a couple of men pulled their mats closer to Reg to share in the frivolity. Paddy's soft brown eyes narrowed as he lit a spindly hand-rolled cigarette. He had a young face under his thick, graying hair, and his big, droopy mustache put Reg in mind of a walrus.

"Give us one of those." The paunchy tattooed man with a receding hairline signaled Paddy's cigarette. "What is it with the bloody Welsh?" Paddy said good-naturedly. "Watch out for Merv." He winked at Reg as he handed Merv his tobacco. "Have the shirt off your bloody back in no time!"

"Whereabouts in Oz you from?" asked a worn-out-looking Englishman as he stood to pull his track pants over his thick waist. He flopped down near Reg's feet. "By the way, I'm Pete, and this frog is Pierre." He flicked his thumb at the huddled sleeping body behind him. "So two Petes really," he cackled.

When Reg saw the mouthful of rotting black stumps, he thought Pete needed to visit Jitesh's dentist. "Brissy—Brisbane," he improvised. "How long have you lot been here?"

"Three and a half years, I think. No, nearer four." Pete ruffled his untidy mousy hair and looked confused. "Got anything on you, man?" His voice turned desperate, and his eyes flashed with a terror Reg thought he'd left at the detention center.

"No, no nothing," he said. "Sorry, mate, four years, eh? How long did you get?"

Pete looked disappointed. "Haven't been sentenced yet," he said.

"None of us have, we're all on fucking remand," an American voice piped up from next to Pete. A guy who looked just like Bob Dylan circa 1965, with dark glasses and wild hair flowing from a paisley scarf, sat up, balanced a packet of cigarette papers on his knees and carefully started to roll a smoke.

"What d'you mean?" cried Reg. "Four years and not even a fucking date?"

"And the rest! Mad Dog's proof of that," said Pete. "Tell him, Dog, tell him how long you've waited."

"Eight years at the end of this month," said the American before he licked his cigarette paper and sealed it.

Reg watched him light the end and blow smoke rings toward the ceiling. "Eight fucking years," said Mad Dog. "The bastards think if they keep me here long enough I'll just die, and then they won't have to bother with court."

Reg's pulse soared. There had to be some mistake.

"Shit," he exclaimed, "that can't be right!"

CHAPTER 28

Jan Edvardsen had never met an Australian. He was a young Swede who looked like a schoolboy nerd and preferred his own company. This lasted only a few days after Reg arrived. Even though Bruce Pennington was loud, Jan found his stories fascinating.

"He's a different bloke since you came." Pete told Reg when they were lining up for lunch with their tin plates. "The friend he got arrested with left months ago. Rumor has it his wealthy parents paid to get him out. Jan's hardly spoken since then, just slept and read."

Jan was waiting for a trial date like all the foreigners in Reg's block. Mad Dog was the Yank veteran and Reg was the Aussie rookie in the multicultural mix. There were around twenty foreigners, including French, Italians, English, Welsh, Irish, and Belgians, and a number of Africans who spoke no English and kept to themselves. Many of the prisoners had already served several years, and none of them had been to court to have their cases heard.

Reg set about getting into a routine to stay healthy and look for ways to make money. Plan A was to wait for a court date and post bail; plan B was that if no court date was forthcoming, then he would bribe his way out. He didn't like to think about plan C, but he had already decided if push came to shove he would have to devise the mother of all escapes. He wouldn't think about that scenario until he'd completely discounted the other two possibilities. His new surroundings were a hell of a lot better than the detention center where he'd spent the first two weeks of his incarceration. He could put up with them for a while if he knew that Annie was okay, that she wasn't suffering. That she was safe.

The big communal cell did have a washroom, albeit shared by 120 men. The plumbing was archaic, with groaning pipes, hole-in-the-ground toilets, filthy sinks, and cold, dirty water. Prisoners who wanted a full-body wash had to take it during the day when the cell was unlocked. They could fight their way to one of the few grimy showers on the ground floor or make an outdoor dash for a prehistoric stone bath. Reg's favorite trick was to strip off, outrun the pack, and then hurl himself headlong in front of the others and give them all a good laugh. He wondered about the toilet facilities in the women's prison. Surely they had only female guards there? What if Annie had to wash in front of leering men? She'd be okay if there were foreigners with her who spoke English, because they would stick together like the blokes in his block.

Prison food was hardly the silver service variety. Meals arrived from the main kitchen, wheeled into the courtyard in big metal vats. Prisoners would line up to have the menu of the day dolloped into their bent tin bowls. The main diet was chapati bread, rice, dhal or black gram made from lentils, and a brown liquid that contained any manner of inedible floating debris. The first time Reg tried to eat the watery soup with strange vegetables and a floating fish head he felt like throwing up. He was reminded of Forbes, the man from the shipping office in Adelaide who had a framed fish, a red emperor, hanging on his wall. The rice was overcooked and sticky, but it helped stave off his hunger. Things would get better, he kept telling himself, but when he thought about the conditions he'd witnessed the first couple of weeks of his incarceration he did not complain.

Every month the prisoners were issued with a couple of hundred rupees' worth of coupons from the kitchen. The highly prized slips could be exchanged for extras like soap, tea, bread, or the hashish cigarettes called "charas" that gave off a sweet pungent odor. The value of the coupons was so low that they entitled prisoners to only about four extra items. Reg soon discovered that the coupon system was the main currency of the prison. Wealthy inmates had cash sent from relatives to purchase extra vouchers or to bribe the guards for cigarettes or special foodstuff from the kitchen to take back to their barracks to consume after hours.

Each day started with a headcount at six in the morning. Then the cell would be unlocked, and prisoners were free to roam the courtyard areas until lockup time at six every night. Jitesh and Weasel, along with other regular guards, patrolled the courtyard, but as soon as the prisoners were returned to their barracks, the overseers became all powerful. The overseer Chopra and his insignificant sidekick, Malik, kept a few provisions under lock and key at the end of Reg's room. They presided over rudimentary tea-making facilities, and operated a little hand-fired burner to reheat chapatis that had been smuggled into the block.

Chopra and Malik were long-term prisoners who'd been empowered to dish out their own form of punishment to whomever they wished, for whatever they wished. The biggest crime in the barracks was talking when the overseers wanted to sleep. The Indian prisoners were mainly compliant, but loud snorers and crazy ramblers regularly got belted with a bamboo stick.

"You treat the overseers with respect and they leave you alone, they might even make you a cuppa," Paddy told Reg. "They think anyone who speaks English *is* English, so don't keep going on about being a fucking Aussie, else they might beat the crap out of you like they do their own people."

One night when Chopra was issuing threats, Reg retaliated. "You come near me with that bloody stick," he bellowed, "and I'll make you eat it."

Everyone who was awake stopped breathing. Mad Dog and Paddy chuckled in whispers. Chopra lay silent in the darkness, humiliated. Pennington was six foot two with two hundred pounds of muscle. Chopra had never seen a white man like him, and he wasn't about to take Reg on.

Toward the end of his second month at the prison, Reg was granted a ten-minute meeting with a lawyer in an office in the administration block. The elderly Indian gentleman spoke good English and took notes. When Reg inquired about their next appointment, the man said he wouldn't be returning until he'd been given Reg's court date. This raised alarm bells for Reg; it might take years to get a date, and what if the lawyer died in the meantime? More important, what were his chances of getting a better deal than any of these other poor blighters he was locked up with? He was hardly in a position to call the Australian embassy.

The inmate advocate service was periodically made available to everyone, although Reg doubted if many of the local prisoners ever got legal advice. On the two occasions that he sat opposite his advocate in an office in the main building, he found the little suited man's smile sickeningly insincere.

"You just have to be patient, Mr. Pennington," said the advocate when he met with Reg the second time "You are part of our system now."

"Can you please just get me some news about my girlfriend Sonia, Sonia Priestly?"

"I'm sorry, Mr. Pennington, I would be jeopardizing my position." The advocate avoided Reg's gaze. Then he said, "You may find some way of getting information," and Reg thought, you're asking me for money, you slimy little prick. "Otherwise you will have to wait for one year, and then you are allowed to write a letter," the advocate continued, wiping the remains of his lunch from his thin, pink mouth.

"A year!" Reg was outraged. "I'm not planning on being here in a fucking year!"

The expert looked taken aback by Reg's outburst. He mumbled something about another appointment as he stuffed his papers and lunch box into his briefcase, and then hurried out of the room.

"Oy! I'm still wanting advice," Reg called after him, but he never saw him again.

That night he lay on his mat, keeping his new friends awake with his incessant questions. He'd been locked up now for over three months, and he hadn't had one decent night's sleep. The room seethed with restless, snoring men. His head was full of tantalizing thoughts: the curve of Annie's neck, steak and fries with a cold beer, the sound of surf rolling onto a beautiful Australian beach. He longed to be anywhere but here, where his skin itched like crazy, and no matter how many times he shook his blanket, he couldn't rid it of wretched crawling bugs and lice.

"Quiet, quiet now," Chopra wailed from the far end of the room.

Paddy whispered, "So if you're ever lucky enough to get a court date, you might get out on bail."

"How much is bail?" Reg wondered, thinking that the money that Annie had left in her backpack probably wouldn't be enough.

"Whatever they come up with on the day."

The Welshman three men away made a grunting noise, then exploded. "Will you two shut the fuck up? I'm sick of you wankers blithering on night after night. You're gonna be in here forever, we all are. Learn to live with it like every other fucker!"

"Nobody learns to live with it, man." Mad Dog's slow, American drawl hung over the room.

Reg listened to his own heartbeat. His whole life might tick away before he was free again. He might die here and never see Annie again. Oh God! What was happening to her? This was his fault, all of it.

"You okay, Bruce?" Jan's sensitive tone sounded out of place.

"Yeah, thanks, mate," said Reg. "Just having a hard time getting my head around this bent fucking system."

He couldn't change the system, so what were his options? Those who couldn't raise bail were kept here until their case was heard, but none of these guys had ever heard of anyone being acquitted. The odds were completely stacked against him. He didn't know if Annie had any money, and even if she did, it had probably been nicked by now. He had to face facts: they might not be able to lay their hands on bail money. There was only one way they could go: they'd have to buy themselves out, and he'd have to find the resources to do it.

CHAPTER 29

Reg had been locked up for five months, and his situation still seemed as hopeless as the day he set foot inside the prison. He'd had no news from his lawyer, he still didn't know how the hell he was going to raise bail money, and he had no idea what was happening to Annie. But at least he did know where she was, because a number of the inmates had pointed out the women's prison, and Reg could just make out the outline of the roof in the distance.

He spent his days with Jan and the others in the big court-yard adjoining his barrack. The area was about the size of six tennis courts. Some of the long-serving prisoners had lost interest in exercising and lay around the yard. Mad Dog was one of them. He stuck with Reg's group, but preferred to sit to the side in the shade and pick out tunes on his old guitar.

One day Reg noticed a couple of older, stout Indian gentlemen were occasionally in the courtyard, men who were billeted in a big adjoining block near the kitchen. The pair tended to keep to themselves on an old, wooden bench beside the wall, deep in conversation. They stood out because of their dress: full-length kaftans that looked new and were adorned with bright sashes. The taller one was particularly flamboyant, with his long, gold medallions and expensive watch. He smoked brown cigarettes with fancy edging, played dominoes, and shared whispered conversations with his friend. Occasionally, the men would look up for a while and peer across at Reg's gang or fix their eyes on small groups of locals milling around the yard. Reg found them intriguing, especially the tall man. He suspected they were in some kind of collusion and wondered what they were talking about.

The yard was a perfect space for ball games. Reg had mentioned this to Jitesh, and when the young guard found them a ball, Reg set about arranging five-a-side football teams and running regular competitions. He soon noticed an uncharacteristically bulky and powerful-looking Indian called Suji. Everyone was wary of Suji, even the guards, and rumor had it that the young Indian had stabbed a man in his block. He would try to impress the stately duo on the bench with his ungainly leaps around the court. Suji had few ball skills and relied on brute strength to intimidate the other players. Most games ended with someone falling foul of him and getting hurt. This was often Jan, who was very thin, and had joined in only because of Reg's cajoling.

"You could take care of him no trouble," Pete said to Reg after Suji's latest temper tantrum. "He's just a big bag of blubber."

The Westerners were slumped in a row against a wall, barechested with their shirts on their heads to block the scorching sun. The air was hot and humid, their conversation intermittent and breathless after a ball game with the locals. The Indians had ownership of the shaded area lined with benches; it was an unwritten law.

They were observing Suji showing off his strength by taking on some of his countrymen at arm wrestling. The two older Indian gentlemen sat in their regular spot, watching the loudmouthed antics of the fiery young braggart. The one with the flashy jewelry fired words at Suji in his native tongue, and Reg's gang wished they knew what he was saying.

"What a tosser that Suji is," said Pete, flopping next to Reg. "He's been hurting their blokes for a couple of weeks now. Insists that some poor weak bastard give him an arm wrestle and then delights in seeing them in pain when he's wrecked their arm."

"I'd like to see someone wreck his arm," said Jan. He shoved his glasses on his nose. "My leg's not recovered from where he kicked it last time." He pulled his trousers up and inspected the damage.

"Just like the schoolyard bully," Reg agreed. "I'd sure as hell like to know what's going on between him and the big bloke with the jewelry. Look at them now. Suji treats him like a god, and so do the others."

"You can see what the pecking order is," said Pete. "All the younger blokes are petrified of Suji. Asshole's built like a fucking tank. Then Suji and all of them bow and scrape to the two big fellows. All very odd!"

The big man with the jewelry started to shout. Suji kneeled by his feet at the bench. When he stood, it was the first time Reg had ever seen Suji look frightened, and they watched him bow his head respectfully, then walk off. Another couple of Indians stood in line to speak to the older man, and one of them kneeled the way Suji had. He swayed and lowered his head, with his hands in the prayer position.

"Why are they all so fucking subservient around him?" said Paddy, stroking his graying mustache.

"It's always been like this," Pete said, pulling on his Arsenal shirt.

"Even the guards are especially nice to that man," added Jan. He breathed on his glasses and wrinkled his nose. "And you might say he's got Weasel . . . how are you saying it? . . . eating from the hand?"

"That's right, buddy. You're sounding like a native," Reg said, and everyone chuckled.

Jan laughed with them. His fair hair waved around his eyes as he bent forward and polished his lenses on his trousers.

"How long . . . how long's the older guy been here, Pete?" Reg asked.

"Couple of years I'd say, on and off . . ."

"On and off?" Reg repeated.

"Bit like Houdini," Pete said.

"Sounds like a Mafia man," Reg said. "And who's the old bloke sitting next to him?"

"If the big one's mafia, the don, then old Big Ears next to him is family," said Paddy.

Weasel blew his shrill whistle to signal everyone indoors. Reg slipped into his shirt and collected the ball, then made his way across the courtyard. The mysterious character they'd been discussing was the only Indian left, apart from Weasel, who always kowtowed to him. The man with the jewelry looked relaxed, almost biblical. His dark beard outlined his swarthy face, and his black hair had a badger's stroke of silver. He reclined in his regal gown, his gold medallions clinking with the rhythm of his nonchalant chewing. As he helped himself to another sweetmeat from an exotic box, his sultry eyes slid sideways beneath long lashes, resting on Reg as he strolled past.

"You play very well." The deep, rich English took Reg by surprise. Reg slowed, wanting to hear him speak again.

"Thank you," he said. "Do you like . . . football?"

"Move on now, Pennington," Weasel yelled.

"It's all right, you can leave us now." The Indian prisoner waved him away, and Weasel slunk off.

"Come sit." The older man patted the bench beside him. "Talk to me about your football. Turkish delight?"

Reg peered at dusty pink cubes nestled in delicate beds of crimped paper.

"Don't mind if I do," he smiled appreciatively as he popped one into his mouth.

He studied the man's face as he savored the honey-scented candy and the way it melted on his tongue. He thought it was a distinguished face, handsome even, in spite of being overweight.

"I want to apologize about our young Suji," the man said. "He gets very heated and hasn't learned the finer points of being on a team."

"Yeah, you might say that," Reg said. "But he's still young," he added diplomatically.

He noticed Weasel standing by the exit. His arms were folded in a contentious stance, and he was glaring at Reg.

"I don't think he'll ever get to your standard. I doubt if he has your strength," said the man, as if he'd given it some thought. "By the way, I should introduce myself properly." His medallions rustled against the starched sash across his chest. "Kahn. Khalid Kahn is my name. And you are?"

"Pennington, Bruce Pennington." Reg hated saying it. If only he could be good old Reggie Spiers again. He shook the outstretched manicured hand that was dominated by an ornate gold ring inlaid with a huge emerald. Reg resolved that if he ever got out of this godforsaken place he would buy Annie one just like it.

"Well, Mr. Pennington . . ." Kahn said as he rose slowly. He organized his attire, then raised his fist to his mouth and coughed—and Reg thought it was the first time he'd seen someone look dignified when they did that. "What I want to say before I leave you is this; I'm having a small celebration dinner this evening in the dayroom and I would like you to join me. You can bring a friend. Would you like that?"

Reg was taken aback. "I'd like that very much, Mr. Kahn."

He could hardly believe what he was hearing. Food. Something different from rice—Christ almighty, this was bloody brilliant. "Thank you very much!"

Weasel saw that Kahn was ready to go, and walked toward them.

"Someone will collect you when it's time," Kahn said as Weasel led Reg away.

"By the way," Reg called back. "What are you celebrating?"

"My release," Kahn told him. "I will be leaving here very shortly."

"Any chance of putting me in your suitcase?" Reg grinned, before an irritated Weasel marched him back to his block.

✈ ✈ ✈

"You're positive he said you can bring a friend?" Jan nervously asked Reg as Jitesh and another guard escorted them to Kahn's block.

"Yeah, but we're hardly dressed for posh nosh, are we?" said Reg, adjusting the waistband of his cotton trousers.

His sandals flopped against the concrete floor as he and Jan walked between the guards across the courtyard. Jitesh unlocked the metal gate to Kahn's compound. They hurried past the laundry and kitchen wood store and took the stairs to the third floor of the big rectangular building. As they neared the dayroom, soft sitar music drifted from the open door. Reg shot Jan a look of disbelief. "Sounds like a real party."

"You have money, anything's possible," Jan whispered excitedly. He was thrilled that Reg had chosen him out of all the prisoners in B Block to take to the special meal.

"Take your hands out of your pockets," Jitesh ordered, and Jan immediately pressed his arms to his sides.

Reg swept his hair out of his face with both hands as Jitesh ushered them into the dayroom. The guests were seated at the end of the long hall, and as the newcomers walked toward them, the diners fell silent, turned, and stared. Jitesh bowed and nervously addressed Kahn in his native tongue.

Kahn was at the head of the table, sitting cross-legged on a maroon velveteen cushion fringed with tassels that matched the batik cloth spread over the low dining table. Reg wondered where the hell all this stuff had come from. Kahn looked even more like a dignitary than usual, his sash embroidered in ochre and midnight blue, his chest and hands adorned with gold. A musician sat on the floor behind him, his sinewy fingers coaxing a soulful melody from the sitar between his legs.

"Welcome, Mr. Pennington," the host announced graciously. "And who is your friend, please?"

Reg was about to make the introduction when Jan spoke for himself.

"Jan Edvardsen, sir. Very happy to be here," he said tentatively. Reg thought he looked like a schoolboy on his first date.

"Come," said Kahn. He gestured with a flourish.

"Thank you," said Reg, overawed by the formality of the occasion.

Two vacant floor cushions were next to Kahn. Reg sat down beside him, Jan on the other side of Reg. Weasel was seated opposite them. He smiled at the newcomers through clenched teeth for Kahn's benefit. Suji was at the other end of the table; his big, sulky face flushed with annoyance. Reg didn't recognize the other guests. They were mainly older Indian gentlemen. Some were adorned in finery, though none as flamboyant as Kahn's.

"Our friend Suji looks a bit irritated," Reg whispered to Jan when he got the chance. Jan wiped his mouth and grinned.

It was a banquet to remember. The smell of spices, curry, and incense pervaded the room. The wine flowed, and for a couple of hours Reg and Jan reveled in their situation. Reg was heartened to see the young serious Swede enjoying himself.

"Eat, eat, and eat," he told him. "It will be some time before we see food like this again!"

It was a sumptuous feast. There were three large platters of different curries: chicken, fish, and beef. Two ornate trays of pilau rice with fresh coriander sat amid poppadoms, naan bread, chutneys, and delicate saucers of pistachio nuts and dried peas. A silver bowl of mangoes, kiwi fruit, and lychees took center stage on the beautiful tablecloth, strewn with frangipani petals. The scent reminded Reg of Annie, and he dearly wished she could enjoy the evening with him.

The music became louder as the evening progressed. The men chattered in Hindi; everyone laughing on cue as raconteur Kahn regaled his followers with humorous stories. Reg and Jan let the warmth of the occasion wash over them like the wine that was going to their heads. Jan declined the offer of a cigar, but Reg smoked his with relish. Then they took their turn when Kahn lit a big, brass water pipe.

"The best you can buy in all of India, my friend," Kahn announced, then sucked the life out of the gurgling machine.

The music got louder. Jan was laughing. Reg looked down the row of chattering men and caught Suji's eye. Reg smiled at him and raised his glass, but the big, sulky Indian looked away.

"And have you enjoyed your evening?" Kahn asked Reg just before Jitesh and another guard came to collect him and Jan.

"Very much," replied Reg, trying not to slur his wine-sodden words. "You have a great place here, with the dayroom and everything. Wish we had all this."

"I dare say that could be arranged; would you like it to be arranged?"

Reg widened his eyes and swallowed, hard, wondering how far Mr. Fixit's authority spread. Then his mind raced with thoughts of Annie. He'd be able to see the women's prison from the covered way outside this very room. Everyone said you could see it easily. Easily, they said.

"You could do that?" he asked, his voice more quivery than he'd have liked.

"Of course," said Kahn, and when Reg stared into his coal-black eyes, he knew that here was a man who could do anything.

CHAPTER 30

By the end of the following week Reg, Jan, Paddy, Pete, Merv, and Mad Dog were billeted in their new block. Their day-to-day routine hadn't changed, but Reg and Paddy were often slipped a few extra coupons when they visited the kitchen. Their dormitory was almost identical to the one in B Block, but noticeably cleaner, with a fresher supply of blankets. And there were fewer local prisoners, most of whom Reg recognized from the courtyard; well-educated men who frequently spoke to the Westerners in English.

Reg's group spent their days in the same courtyard they'd used before. But their evenings were sometimes very different—when they were invited to join Kahn and his underworld dons in the dayroom for an evening meal. Delicious curries, hashish, and music flowed, and Reg and company, who thought of themselves as the B Block boys, had never been so well fed.

Kahn and his colleagues were happily ensconced in the dormitory opposite Reg's. Nobody could see into it because a fancy curtain was draped on the other side of the gate. Reg suspected that, however many men were inside, their number was small, and they probably enjoyed every luxury denied the vast majority of prisoners. Paddy was convinced Kahn slept in a bed. Jan suggested that if no beds were available, the privileged few at least had mattresses.

One unbearably hot afternoon Reg was irritable and restless. So far he'd only been on the undercover area on the third floor in the evening, and he desperately wanted to get a good view of the women's prison. Dark clouds were gathering, and darts of rain began pelting the dry compacted earth. The droplets became a downpour, and the men ran for cover.

"Back," one of the guards shouted, and everyone filed despondently up the stairs.

Reg wasn't ready to go back to his dormitory. When he got to the second floor he noticed Jitesh was substituting for the regular guard at the door leading to the dayroom. Perfect. He wouldn't even have to give him any cigarettes.

"Just half an hour. Go on mate, thirty minutes," he pleaded.

"Otherwise I'll come and get you," Jitesh agreed, and reluctantly unlocked the door.

Reg winked at him playfully. He took the stairs two at a time, bypassed the dayroom, and strode along the open corridor, swinging his arms as he inhaled the warm air. The atmosphere was moist and fresh, livened by the rain pounding the waist-high wall onto the passageway ahead. The wall was edged with bars that extended to the roof. It was those wretched bars that stopped him from hooking his leg over the wall and scaling down.

He gazed longingly at the parallel terrace of the women's prison, about seventy meters across the way. Where was she? How long until he'd see her again? Then he slowed, focusing on the solitary figure of a woman with sandy red hair.

I've conjured her up, thought Reg. She isn't real.

Her hair shimmered orange and gold through the driving rain.

"Annie," Reg hollered at her through the bars.

She didn't stir.

"Annie, Annie," he bellowed over the hammering rain, his heart racing.

The young woman swung around and looked directly up at him. She swayed for a moment, and then grasped the bars of her cage to steady herself.

"Reggie!" she wailed as they fixed their eyes on each other across the watery divide.

Raindrops splatted Reg's face and ran into his eyes. He wiped them away, laughing and crying.

"I love you. It won't be long. It won't be long, Annie!"

✈ ✈ ✈

Four days later, one of the guards smuggled a letter to Reg:

Dear Reggie,

I couldn't believe it when I saw you on the terrace. It was a good day to see you because I was feeling a bit depressed, I miss you so much and I can't stand this place much longer. We're only allowed to go up there if we're sent on an errand and a girl I've met told me that your building is the men's prison but every time I've looked over nobody is there. I don't even know if you will get this.

I have to keep away from some of the women because they're as rough as the blokes. There are a couple of gangs and when I first arrived they all kept touching my hair, but I think the guards have warned them off me. Ira is in my cell with four other girls that speak English. She talks to the others in Indian and then tells us what they are saying.

The lawyer reckons I'll get bailed before you and I've given him all the cash I had for when the time comes so keep your fingers crossed that he's honest. I figured it would be safer because everything gets nicked here. What I'm worried about now is that we won't have enough bail money for you, and it's not as if we can phone Australia and ask our families to help us out!

By the way I've lost tons of weight, not on purpose, I just can't stand the sludge they serve up but you're probably having the same. Love you Reggie, can't wait to see you again. If I'm out first don't worry, I'll be waiting for you.

Big kisses from your Sandy girl,

Annie xxx

Annie was released from the women's prison after serving six months. Reg spoke to her from the top of his building several times again before she left, and received another letter from her after she'd gone. She reassured him that she had met with his court-appointed lawyer, who was confident that Reg, too, would be freed in a few months, and she'd secured the funds to post his bail when the time came. This worried him. If Annie was conducting little drug deals around Bombay, she'd get no sympathy if she was caught, and she could end up back inside.

She said how much she loved and missed him, and that he should concentrate on looking after himself so that he was in good shape for his release. This was easier said than done. Boredom was the main enemy of Reg and his mates. Time outside for recreation helped, but there were only so many exercise sessions, arm-wrestling competitions, and ball games that they could maintain enough interest and stamina for.

One evening, when Reg was enjoying one of Kahn's special dinners in the dayroom, his host took him aside.

"Are you a betting man, Mr. Pennington?" he asked.

Reg was taken aback. Was it a trick question?

"I probably am." Reg paused. "Of course I am," he laughed. "Why d'you ask?"

"I may have a proposition for you in a few days, but it's a proposition for a betting man. Do you think you might be interested?"

Betting usually included money; the very thing he and Annie would need when they hit the road again.

"I do, Mr. Kahn," he said. "I am very interested."

"What's in this for you?" Reg asked Kahn when he was alone with him in the courtyard a couple of days later.

"Let us say, amusement. It should make a good contest."

"Mighty load of work for a bit of amusement."

Kahn opened a new box of Turkish delight and offered it to Reg. "It will be a good show for the gamblers. There are plenty of those here."

Reg's eyes lit up. "Thanks," he said. Kahn took a candy for himself and studied it before slowly putting it in his mouth.

"And you think it could earn me a bit?" Reg asked with his mouth full.

"If you win." Kahn stopped chewing and spoke with a lump in his cheek. "It's a wager, but if you lose, nothing changes."

"I won't be losing, no way." Reg was emphatic.

"And that's why I'm going to bet on you, but Suji doesn't need to know that. He will have plenty of support."

Kahn straightened his gown across his lap and nodded at Weasel. Reg knew this was his cue to leave.

"I'm grateful . . ." he started to say.

"Don't be grateful, Mr. Pennington," said Kahn, his voice cautionary. "Just make sure you win. You have eight days to prepare. Use them wisely."

"I sure will," said Reg. Shit! he thought. Talk about pressure!

Weasel was in a bad mood. He'd got wind something was going on and hated not being privy to the facts.

"Just think," he said snidely as he unlocked the heavy metal door of Reg's dormitory. "When Mr. Kahn leaves, you'll be just another prisoner."

That's what you think, you little rat, thought Reg as the bolt cranked behind him.

"You said you'd spill the beans today, Oz, so come on, out with it," Pete cornered him as Reg flopped onto his mat.

Pete shifted his own mat closer to Reg's and made himself comfortable. Reg propped his back against the wall and dangled his hands over his bent knees.

"Yeah, Bruce." Jan looked up from his book and sniffed. "You and Mr. Kahn are looking cozy lately. People are starting to talk."

"You're teaching this boy too much bloody English, Pete," Reg joked. "I was going to tell you blokes about it anyway."

Mad Dog sat up and turned to face the group, clutching his guitar. His hair was particularly disheveled, and his black shades were about to fall off the end of his nose. He began to strum his usual out-of-key chords, accompanied by breathy vocals nobody could understand. Jan raised his eyebrows. Exasperated, he dumped his book, pushed his glasses onto the top of his head, and rubbed his eyes, then widened them as though he was having trouble focusing.

"Don't start without me," said Merv, squeezing in between Mad Dog and Paddy.

He spread his long, tattooed frame across the floor.

"Come on, Oz," Paddy muttered. "Let's be having it."

"Now is as good a time as any to fill you blokes in," Reg agreed.

"Speak up then," said Paddy. "I can't hear a damn thing. For fuck's sake, Dog," he yelled. "Will ya shut that whiney crap up, it's getting on my fucking nerves. Dylan beat you to it. Get over it, you sad bastard."

A couple of locals who were chatting with their own countrymen glanced Mad Dog's way. He sighed impatiently, laid his guitar across his knees, and used it as a table to roll a smoke.

Reg's group turned quiet, all eyes were on him.

"Okay, I'm going to explain to you how this will work," he said. "I'm taking on Suji in an arm-wrestling competition, first thing next Friday."

"Bloody hell!" said Pete, his black teeth on show. He looked at the others to gauge their reaction.

"Why?" asked Jan. "Why does Kahn want you in this arm contest?"

"He's going to run it like a bookie, proper bets and everything. Might even put money on myself," Reg joked.

The others looked confused.

"How will the money thing work, man?" Mad Dog asked in his usual bleary, spaced-out voice. A cigarette dangled from the side of his mouth as he turned his guitar around and softly resumed his chords, hoping no one would notice.

"Keep it like that, Dog," said Reg, looking both ways, "so that lot can't hear everything. Right, you guys, Kahn's going to make the betting two to one on Suji."

"That's fucking rubbish odds!" spat Paddy.

"Remind us how the odds thing works," said Pete.

Reg studied the group to check everyone was concentrating. "Think of bets as units, although obviously people can bet however much they like," he said. "So it's two to one on Suji. He's the favorite. So a bet of two units wins one unit and the original stake."

"If he wins," said Pete.

Reg nodded. "But if you bet on Suji and he loses, you get sweet fuck all."

"Ha!" cried Pete. "How beautiful would that be? If Oz wins and all the locals have got their rupees on Suji baby. We could clean the bastards out!"

"Keep your voice down," urged Reg, "they don't know about this yet."

Paddy sat up and scratched his head. "I might try to flog some of my coupons."

"You and me both," said Reg. "I'm stockpiling the little beauties, and it's a sad day when a man can't back himself."

Jan started to scribble notes on the inside flap of his paperback. "So Bruce, how does the unit thing work for a bet on you?"

"Because Suji is the favorite, you can make more by betting on me if I win than by betting on Suji and he wins. Get it?" Reg searched their faces.

Mad Dog strummed louder. "Cool," he crooned.

"You've still gotta win though," said Pete. "He's a big bastard to beat."

Paddy said, "If anyone can do it, Oz can. He's a fucking freak with his one-armed push-ups. Not of this world, I tell ya."

"And whoever wins gets whatever's left in the pot after everyone's been paid off," Reg's voice raised with excitement. "It doesn't taken an Einstein to work out which way most of the bets will go."

"But if Suji wins and only a few people have bet on you, where will the money come from to pay them?" Pete asked.

"Kahn's minted, man," said Paddy. "Obviously bankrolling the whole deal. Might seem nice now, but I tell ya, there's menace behind that Turkish delight."

"There's one thing only that is a worry to me," Jan said thoughtfully. "Who is having control for the betting?"

"Kahn," said Reg, "like I said."

"Yes, Kahn but . . ." said Jan. "But Bruce, Paddy's right . . . can you trust him?"

News of the arm-wrestling competition between Oz, the buccaneer white man, and Suji, the biggest of the local inmates, spread like wildfire through the prison population. Reg was confident he had the vote of his mates. If not, better yet, his pot would be even bigger. Someone from the kitchen told Paddy he thought a few of the locals might back Reg, although they'd probably keep that to themselves. Even though his opponent was bigger, Reg was hoping he wouldn't have the brute strength to pin him down. He remembered Australian blokes built like Suji, some from his athletics club in Adelaide. When it came to lifting weights, they were often outclassed by smaller, stronger men.

Prisoners seemed to find money from nowhere, even though they were supposed to have only what was sent to them. Kahn had acquired a massive hinged box. Reg saw inside it once. There were special compartments where the Indian stored money and receipts. He'd stopped playing dominoes and cards altogether, and devoted his time on the courtyard bench to checking documentation and balancing his books.

The guards seemed to be looking forward to the competition as much as the prisoners. Pete heard a rumor that some of them were betting on Suji. The guards were paid a pittance and were always on the lookout for ways to supplement their income. A couple of them had even put up posters they'd made with cartoons of the opponents. Kahn, Weasel, Reg's supporters, and Suji's supporters would gather in the courtyard for the big event. The excitement soared; it was the hottest ticket in town.

The football matches in the courtyard had been temporarily suspended so Reg could prepare for the contest with push-ups and arm-building exercises. It was particularly hot, and he trained in his underpants while Jan and the others slumped against their usual wall, discussing his chances. Paddy had volunteered as Reg's personal trainer and reveled in his new role, prancing around the courtyard firing instructions. Paddy had trained amateur boxers in his hometown of Port Rush a few years earlier. Apart from Reg, he was the only prisoner in their block with links to sport, however tenuous. Pete pointed out that he had earned a certificate for swimming the breaststroke at his primary school, but the consensus was that his swimming career was too long ago to count.

Reg's group wanted to donate their chapatis to him. Paddy said he should eat more of the ominous slurry called black gram, reputed to be highly nutritious.

"No more food or I'm gonna be sick," Reg told everyone the day before the contest.

"Word is they're building Suji up," said Pete. "Bastard's been eating like a king, probably got a steak for breakfast this morning."

Reg had trouble sleeping on Thursday night. He kept trying to imagine how Suji would play it: slowly or in one big thrust? Then he thought about what Jan had said. What if he won but Kahn made off with their winnings? Later, in the darkness, he heard Pete's voice.

"Psst . . . Dog, what you got on Oz tomorrow?"

"Fucking everything. If he loses, I'm gonna have to sell my fucking guitar!"

CHAPTER 31

The day of reckoning had arrived. Everyone was in the courtyard except Jan and Reg. Jan wanted to support Reg; until now it had felt like Reg was looking out for him, but he was having a hard time hiding his nervousness. He hated confrontation of any kind. He'd watched Suji arm wrestling several times and didn't like Reg's chances.

"You feeling all right?" he asked.

"Ready as I'll ever be," said Reg.

He didn't let on about the churning in his stomach or his fear that Suji might have something up his sleeve. Or his biggest worry of all, that Kahn might double-cross him. Paddy had warned him, just as Niko had warned him about Kurt Danson. No point in dwelling on that now, he just had to get down there and wipe that smirk off Weasel's face and take Suji down. He'd sort the rest out later.

The unlikely duo—the big athletic contender and his frail, bespectacled young friend—walked the gauntlet. Out of the dormitory, they hovered in the hallway while Jitesh relocked the last heavy metal door. The excited hum of the courtyard assembly flooded the stairwell.

Reg peered down the dark staircase he took every day. It looked steeper now. The open door at the bottom revealed a stark patch of dry, red, sunlit earth. He stood for a moment, staring down at the unknown: a threshold, beckoning him to meet his fate with Suji.

"You go first; good luck, Mr. Oz." Jitesh flashed a toothy grin.

"Thanks, Teshy, hope I don't bankrupt you," said Reg.

He knew Jitesh liked him, but Christ, he wasn't expecting his bet!

"Good luck, Bruce," said Jan.

Reg shot him a smile and steadily descended the stairs. Every slow footfall was marked by three beats of his pounding heart.

I'm doing this for you, Annie.

His senses heightened as he was enveloped by the bright heat and bustle of the courtyard. A large group of prisoners had assembled in the Indian section, jostling for a bird's-eye view of the proceedings. Reg faltered for a moment, overwhelmed by the occasion. Then a guard blew a whistle, and the spectators turned toward the latest arrival: the blond foreigner who dared to take on the biggest man in the prison.

The babble dissipated into whispers as news spread that Suji's opponent had arrived. The sea of men parted, giving Reg a view of the makeshift table where Suji and Kahn were waiting. Suji lifted his huge frame as Reg approached, raised his arms, and flexed his biceps. The prisoners erupted into a frenzy of cheering and chanting.

"Su-ji, Su-ji . . ."

Suji was sporting a purple headscarf. Reg thought it looked ridiculous; he must have pinched the idea from Mad Dog. The Indian's face radiated contempt, eyes like cold, black slits behind big, round cheeks and overhanging brow. His jaw fell open as the assembly cheered him on. He flexed the muscle of his upper lip and glared at his opponent with a mocking sneer.

As Reg neared the table, lines of heads followed him. Support for Suji became scorn for his adversary, and booing and hissing erupted. Reg wouldn't let it psyche him out; he would keep his head high like a proud Aussie gladiator who meant business. He strode with confidence, slowly but surely, and took his position opposite Suji.

Kahn was the adjudicator and faced the audience with Suji on his left and Reg to his right. He rose and adjusted his sash, the midnight-blue-and-ochre flamboyance he'd worn for the special dinner. He raised his arm with his palm toward the spectators as if he were the pope blessing his congregation. The courtyard fell silent.

Reg scoured the crowd, which seemed even bigger now that he was in the middle of it. Several guards dotted the first row, no more than one meter from his table. Weasel stood directly opposite Reg, with his arms folded. His mouth was twisted in a supercilious smile, suggesting that he was convinced Reg was in for a hammering. Reg took a deep breath to steady his nerves. Where the hell was Jan and the others? There Jan was, with Pete, Mad Dog, Paddy, and Merv, and all the Westerners. They were vastly outnumbered, squashed at the side by Suji's gang. Pete showed him a fist.

"I think most of you know Mr. Pennington," Kahn continued. He held Reg's arm high in the air.

Reg looked into his face. Kahn smiled at him with his eyes, but his mouth didn't move, and Reg hoped this was a good sign.

The crowd started cheering again when Kahn raised Suji's arm. "Su-ji, Su-ji . . ."

Then came the chanting from Reg's band of supporters at the side. "Oz, Oz, Oz, Oz . . ."

Reg waved his other hand at them and beamed appreciatively.

Kahn looked delighted as he lowered the arms of the contestants—his little extravaganza was going splendidly. Reg was surprised when Suji began to peel off his shirt. God, how huge was he? The width of his upper arms had to be at least twenty inches. His chest was decorated with a garish tattoo with an Indian inscription at its center—Reg wondered what it meant—circled by two menacing daggers that bulged when Suji flexed his pectorals. As his compatriots cheered even louder, Suji shot Reg a smug look of contempt.

Reg thought there was nothing for it but to take off his own shirt. When he pulled it over his head, he felt pale and insignificant next to the big hulk of a man on the other side of Kahn. His friends cheered again, but it sounded paltry against the hysteria of Suji's rabble.

Bloody well get on with it, thought Reg.

"Places, please, gentlemen," Kahn said.

He remained standing as Reg and Suji took opposite seats at the small table. Someone coughed, breaking the silence.

"Gentleman, first you will position your hands and arms. When you are both ready, you will not be allowed to exert any pressure until this cloth has landed on the table. Do you both understand?" he said, flourishing a white silk handkerchief above their heads.

"Sure do," said Reg, grateful that the proceedings had rules.

Suji hunched his shoulders and gave a half nod as though he thought Kahn's regulations were tiresome.

"Suji?" Kahn said.

"Yes," Suji mumbled.

"If someone has an unfair advantage, I will stop the contest immediately and we will start again. Begin," Kahn directed them.

Reg looked into Suji's dark narrow eyes and couldn't detect one glimmer of apprehension. When they locked hands he was immediately aware of the man's huge palm and thick fingers and the length of his forearm. Then the lopsided gloat of his mouth.

Take it steady, Reg told himself.

He kept Suji's hand in a firm grip. Both men looked sideways to the white handkerchief between Kahn's thumb and forefinger. The tension of the crowd was palpable; men fidgeted and cleared their throats. Reg gazed at the folds of fabric inches from his face, distracted by the letter *K* embroidered in the corner of the dangling cloth. He felt his heart beating. He heard Suji's breathing, and his own, as they waited for Kahn to release the cloth.

The instant the cloth brushed the table, Reg unleashed the explosive strength of a power athlete. Hyped up on adrenaline and desperation, he thrust his opponent's forearm backward with one mighty downward swoop. The crowd gasped; Suji had been taken by surprise. His reaction saved him, although his hand hovered precariously under Reg's, six inches from defeat.

Suji resisted the full force of Reg's strength. Their hands locked in a static battle of wills, a stalemate. The restless tension of the crowd permeated the arena. Two men at the back called out in their native tongue. Reg heard his own people.

"Come on, Oz!"—sounded like Jan's voice. "Watch him!"—definitely Pete's.

Reg smelled the sweetness of Turkish delight as Kahn crouched low to check the contestants' arm positions. Then Reg registered the pungent odor of Suji, whose thick forearm quivered beneath his, and stared into his huge, grimacing face. It was frozen like a mask, screwed up with pain, eyes half-closed, mouth clamped into a gash. The dark plump skin glistened with a thick sweat. After two minutes of locked torture, Reg's arm felt on fire. Lactic acid swamped his muscles as he felt his power drain.

Hold on. Just hold on for Annie . . .

He dared not risk another thrust until he was certain Suji was spent. He'd arm-wrestled enough athletes at his club to know that this part of the competition was as much mental as physical. He felt Suji's resistance dwindling, but was it enough? Reg was banking on the one factor that had given him confidence coming into the competition—Suji was built for power, not endurance.

Reg had both. He looked into Suji's face to read how much will the Indian had left. Suji opened his eyes just wide enough for Reg to catch the telltale signs: anxiety, disbelief, resignation, and the foreshadowing of the humiliation he knew was to come. Suji's supporters sensed their man was retreating. They lifted their voices to urge his return, and the arena exploded in shouting.

"Su-ji, Su-ji . . ."

Reg watched a big bead of sweat run across the brow of his adversary. Suji grunted and made one last effort to force Reg's hand back to the vertical position. The instant he withdrew the pressure, Reg's adrenaline propelled him. As if lightning had struck his forearm, he slammed Suji's arm on the table with one huge thud.

Suji's throng of supporters gasped in shock. Reg's little group cheered loudly. Reg looked at Weasel. His eyes were sharp with fury, and his eyebrows darted up and down. He gabbled angrily to anyone who would listen, as though he suspected foul play. Suji's followers knew it was no mistake; the foreigner had beaten their man fair and square. Their voices got louder, some whining, others yelling in angry disbelief.

Weasel blew the whistle. He sensed he could have a riot on his hands and wanted the prisoners back in their blocks. Kahn's eyes glowed with satisfaction. Suji was slumped over the table with his head in his arms. Jan was waving, and Pete and Paddy were doing some kind of dance. The courtyard had broken into mayhem, but Reg had one thing on his mind. He turned to Kahn with searching eyes.

Kahn's voice was deep and reassuring. "Tomorrow," was all he said. It was all Reg wanted to hear.

CHAPTER 32

Reg's first thought when he woke the next day was that "tomorrow" had arrived. His own people had treated him like a celebrity after he'd nailed Suji's hand to the tabletop, but he could tell that many of the locals were furious by the resentment on their faces. His group's initial elation over his victory was quickly replaced by a nagging sense of unease.

"I'd have paid to see Suji's face when you had him, though," Pete laughed. "Weasel was bloody livid!"

"Yeah, but what happens now?" Jan was cautious. "When do we get paid? And will they be mad at us?"

"He's right," Paddy warned. "We should watch our backs. You the most, Oz."

Reg didn't feel like playing football when they went down to the courtyard, but he took the ball from Jitesh anyway. Kahn was nowhere to be seen, and neither was Suji. The younger Indians who usually played football refused all invitations for a game and lined the shaded benches, whispering. Some leaned with elbows on knees, their disgruntled stares fixed on Reg's contingent.

"Different atmosphere today," said Reg.

"What do you expect, you've bankrupted most of these lads," said Merv. "Don't be surprised if they don't want to play anymore."

"Sore losers," Reg quipped, kicking the ball against the wall.

Later that afternoon, Pete and Paddy were kicking the ball to each other when Kahn's gentleman friend appeared. He was carrying the big ornate box Kahn had used for storing the betting records and money. Reg and his mates watched him settle on Kahn's bench, the box on his lap while a guard unfolded a card table for it. After fiddling with the lock, the man guardedly lifted the lid. A couple of his younger compatriots sprung to their feet and hovered around him. Reg and Jan laughed when he shooed them away.

Pete panted as he ran back to Reg and Jan. "Did you see that? They haven't noticed they bet on the wrong bloke!"

The man with the box looked tentatively over to Reg's group and beckoned them.

"Pay day, boys," said Pete.

They all traipsed across the yard. Reg hung back and let the others collect their winnings first. Even Mad Dog braved the sun, striding purposefully to claim his windfall. When he was given his money, he stuffed it into the pocket of his pants. "Reckon I've got enough for another guitar!"

"For fuck sake, no," Paddy joked.

Reg waited until last. He'd bet all his money on himself, even though it wasn't much. The elderly Indian counted out eight hundred rupees. Reg brushed his hair off his sweaty forehead and looked into the man's eyes.

"Kahn," he said. "Is Kahn here today?"

"Kahn?" the man said. "Kahn won't be coming today."

"Are you sure?"

"Quite sure," the man said.

He rose, took the box and left. A breeze rustled some leaves around the bench where he'd sat, his robe billowing as he scurried away.

Reg followed him toward the building. Weasel stood at the entrance to the block in his usual pose, arms folded, the peak of his cap shading his narrow, furtive eyes. He followed Reg up the stairwell to where Jitesh was waiting.

"Mr. Pennington," he said when they reached the top. "I presume you are still riding high from your victory?"

"Something like that," Reg cringed.

Weasel turned to Jitesh. "I expect our champion would like to relive yesterday's glory," he said with a crooked smile.

"Yes, sir." Jitesh stood to attention.

Weasel looked into Reg's eyes, in a way he'd never done before. "Someone is waiting to speak to you in the dayroom. Ten minutes, no more." He nodded at Jitesh, and the young guard made heavy work of unlocking the door to the stairs up to the third floor.

"Thanking you," Reg said matter-of-factly, thinking that Kahn probably wanted to congratulate him on his victory and wish him well.

Reg smiled to himself; he liked a man with good manners.

"I thought Kahn had left," he told Jitesh as they walked along the corridor where he used to talk to Annie.

"I know nothing about that," said Jitesh. He seemed pensive. "You might only want to stay a few minutes," he said when they reached the door of the dayroom. Then he hurried away.

Jitesh was different and so was the dayroom. It seemed bigger and emptier than Reg remembered it, and where the hell was Kahn? He felt uneasy and heard a door bang down the corridor. Surely his ten minutes weren't up already? He'd felt hot a moment ago, but now a chill seeped through every part of him.

You bloody idiot . . .

The sound was low at first. It soon clicked into the faster, louder gear of an army of strident footsteps, fast approaching in Reg's direction. He grappled to make sense of what was happening. Jitesh had tried to warn him, but he'd been too bloody preoccupied to cotton on. Now the voices were getting closer, and they didn't sound in the mood for a tea party. What the fuck was happening?

Reg moved to the back area of the room and had started to look for something to defend himself with when the dayroom door was thrown open. A gang of men burst into the room—at least a dozen thugs who looked like they had a score to settle. Reg recognized some of them, local street people who'd been given passes to look around the prison earlier that day. Three of them were at least as tall as Reg, a couple had tattoos, and most had mean faces and wild, angry eyes. Worse still, some were brandishing weapons, planks of rough timber.

They raised the makeshift clubs above their heads, taunting and laughing at Reg in a ghastly chorus. His heart pounded. He dashed to the narrow podium at the back of the room and grabbed the only objects available to defend himself: long hessian bags with weights at the bottom, used by young Indian prisoners who swung them around their bodies in a mock combat. He snatched two, one in each hand, and twirled them like a pair of nunchuks.

"Come on!" he taunted, noting to himself the open door behind them and preparing to fight his way through the horde to reach it.

He lunged at the men, lashing them with his makeshift weapons. He summoned every anger he'd ever felt: for his dad who had worked so long and hard; for the one magnificent throw of the javelin that had eluded him; for the bastard who'd betrayed them in Adelaide; for Kurt fucking Danson. A couple of the thugs scoffed and jested in their native tongues. "This lone, mad Australian lunatic thinks he can take us all on!"

"Arrrrrrrrr," Reg gave one long, piercing primordial roar as he leapt into their midst, flailing the heavy bags. His movements were almost graceful, like a dancer's, but fast and decisive, pounding the torsos and heads of his adversaries. He battled furiously, fielding the men's blows as he thrashed his way through their ranks like a wild animal. One of the big men grabbed a heavy piece of wood from the floor and swung it back, ready to strike. Reg saw it from the corner of his eye and quickly ducked.

He was too late. "Whack!" The timber struck his cheek and spun him sideways.

But it didn't stop him. He dodged and wrong-footed his opponents, dropping the hessian bags as he kicked and elbowed his way through the scuffle of the last three men between him and the door. In one desperate lunge he burst through the door and slammed it shut. There was a loud thud as the gang hurled themselves against the inside of it. They were trapped. They hammered to be let out but it was going to take them a while; Reg had secured the metal latch.

He heard them banging and kicking as he hobbled back down the walkway. His cheek was smarting, there was a loud ringing in his ear, and he had the salty taste of blood in his mouth. His legs quivered as he tried to hurry down the stairwell, and when he saw Jitesh's face as he unlocked the metal gate, Reg knew he looked even worse than he felt.

"I'll take you to the hospital wing!" The guard's eyes were wide with shock.

Reg shook his head. "Dormitory," he whispered as he wiped blood from his mouth.

"Sorry, Mr. Oz." Jitesh looked sheepish when he locked him into the big cell.

"What the fuck happened to you?" Pete and the others crowded around as he limped into their midst.

Jan was upset. Mad Dog said he couldn't look because blood made him queasy.

Paddy inspected Reg's wounds. "Dropped your guard, thought you could do it without your trainer this time, did ya?"

"You won't be playing football for a while," said Pete. "The bastards have busted you up pretty bad."

CHAPTER 33

When Annie had been released on bail from the women's prison, she'd lost weight. Unbeknownst to Reg, she'd visited a hospital in the city, where it was discovered she had a recurring blood disorder she'd suffered from as a child. After she was discharged, she was put in the care of a group of nuns who ran a charitable facility connected to the hospital. While being nursed back to health, Annie spent long days of nostalgic contemplation, thinking about everything she and Reg had left behind in Australia.

The nuns were very kind to her, and in the warm glow of their concern, she disclosed more details of her plight than she'd intended. The sisters urged her to contact her mother to let her know that she was safe. When she felt strong enough, Annie discharged herself from the nursing home, leaving a letter for them to post. She told her mother:

> What fate awaits me I've no idea. I just figure I've little to lose and if things go right, lots to gain as regards freedom. Others have made it, why can't I? The "risk" is worth it to me. I just wish it didn't have to be this way—the whole thing is snowballing—I've no means to stop it.

Annie returned to the area near the hotel where she'd stayed with Reg and Niko and was befriended by a young American woman she met in a cafe. They shared a squalid little apartment, and Annie spent months living off her wits. She supported herself by purchasing hash from street traders she knew from her early days in the city and reselling it for a profit to young Western travelers in the local cafes and bars.

Every week she would phone her court-appointed lawyer from a phone box nearby, desperately hoping for news of Reg's release. She could hardly contain her excitement when she finally received the joyful news that, twelve months after they were arrested, Reg had been granted bail and was about to be set free.

✈ ✈ ✈

"Mr. Oz, Mr. Oz."

Reg opened one eye.

"Mr. Oz, your solicitor man is waiting, you have to bring your box and he says hurry, he has to go to court."

"Fuck, what time is it?" Reg rolled over and slowly maneuvered himself to a seated position. "Okay, okay," he said. "Where am I going?"

"Leaving, it's your leaving day."

Reg tried to absorb what Jitesh was telling him. "This better not be some kind of sick joke," he mumbled, but when he looked into the young guard's earnest face he knew it wasn't.

Joyous thoughts of Annie and a whole world of possibilities raced through his mind as he threw a few belongings into his box. A couple of prisoners stirred. Pete was snoring.

"Jan, Jan." Reg kneeled and gently shook his young cellmate.

Jan's eyes opened immediately. He lay still and his arm shot sideways to collect his glasses.

"Listen buddy, I think I'm on my way now," whispered Reg.

Jan twitched when he saw Jitesh towering over them. Disappointment clouded his eyes, and his bottom lip turned inward as he tried to put on a brave face. Reg felt his sadness.

"I'll write and see how you're getting on." He gave Jan's arm a mock punch. "Hey, you're gonna get out of here soon. Who knows, you might even come and visit me in Australia."

"Hurry, Mr. Oz," Jitesh said.

"Go," urged Jan.

Reg shook Jan's shoulder and wished he could take him with him. He didn't look back as he shuffled through the patchwork of sleeping men. He thought he heard the faint strains of Mad Dog's guitar as Jitesh locked the door behind him for the last time.

✈ ✈ ✈

The lawyer was waiting for Reg in the reception area of the main building. He reminded Reg of an older version of Jitesh, long and gangly but with graying hair. His ill-fitting suit looked borrowed, and his trousers were so short they revealed an expanse of white socks.

"I've got to do this quickly," he said anxiously as he sifted through his papers. "The court case is in two months. You can go now but not with your passport. Bail has been paid."

"Paid?"

"Yes, paid by Miss Priestly. This is where you come to see me. Phone for the time." He gave Reg a card and threw his papers into his briefcase. "See you next week, Mr. Pennington, with Miss Priestly." He quickly shook Reg's hand.

"Where is Miss Priestly?" asked Reg.

"Outside, waiting outside," the solicitor called back impatiently as he hurried away, and Reg's heart surged with joy.

The admissions officer took Reg into an adjoining office, where he was given the backpack Bhatti and Chandak had confiscated a year before. Port Cochin seemed a lifetime ago. He was allowed to use the toilet while a guard waited outside. He tipped the contents of the backpack onto the floor and rummaged through the few musty creased clothes that were left, cursing when he realized half of his belongings were missing. He hurriedly pulled on a pair of jeans and a T-shirt and used his rusty razor to shave off as much of his beard as he could manage. He stared at himself in the mirror. God, he looked a sight! What would Annie think?

Weasel hovered by the duty officer's desk. He puffed a cigarette and handed Reg a form with a copy of his passport to sign.

"We will probably be seeing you again shortly," he sneered, as Reg scrawled Bruce Pennington's signature.

Not bloody likely, thought Reg.

He stepped into the sunshine, savoring his first long breath of freedom. He strode joyfully, scarcely believing that the long wretched hours were behind him and he was about to see his beloved Annie. He suddenly stopped, dropped his bag, and removed the solicitor's card from his pocket. He glanced at the name and address.

His hand clenched as he crumpled the card in his palm, thinking that wherever he was going, he definitely wouldn't need it.

"Bull's-eye," he muttered as he chucked it in the bin, and raced off to find Annie.

She was waiting outside the main gate. Reg spotted her among the milling locals and men in suits long before she saw him. Her hair was scraped back in an untidy ponytail. She'd lost weight, and looked so forlorn in her knee-length kaftan and sandals that Reg was put in mind of Orphan Annie. She buried her head in his chest as he threw his bags on the ground. He scooped her into the air and swung her around. When he put her down, he took her face in his hands and their mouths met in a long, heartfelt kiss.

Reg held Annie at arm's length and smoothed her flyaway hair. "God, I've missed you. Let me look at you now!" The sun caught the side of her face, and he thought she looked older. She could age all she liked; she would always be his beautiful Annie.

"I was beginning to think you were never getting out," she said, her eyes welling.

"You don't get rid of me that easily!" He threw his backpack over his shoulder. "Let's get out of here, darling. Before they change their minds."

They picked up a pace down a side road, along a small wasteland of vacant buildings and sprawling weeds. Reg walked around Annie so she was on the inside of the path. She'd always liked the way he did that because it made her feel protected.

"Where we going?"

"To get the bus," said Reg. "But not immediately!" He laughed and nudged her off the path into the undergrowth.

"What?"

Then she saw his mischievous face and knew what he had in mind. He hurried down the bank and flung his backpack behind a corrugated shack. Annie giggled and followed suit, and they fell on the rough ground between their bags. It was strewn with twigs and leaves and rubbish. They didn't care. Goats chomped and grazed nearby. Cars passed by overhead. Reg leaned over Annie and released the tie of her ponytail. He'd lived on the memory of the smell of her hair, and now it fell around her shoulders. She covered him with little kisses, oblivious to the sounds and movement all around them.

Later they lay on their backs and stared at the sky. Annie stroked Reg's hand, sunlight flooding her vivid green eyes as she gazed.

"Did you mention a bus, Mr. Pennington?"

"Yep." He planted a last kiss on her forehead. "I'd better put my trousers on first."

"I think you should go like that."

"Might have to," laughed Reg, "because I can't bloody well find them . . ."

CHAPTER 34

As the scheduled date for Reg and Annie's court appearance drew closer, Reg became more determined to leave Bombay. Their lawyer had told Annie that their chance of an acquittal, based on the evidence from Bhatti and Chandak, was extremely thin. To make matters worse, the young woman Annie had shared their shabby two-roomed apartment with had skipped town. Reg and Annie were responsible for the full rent, and their meager funds were dwindling fast. Reg worried that they might be under some kind of surveillance, and warned Annie that they needed to be extra vigilant about where they went and whom they associated with.

One evening they sat in one of their regular bars, on the lookout for an opportunity to make money, when Annie recognized a well-dressed local man who was a friend of her previous flatmate. The man had been observing them from another table, and when they stood to leave, he beckoned them over. He introduced himself as Amit, and ordered a round of drinks. Reg's ears pricked up when Amit told them that Annie's friend had done a few jobs for him in the past. Reg said he would willingly do a "few jobs," especially if the pay was good enough to set him and Annie up elsewhere.

Reg arranged a meeting with Amit and his associate. The friend was a tall dark figure in a snazzy suit, a lounge lizard who drank in more-expensive bars than Reg and Annie could afford. Reg asked the man his name, and he said he didn't have one, holding Reg's gaze to make sure he understood. Reg agreed to make a couple of deliveries to some of the plush hotels around the city.

Over the next couple of months, he would make deliveries, collect the payments—big wads of notes held together by thick elastic bands—and take them straight back to the man with no name.

On the night of Reg's last delivery he was feeling downright nervous; their court case was due in a couple of days, and they needed to get out of town. After a few drinks with Amit and his nameless colleague, Reg confided in them about his predicament. Amit offered to help by driving them to the bus station, and said he hoped that Reg would continue doing business with them when he returned.

Reg and Annie planned to leave Bombay the following day to avoid going to court to answer their charges. By now they'd lost touch with the lawyer, who didn't have a clue where they were staying. In the early evening of the next day Amit knocked on their door and asked if they were ready. He helped them cart their duffle bag and backpacks down the narrow little staircase to his car. He put their big bag in his boot, and Reg and Annie squeezed into the backseat with their backpacks. Amit sat in the driver's seat next to the man with no name, and they drove for half an hour through the city traffic to the bus station.

Reg and Annie couldn't understand the information blaring from a loudspeaker over the huge forecourt of the station. The area throbbed with people and luggage. Belongings littered the crammed ticket offices and bus bays. Congested lines of jabbering passengers waited to board the buses. An old man sat talking to himself, sandwiched between the brightly colored silks of two women's saris.

Annie stood bewildered amid the commotion. Reg glanced sideways, leaned close to her and whispered. "It's swarming with cops."

Amit reached into the inside pocket of his smart blue lapelled jacket. "Tickets, and something to sell at the other end," he said, handing Reg two dockets and a fat envelope. "Bay seven, this way."

Reg and Annie followed the two men through rows of passengers with unwieldy chattels. They finally came to bay seven, where a large, old bus with a "Goa" sign on the front was parked.

"Wait here," said Amit, as he and Nameless leapt aboard the bus. They strode to the back of the aisle, and pulled two unsuspecting locals out of their seats. The disgruntled passengers, an elderly man and a young woman, quickly disembarked, followed by Amit and his nameless friend.

"Don't think about it," Amit said, when he saw the look of shame on Annie's face. "Your need is greater than theirs." He turned to Reg, "Lots of people like you in Goa," and flashed him a knowing smile.

Reg shook the men's hands, told them how much he appreciated their help, and watched them disappear into the crowd. He followed Annie up the steps of the bus, and they showed their tickets to the young driver.

"Phew," Reg sighed as they slumped into two vacant seats near the back.

Annie laid her head on his shoulder. "Yeah, but I hate the way we got here, it's bloody unfair." Reg sighed and kissed the top of her head. God, he'd missed her when he was in jail.

Their driver beeped the horn, and the bus rattled toward the outskirts of the city. They'd been up late the previous night worrying about where they were going, and they dozed through the first hours of their journey.

Meanwhile, in Adelaide, Annie's mother had received the letter her daughter had sent from the nunnery in Bombay. Annie's mother had managed to find the phone number for the nunnery and had spoken to a sister who had confirmed that Annie had left. A distraught Mrs. Hayes had contacted the Australian Federal Police and told them what was in Annie's letter, including her daughter's insistence that she and Reg had no intention of appearing in court to answer their charges. The police had in turn informed Interpol of this latest twist in the Spiers case. But by the time the Indian authorities learned that Bruce Pennington was really Reg Spiers, and Sonia Priestly was really Annie Hayes, the pair were just waking up from a peaceful nap on the road to Goa.

"Hey, something smells good," said Reg, stretching awake.

A couple of village women had boarded the bus with baskets of hot food. Annie bought two *vada pavs,* rolls filled with a fried, spicy mashed potato, two crispy cauliflower *pakoras,* and a bottle of fruit juice.

"How long till we get to Goa?" she asked after they'd devoured the food.

"Ages, I remember seeing it on a map. It's gotta be the best part of four or five hundred miles. We won't be there till early morning."

Annie groaned. "Better be worth it."

The bus jangled down the road, slowing for oncoming vehicles along the twists and turns of the undulating terrain. Annie slept a few more hours. Reg managed only to doze; he worried about their situation. They weren't technically on the run until they failed to show up for their trial, but how would they explain not having passports if they were questioned by the police?

The miles lapped the last light until Reg could see himself in the window among a myriad of pinprick stars. His face was pale and ghostly, and he hoped his long hair didn't make him look like a troublemaker. The last thing he wanted was to stand out in a crowd. They'd have to watch their step if they didn't want to land back in jail. He wondered what Niko was doing at that moment, if he was still in India.

The coach shook as they crunched over the stony ground of a car park. Annie stirred.

"Are we there?"

"No," Reg told her, "but if you want the loo, this might be your last chance for a while."

The driver sighed as he turned off the engine opposite a primitive toilet block. He pointed to his watch to tell them to be quick. Reg and Annie were last in line to use the disgusting hut. She waited for Reg, keeping her eye on the bus. The driver's cigarette glowed as he sat on the steps of his vehicle. Suddenly, a car swooped out of the night and pulled alongside him. The driver stood up, and she watched in horror as two policemen got out of the car and followed him onto the bus.

"Reg," she hissed under the gap of the toilet door. "It's the cops."

"Shit!" He was still zipping his trousers when he burst out.

The bus interior lit up. One policeman was walking up and down the aisle and talking to the passengers, looking at papers.

Reg's mind swirled; they had their backpacks with the money he'd made recently, but he sure as hell wasn't going to give up the duffle bag. It contained every stitch of clothing they owned, including new things they'd bought to replace what they'd lost in the prison.

"As quietly as we can," he whispered. He grabbed Annie's hand and whisked her into the night.

They circumnavigated the bus, staying wide of it until they reached a clump of trees. Reg peered from the shrubbery and saw that the officers had finished their rounds but were still on-board talking to the driver. The bus would probably leave as soon as the police got off, and that left him with only one option.

"Now," Reg hissed, and they took off again.

They darted around the back of the bus, then up the side, crouching low. They stealthily crept around the front. Annie felt her heart pounding. Her wide eyes met Reg's as they listened to the men talking as they disembarked. Then the stones crunched under their shoes a few feet away. The bus started as the car door slammed.

The police vehicle idled for a moment, then it moved slowly past the huddling pair. Reg pulled Annie around the corner of the bus and rushed her up the steps.

"Thought you were leaving without us," Reg rasped at the driver.

The man hadn't even noticed they were missing, and nodded sheepishly.

A relieved Reg and Annie flopped into their seats, their faces flushed. They stared at each other.

"Hope it's a bit calmer in Goa," Annie panted.

"We have to get new passports, though," Reg said.

"God, Reggie," Annie moaned. "When I think of the trouble we went to for those. Who the hell are we gonna be this time?"

CHAPTER 35

His real name was Mike Goodall. Someone had dubbed him "Ezy" when his travels landed him in Goa three summers before, and the name stuck. He had intended to spend a few weeks before heading back to London. Time grew with the length of his silver hair. Soon enough, the sight of Ezy on his scooter speeding across the sand with his silver locks streaming behind was a regular feature of Calangute Beach. And he was easy—easy come, easy go—a devotee of the laid-back communal lifestyle that had lured dozens of young and old hippies to Goa. Some were transient. Others, like Ezy, had made it their home.

It suited Ezy that nobody around Calangute Beach asked too many questions. If quizzed by tourists in the numerous beach cafes and bars about what he did for a living, he'd joke that he was in "communications." His communication was largely limited to telling potential customers the price of what he was selling, and his business dealings were usually done by lunchtime. That left the afternoons free to chill out with friends and enjoy the fruits of his labor.

This morning was hot with a light breeze. Ezy crammed his canvas shoulder bag with merchandise and took his normal route out to the village on his red scooter. After he'd rendezvoused with a few contacts, his bag felt lighter. He undid the top button of his cheesecloth shirt and headed back along the main road. He'd just spluttered up the brow of the hill when he passed two young Westerners with backpacks traipsing in the same direction. He pulled alongside them.

Ezy was the self-appointed tourist guide for newcomers. "Need any help?" he asked in his friendly, Cockney accent.

Annie studied the tall, middle-aged man. His silver mop was almost as long as her hair, and it made his leathery face look very tanned. She'd never seen so many patches on one pair of denim jeans.

"Sure do," said Reg. Ezy didn't look like the sort of bloke to be checking passports. "Thought we'd take a look at Calangute Beach. Worth seeing?"

"You'd better believe it! Just keep walking, then take the left fork and there's a little bar just before the beach. I'll be there having a beer. Give you the lowdown if you like."

"Great," Reg said.

Annie nodded. "Thanks."

"This is more like it," said Reg when they found the beach.

They'd seen plenty of beautiful coastlines in Australia, but the kilometers of white sand and swaying palms spilling into the Arabian Sea captivated them. The shoreline curved into a large bay, bordered by a wooded headland dotted with assorted shacks and hawkers' stalls displaying handicrafts and produce.

"He's right. It's beautiful," Annie said when they were walking into the bar to find Ezy. "Oh Reggie, let's stay here. We've earned some peace."

✈ ✈ ✈

"So how long you guys sticking around?" asked Ezy when Reg brought the second round to the table.

Annie looked hopefully at Reg. "Depends on how much it costs," she said. "Where does everybody live around here?"

"If you're staying more than a month, you don't pay tourist prices. There are some great little shacks almost on the beach. Going for next to nothing."

"Nothing sounds better," said Reg. Annie straightened, very interested.

"The guy around the corner from mine has got keys to one farther up. Wanna see it?" Ezy asked.

Reg swigged his beer. "Sure do, buddy," he said as he put the empty bottle on the table. "Ready when you are."

✈ ✈ ✈

Annie thought the one-bedroom timber bungalow was perfect; the first place she and Reg had ever had to themselves. It nestled on the corner of a sandy path, no more than a hundred meters from the beach. There were two steps up to the timber veranda, where Annie insisted they dump their shoes. By day they could lounge on the deck and watch the children frolicking along the shoreline. At night the rhythm of the restless tide would lull them to sleep.

"You know that Bogart film, *Casablanca*?" Annie said one evening.

"Yeah," said Reg. "What about it?"

"Can't stop thinking about it."

"Why?"

"Because . . . because we'll always have Goa."

"That's nice," Reg smiled. "And each other."

He looked for work; most of the cash he'd earned in Bombay had gone as a down payment on their bungalow. Jobs in the outlying towns went to locals, and bars operated by Westerners rarely hired newcomers. There wasn't time to develop a comprehensive business plan, so he concentrated on what he knew best.

"Have you thought of expanding your business enterprise?" he asked Ezy at the end of the first month in Goa.

"How d'you mean?" Ezy's tone was cautious.

He had kept his routine simple to avoid the stress of working with other people. Every Friday he bought blocks of hash from a contact in a nearby town and prepared them for sale at his old wooden table. He'd measure and cut them into neat little portions to sell to friends or tourists in the beach bars and clubs in the village.

"Give me one week working with you," Reg suggested. "You'll make more with me in seven days than you make on your own in four weeks."

"For Christ's sake! Don't push our luck!" Annie protested when she and Reg were alone. "Look what happened at Port Cochin—I'm not going through that again!"

"We've got to eat, Annie, and pay the rent," Reg insisted. "If you want to settle for a while, we need a regular income. It'll be fine, we're talking small-time stuff here."

Ezy couldn't resist Reg's offer. Before long they'd established a profitable operation that included the neighboring towns of Arpora-Nagoa, Saligao, and Candolin. He increased his Friday order sixfold. By Saturday lunchtime, the pair had finished cutting the blocks into a hundred neat portions.

Reg rented his own scooter; lime green to match the Indian shoulder bag Annie had bought him. Soon people grew accustomed to the red and green scooters zipping around the narrow dusty streets of the neighborhood.

Ezy was delighted. "You've made an entrepreneur out of me, Brucie," he joked.

Annie often accompanied Reg on his local deliveries. One evening they visited Adele and Jeana, French Canadian twins who had arrived at Calangute the week before. Their house was identical to Reg and Annie's, but nestled in a more secluded area farther back from the beach.

"Come in, Bruce," a woman called when they rang the brass cowbell by the door.

The lounge had a strong smell of ink and four small tables in some kind of production line. One table held piles of different cards and paper, an assortment of rulers, straightedges, knives, and scissors. Another was covered with printing paraphernalia: sheets of templates and stencils with bottles of ink in assorted colors. Jeana sat cross-legged under a long kaftan at the third workstation. Her double, Adele, pored over a pile of documents on the end table. She worked by hand. As she peered through a magnifying lens, her large hooped earrings made little chinking sounds against the glass.

"With you in a minute," she called without looking up. "This one's giving me the shits."

Later they all sat on the sofas. "I had no idea you girls were so industrious," said Reg. "Can you produce any kind of passport, or only certain nationalities?"

"At the moment English, French, Canadian, Australian, and New Zealand," Adele said. Jeana added, "Should have American next month when I've fine-tuned the details."

Annie thought Reg was joking when he said he wanted to

order a French passport. When Adele delivered it, his sleek new Bordeaux-red passport with the French coat of arms bore the name of Patrick Albert Claude Ledoux.

Annie said she thought it was a ridiculous idea.

"Don't you see," Reg said. "That's why, because it *is* so unlikely. Who'd ever think an Aussie fugitive like Bruce Pennington would masquerade as a Frenchman!"

Annie settled for being Annette Joyce Chamberlain from New Zealand.

"Like we haven't got enough problems," she complained. "You wanna be bloody French!"

They'd been in Goa for six months, two weeks, and three days. Annie kept a diary. She recorded all the lovely things they did: their long walks along the coast, meals with Ezy and his mad bunch of friends, the ornaments she'd bought to make their little beach shack a home. They'd buy a place of their own someday. In a year or so they'd be able to go back to Australia. Perhaps not Adelaide to start with, but it wouldn't take long to establish themselves again. They would find Niko and Cheryl and everyone, and before long they'd all have kids and be godparents. But when she looked back at all the madness, she would remember today, this here and now, because it was perfect and she was truly happy.

She ran her fingers through the warm sand next to her face, luxuriating in one last stretch before sitting up to survey the scene from their usual spot on Calangute Beach. A new breeze played with the russet strands of her hair, a deeper red now, dyed with henna bought at one of the local stalls. She focused behind her sunglasses on a distant bird, hovering above the horizon. Reg stirred from sleep as she stroked the long wisps of sun-bleached hair from his eyes.

"Five minutes, then a beer," he mumbled.

She sighed, thinking about how they'd argued about his French passport a few weeks ago. She turned to him and found him gazing up at her.

"How long have you been staring at me?" she asked.

"Ages, wondering what you're thinking about."

"Nothing important," she lied.

Their regular beach bar seemed more crowded than usual. They squeezed into opposite seats and ordered beers. The remnants of the sun cast long shadows across the table as Annie stooped to take a shawl from her bag. The man behind her cleared his throat. Reg watched him lift his crinkled newspaper and shake it open. He couldn't see the man's face, just the back of his left hand clutching the front page of the *Bombay Times*.

"What's up?" Annie asked when she saw the glazed look in his eyes.

"I'll tell you later," he said, in a way she knew meant, "something's wrong!"

The shock disoriented Reg. He looked at the large black headline on the man's newspaper again. It floated across the white background. He wanted to believe it was a mistake, that it didn't read "FOREIGNERS ABSCOND TO GOA." But there was no mistaking the photographs: two enlargements of their passport photographs they had to leave when they were bailed out in Bombay. Reg's mouth turned dry. His heart pounded as he put a few coins on the table and stood and leaned over Annie.

"Keep your sunglasses on, we're going now," he said under his breath.

She rose slowly, walked around the table, and followed Reg onto the beach. She paced to keep up with him, not daring to look back.

"For God's sake, Reg, tell me what's going on!" Annie demanded when he closed the door of their house.

"I'm trying to think! Just seen the front page of some guy's bloody newspaper, haven't I? I was staring at two huge fucking mug shots. Us! Foreigners abscond to Goa, that's what it said. Don't ask me how they bloody know!"

Annie slumped in a chair and folded her arms.

"Okay, it's bad, but not really bad. We could go away for a few days and when we come back it'll all be forgotten. People will believe us, that it must have been someone else."

"Don't be ridiculous," Reg blurted as he raced into the bedroom. "One similar face, maybe, but not two. We're out of here!"

Annie stomped after him and watched him grab bags and clothing from the cupboard.

"I'm sick of running Reg! Where the fuck can we go this time?" she yelled, chucking clothes on the bed.

Reg's eyes darted around the room as he grabbed shoes and jewelry. They softened when they settled on Annie's teary face. He hugged her tightly.

"We'll work that out on the way. We'll get through this, I'm not risking us being sent back to that place."

Annie stuffed clothing into bags. "I'm not as strong as you!" she wailed. "I get happy, then there's the ticking time bomb and I'm nowhere again. I can't do this anymore!"

"We can't talk about it now, Annie." Reg stared at their belongings. "And we can't take all this. Forget the duffle bag, it won't fit on the bike. Just the backpacks."

He lifted the mattress, grabbed their envelope of rupees, and shoved it in his bag with his notebook and their new passports. He scribbled a note, "Hope our paths cross again someday, buddy," and rested it against a candle on the table.

"Don't leave Oscar, you'll regret it," Reg said as he saw Annie agonize over what to leave behind.

She bit her lip as she pulled out a bottle of shampoo and a jumper before squeezing the floppy koala in the side of her bag.

She threw the strap of her bag over her head as they raced down the steps of the porch. It was almost dark now, and when she climbed onto the scooter behind Reg, she found it hard to balance. He revved the engine. The bike accelerated and Annie lurched backward. They wound through a trail along the lush headland path past Ezy's little timber shack.

"Thanks, mate," Reg muttered. He wished he'd left the note on Ezy's porch.

They traveled inland, where the forest grew denser and the narrow sandy path gave way to bushes and stones. The bike sputtered under their weight as they traversed a slope. Annie clung to Reg, head down, arms encircling his torso. She gulped mouthfuls of air as they hurtled through the undergrowth.

"We're too loaded, lose something!" Reg yelled over the noise of the vibrating engine.

Annie struggled to balance as she ripped open the zipper of the bag sticking into her stomach. She groped inside as they hit a rock and she flew upward. She flung socks, shoes, and T-shirts into the bushes. God, would they have anything left? Air whipped her face and billowed her hair as she clung to Reg for dear life.

"Where are we going?" she shouted.

"The airport."

"Where?"

"The airport."

"Where are we going then?"

The scooter jolted on a rock and skidded sideways before Reg brought it to a standstill.

"Wherever we like," he said.

"Where would you like to go?" panted Annie.

Reg thought for a moment, catching his breath.

"Africa." His voice was calm now. "You always said you wanted to go to Africa."

CHAPTER 36

The airport official barely looked at their passports. Reg zipped them into the front compartment of his backpack as they strolled through the passport control section of Mombasa Airport. Reg and Annie had reinvented themselves. Patrick Albert Claude Ledoux had undergone a transformation in the men's washroom before boarding the plane. He was clean-shaven, his hair styled in the crew cut he'd sported years ago.

Meanwhile, his girlfriend, Annette, had been experimenting with hairdos in the women's toilet next door. Her red tresses were piled on top of her head in a chic bun, softened with loose tendrils around her face. She'd matched her sophisticated new look with a sassy cinnamon lipstick she'd splashed out on in the duty-free perfumery, and large hooped earrings the twins had given her. The beach had baked their skin golden brown, and as they left the Mombasa airport in white T-shirts and jeans, Reg was hoping they could pass themselves off as well-heeled tourists.

Their latest plan was to trek overland from Mombasa to Cape Town and make some money on the way. They had to make something. Although they looked like a wealthy jet-setting couple as they donned their sunglasses that morning, most of their money had been spent on airfares, and funds were running low.

"Taxi," Reg called. They got in the second cab.

"Can you recommend a hotel?" he asked the driver.

"Shall I take you there? Best hotel in Mombasa." The driver's big white smile was hopeful.

Reg looked at Annie and she shrugged her shoulders. "Why not?" she said. She'd been forced to leave everywhere she loved, why should she rough it?

Reg felt the same. "Lead the way, pal."

"Welcome to the Palms Hotel," the concierge greeted them as the bellboy carried their backpacks across the foyer.

"Will you be staying long, Mr. . . ." The clerk flicked the pages of Reg's passport. "Mr. Ledoux?"

Reg smiled at his beautiful girlfriend. "Couple of weeks, darling?" Annie nodded. "Our other luggage will be coming later," added Reg, thinking how out of place their backpacks looked for a pair of up-and-coming professionals.

The bellboy showed them to their suite, and Reg slipped him a smaller tip than he'd have liked.

"I can't believe this!" Annie dived onto the bed. "This could be great," she said when she'd stopped bouncing. "Let's go and look at stuff and be tourists. Can we have some fun?"

"A couple of days, then we'll head south," Reg said as he lay beside her. "Stay on the move, and make our way overland to Cape Town."

"Don't want to think about leaving. We just got here," said Annie, running her fingers across the gold brocade bedspread.

Reg sighed and put his hands under his head. "Shit, Annie, will you just look at this place," he said as he surveyed the curtains with tasseled tiebacks, matching bedcover, and elaborate walnut furniture. "Let's enjoy it while we can."

On the first two mornings, Annie rose early and crept into the bathroom while Reg slept. She liked to fill the tub, add the complimentary bubble bath, and fantasize about being Annie Spiers from Adelaide while she wallowed in the foam. After breakfast in the dining room, they planned their day like regular tourists. They explored every corner of the old Arabic town, Nyali Beach, and Fort Jesus. On the fourth afternoon, they wandered across the lush lawns of the Gedi Ruins and mingled with sightseers beneath the old stone skeletons of buildings.

"I'd never find a job in a place like this," said Reg.

Annie looked disappointed. "Are we doing a runner?"

"We have to keep moving, Annie, we don't have enough to hang around."

"Just two more days, two more." Annie drained her drink. "Then reality."

Every Saturday night was a dinner dance at the Palms Hotel. Annie had only one dress: a long, slinky Indian thing she'd bought at a market in Goa. Reg had managed to hold on to one semismart shirt. But the shirt and the dress were a crinkled mess at the bottom of their backpacks.

"We could just have dinner sent to our room," said Reg when he saw the state of their clothes.

"Oh no, let's go to the special dinner," pleaded Annie. "I'll stick them in the laundry service, they'll have them back by five."

✈ ✈ ✈

The jazz band in the dining room played a smoky version of "Girl from Ipanema." Reg and Annie wound their way through the softly lit tables. Her dress and his shirt looked as good as new. Annie was wearing makeup, with her hair swirled to the side in a sparkly clasp to show off her hooped earrings. The stunning redhead got admiring glances from several male diners. A table of four women dissolved into giggles. One craned her neck to get a better view of the handsome, tanned blond stud in the white shirt.

"If only they knew," Reg whispered across the breadbasket.

Annie grinned behind her menu. "Very posh," she said as she tried to decipher it. "Classic chicken gumbo sounds good."

"Wine, sir?" the waiter asked.

"Just a beer, thanks," said Reg.

"Oh go on, let's have wine," Annie insisted.

"The lady wants wine, so that's what she'll have," said Reg affably. "Leave it up to you," he told the waiter. "Something to go with chicken, the gumbo."

"Very good, sir," the waiter was flattered at the confidence placed in him, and sauntered off in time to the music.

Annie flashed Reg an excited little smile.

"Might as well have what we want," he lowered his voice. "It'll have to be on the house."

"You'll enjoy the gumbo, it's very good here," a plump middle-aged woman with a German accent called from the adjacent table. Her gaudy necklace jangled on her ample chest.

"Oh really, well, thank you," said Annie politely.

"You're from Australia aren't you?" the woman continued. "Looks like a fascinating place."

Annie had to check herself. "New Zealand," she said. "How about you?"

"Just outside Munich," said the woman's partner.

He was a droopy-faced man with fluffy gray hair, and his white tuxedo jacket made Reg feel underdressed.

"But we live here now. Just having a weekend to celebrate our wedding anniversary," the man told them.

"I'll drink to that," Reg announced as he raised his glass.

By the end of the evening the Schneiders had insisted that Reg and Annie join them at their table. After two bottles of wine, Annie was having difficulty fielding their questions. Reg came to her aid.

"My real estate company has been doing well, but I was suffering from burn out, you know how it is," he told them. "So my business partner in Auckland agreed to hold the fort so we could take a break."

"How wonderful!" Agnes Schneider said as she sipped her third brandy. Annie gave Reg a little kick under the table.

"What a shame we leave in the morning, we would have liked to hear more about New Zealand. Wouldn't we, Errol?"

"We certainly would," Errol agreed. "Where are you folks heading next?"

"Dar es Salaam, tomorrow probably," said Reg. "No point in flying everywhere, you miss it all."

Annie stared at him. What happened to her two more days?

"We're meeting friends at Diani Beach tomorrow," Errol said. "It's only an hour or so, but you're welcome to ride with us, it'll get you off the island."

"Indeed," said Agnes. "If you don't mind an early start."

Reg looked at Annie, eyebrows raised. "What d'you think, Annette, should we burden these good people?"

Annie tried to sound enthusiastic. "If it's not too much trouble."

"No trouble at all, so we're taking that as a yes," Errol Schneider said. "Good to have your company," he added as he signaled for them to raise their glasses again.

Reg tried to marshal his thoughts as they made their way back to their room.

"We can't leave our passports," he said, steering Annie to the reception desk.

"Wonder if you could help me?" he asked the white-shirted, black-waistcoated young man behind the counter. "We have to take our passports into the consulate office tomorrow to get some documents stamped."

The clerk checked his records. There was no deposit on Mr. Ledoux's room, and handing back passports to guests who hadn't settled their bills was forbidden—unless they offered some kind of surety.

Reg read his mind and turned to Annie. "We could leave something, couldn't we, darling, as a sign of good faith?"

Annie rolled her eyes, peeved that she was always the one who had to make sacrifices.

"Sure," she said, forcing a smile.

She tugged at the diamond ring on her wedding finger. Reg had bought it for her on one of their trips; it was the only valuable thing they owned. It refused to budge, and she had to lick her finger before it would slide off.

She placed it in front of the clerk. "That will be fine, sir," he said, barely looking at it.

He disappeared into a back office with the ring and returned moments later with their passports.

"Thanks, have 'em back tomorrow," said Reg, relieved to have one less thing to worry about.

At seven the next morning Reg and Annie padded down the corridor with their bags and shoes. When they heard the rattle of a cleaner's trolley behind them they dashed around a corner. Reg had located a side exit the previous evening. They avoided the main foyer and sneaked down a passageway to the tradesperson's entrance. Muffled voices sounded from the kitchen as they passed. They quickly shuffled their bags through the outer door and darted down the path. The tall lattice gate at the end was locked. They slipped into their shoes, Reg hurled their bags over the railings, and they clambered after them.

They'd given the Schneiders the excuse they'd be breakfasting in town so they wouldn't have to leave the hotel with them. Errol had said it would be no trouble to collect them down the road.

"Traveling light," he noted when he wedged their backpacks into the boot of his black Daimler.

"Don't remind me, still in negotiation with the airline," said Reg. "Typical of those idiots, lost everything."

He felt unsettled as he climbed into the backseat beside Annie. Lying had become automatic lately, but he consoled himself with the thought that normal rules didn't apply to special circumstances such as these. Half an hour into the journey Reg regretted that he'd accepted the Germans' offer of a lift, as he answered their incessant questions about property investment. By the time Errol dropped them off, Reg had established himself as somewhat of an expert and had made a mental checklist of everything he'd told them. They collected their bags from the boot, wished the Schneiders well, and thanked them for the ride.

Reg and Annie quickly found a little cafe and were just finishing coffee and sandwiches when Reg overheard the waitress chatting with a priest at the next table. Priests had been good to Reg in the past, and while the waitress busied herself, he struck up a conversation with him. By the time Annie had finished her coffee, Reg had organized their next lift south, to Lunga.

Reg sat in the front passenger seat of the little car, quizzing the balding Englishman about his Kenyan Catholic ministry. Annie sat quietly in the back, gazing at the wide landscape and the towering baobab trees along the way. The car shook as the road became stony and pitted, and Annie wondered how the hell they were going to lay their hands on enough money to get them to Cape Town.

Chapter 37

The air was hot and moist as Reg and Annie trudged down a busy street in Dar es Salaam. The kindly priest had dropped them at Lunga, where Reg had almost drained his wallet to purchase their train tickets. Their finances had been reduced to a few coins, and now the light was fading and they desperately needed somewhere to spend the night. Reg remembered the priest telling him that Dar es Salaam meant the "abode of peace." That was what he wanted now, peace. He dearly wanted to rest and take stock of their situation. He couldn't make important decisions when he felt so worn out.

Little shops and stalls were sandwiched between modern office blocks and apartment complexes. Older buildings looked Indian or Arabic; the bleached hues of horseshoe arches and embossed columns were iridescent in the fading light. They passed counters of fruits, sweetmeats, and breads, and the sight and smell of them made Reg and Annie even hungrier.

The locals beckoned them to see their wares, woodcarvings, beaded jewelry, and handicrafts. It was unusual for Annie not to want to explore, but her body ached so much that all she wanted to do was lie down. Reg was tempted to check into a hotel, but they looked more like hippies than wealthy tourists.

"Look Reggie!" Annie pointed.

"That's it!" Reg exclaimed. "That'll do nicely. Whenever you're in trouble look for God."

He grabbed her hand and pulled her along the street with renewed energy.

Annie adjusted her backpack. "Hang on, this is heavy!"

He pulled it off her back and lifted it onto his right shoulder, striding ahead until they arrived at the ornate entrance of a Hindu temple. They caught their breath at the doorway of a courtyard, and then filtered into the straggle of early evening devotees.

"They don't kick you out of these," whispered Reg. "Kurt told me about one in India where he slept for two nights."

They removed their shoes at the doorway of the main hall and walked gratefully into the tranquillity of the sweet-smelling interior. The floor was sparsely lined with Indian worshippers, the back wall flanked by statues of Indian deities. The only one they recognized was the god Shiva. Reg soon spotted what he was looking for, a small anteroom to the side with a disparate group of misfits lounging on mats.

A dark-haired young American with John Lennon glasses looked up from his book. "Hey guys," he smiled. "Welcome to the Hindu Hotel, food isn't included but it's mighty comfortable."

"Brilliant, mate," said Reg as he offloaded his bags. "Hope you don't mind two more."

They squeezed in between the hippie and an old woman in raggedy clothes who reminded Annie of Bethra. They were more tired than hungry. It was getting late, and it wasn't worth losing their position on the mat to do anything else that day.

✈ ✈ ✈

Reg found the chanting soothing, but when he woke the next morning the temple seemed empty and austere. He panicked when he saw the hippie had gone. He sat bolt upright, then sighed with relief when he saw their backpacks. If they lost their passports now they were well and truly stuffed.

"Annie," he whispered and gently shook her shoulder.

"Just a few minutes more," she murmured.

"I'm gonna try to find us something to eat. Watch the bags. Won't be long."

He stepped into the early morning streets and turned left. Desperate for a pee, he created a commotion when he relieved himself behind a disused hut and a barking dog tried to hurry him along. A door flew open and a big dark woman with a coiled headscarf threw a bucket of water across the road. Reg sidestepped the flow and detoured down a narrow lane toward the sound of voices. The shabby tenements opened onto a square crammed with merchants setting up their stalls.

Reg ambled down the aisles, surveying colorful displays of fruit, vegetables, dried beans, and breads. He tried to focus on what he wanted and plan how was he was going to steal it. Excited children called him to their tables, pricking his conscience—he was uncomfortable nicking stuff from people so poor. He would do it only this one time.

He had to take something back for Annie, but how the hell was he going to get it? It occurred to him that although he was a criminal, he'd never actually stolen anything—except fruit off neighboring trees when he was a kid, but he didn't think that should count. If he grabbed what he wanted and made a dash for it, he could probably outrun every male around, but he might run straight into the arms of the law. Annie would be at the temple for days. He would never return . . .

The market busied as Reg weaved through the crowd. He slunk to the corner of a table, grateful for the large pockets on the legs of his khaki trousers. He'd have to make his move soon. Annie would be worrying, but he didn't want to return empty-handed. He glanced along a row of chattering stallholders before gliding his hand over the produce and touching a small piece of fruit. The merchant glanced his way before counting coins into the palm of a young woman. Reg's pulse quickened as he pretended to test the ripeness of the fruit.

"It's a marula, man."

Reg froze. His mind spun possibilities, from the Australian feds to the Bombay police. Then he recognized the distinctive voice and turned slowly. He met Paddy's laughing brown eyes and the familiar bushy, gray mustache.

"It's a kind of melon, they're bloody good," enthused the Irishman.

Reg almost lost his balance with surprise. "What the fuck are you doing here?" he asked, so loudly that nearby morning shoppers stopped to stare at the two excited foreigners.

Paddy chuckled and shook his head in disbelief. "Hey, is that any way to greet your old trainer?" he asked a dumbfounded Reg.

"C'mon buddy, let me get that for you." He leaned and whispered in Reg's ear. "You weren't looking like you were too keen on paying for it anyway."

"That obvious?"

"Enjoy prison life, do ya?" quipped Paddy.

He groped in his trouser pocket for some loose change and handed it to the stallholder, who hadn't taken his eyes off the fruit since the Irishman had arrived.

"So how'd you get out?" Reg asked him when they were sitting on a nearby wall.

"Let's just say I used my last wish with the leprechaun," beamed Paddy. "Case finally got heard and all their witnesses had flown. It was fucking beautiful."

"Great stuff. Anyone else out?"

"They were all still there, but it just wasn't the same after you left. Jan went back to his old quiet self like before you arrived. Still training?" Paddy grinned.

"Can't say it's been a priority," said Reg, trying not to picture Jan.

"Slacker. Be honest, you tracked me down to train you for a comeback. My rates don't come cheap, I can tell ya."

"Rules me out then," Reg smiled. "I'm skint."

"Where you headin'?"

"Kimberley, then the Blue Train to Cape Town if I can make enough for the bloody fare."

"With your missus, she still with you?" asked Paddy.

"Sure is. Christ! I've gotta get going, she'll be wondering where the hell I am." Reg jumped up. "Thanks for the . . . whatever-it's-called. It's bloody welcome."

Paddy stood beside him, flipped open his denim jacket and retrieved a wad of banknotes from the inside pocket. He skimmed a few off the top and handed them to Reg. Reg tried to refuse the money, but Paddy insisted.

"No arguments, old friend," he said. "I'm okay at the moment."

"Thanks, mate," said Reg. "Great to find a pal when you need one."

Paddy lowered his voice. "Before you go," he whispered. "Last week I met a bloke, he'd just come from Cape Town. Done a lot of business in your industry."

He checked that nobody was in earshot.

"Apparently Sri Lanka's the go-to place right now. Plenty of people looking for a safe pair of hands, if you know what I mean."

Reg knew exactly what Paddy meant. He thought of nothing else as he hurried back to Annie with a new spring in his step, money in his pocket, and a most unusual breakfast.

CHAPTER 38

The ticket bays bustled with travelers. A young woman in a sari behind Reg and Annie rocked her crying baby. Annie clutched the carrier bag of goods they'd just bought at the Dar es Salaam market: cakes of Lux soap, pens, and coffee, things they'd been told were useful for getting seats on trains. When it was his turn, Reg stepped up to the counter and asked for two tickets for Kabwe.

"Kapiri Mposhi, then bus to Kabwe, come back tomorrow," said the pockmarked clerk.

Reg lifted his backpack off his shoulders.

"Tomorrow's too late."

"How much d'you have?"

"What's that got to do with no seats?" Reg was indignant.

Then he remembered their bartering items and took the plastic bag from Annie.

"Not all of them!" she blurted, retrieving a bottle of shampoo and a tin of coffee.

Reg put the bag with the remainder of the items on the counter. The clerk examined the contents.

"Money?" he asked.

Reg placed some of the notes Paddy had given him on the counter. The clerk stared at him blankly. Reg offered him another one, and the man disappeared with the money and the bag, reappearing moments later with two tickets.

Reg and Annie hurried off to find their platform, and waited on a bench until they were allowed to board the train.

"Even though we've got money," Reg was thinking aloud, "we

should spend wisely. It's going to be a long journey."

"It really pisses me off," said Annie. "The way you give something extra, and they suddenly magic you up a ticket." She shook her head. "It's just not fair."

"Forget fair," said Reg. "Fair just doesn't come into it. We left fair behind a long time ago."

First-class passengers had little rooms with beds, but Reg and Annie were seated with the locals. They bought drinks and sandwiches from the dining carriage and bags of delicious, hot sweet potatoes from villagers who boarded the train along the way.

The locomotive purred through long, dark tunnels, chugging into the light atop mighty bridges as it ate up the miles. They spotted elephants and giraffes meandering across the Selous Game Reserve. Annie longed for a pair of binoculars to view the wild, mysterious landscape as it rolled past their window beneath a big Tanzanian sky.

The journey took the best part of three days. Their juddering carriage melted into long, dream-filled sleeps and black starry nights, during which they talked until glorious sunrises, swapping theories about what might have become of Niko and their perfect life if they ever got back to Australia. They woke to a wide brown landscape, patched with undulations of lush bushland, and huge birds perched on graveyards of broken tracks and rusty old railway wagons. They joked with a big uniformed official who stamped their passports for Zambia long after they'd crossed the border, and finally arrived at the station of Kapiri Mposhi late in the afternoon.

Tired from sitting so long, they dawdled in the station toilets, and by the time they reached the car park a small bus with a Kabwe sign was just pulling away. They couldn't be bothered to go back and ask when the next one was due, so they decided to thumb a lift. Reg was hoping some friendly motorist might offer them a bed for the night. The day faded with a trickle of cars and trucks. He tried standing in the road with his friendly hitchhiker smile, but nobody offered a ride.

"These bloody mosquitos are driving me nuts," Annie complained. She'd spent the last hour swatting her bare legs.

Dusk was thick with insects and the code of crickets. Stones crunched underfoot as they lugged their heavy backpacks. Reg grew uneasy. "I don't like this, Annie," he said. Then the headlights of an approaching vehicle lit the road. "Get down," he shouted as he yanked her into the bushes. They crouched low, peering as a truckload of yelling men sped by.

Reg said, "I've got a bad feeling about this."

He threw the bag off his shoulders and rummaged through it in the darkness.

"Got it," he said. He retrieved a small torch. The beam flickered as they pushed through the waist-high scrubland. They came to a clearing. A distant owl hooted and the undergrowth seethed with wildlife.

"We're okay here," Reg whispered.

He was just about to look for something to sit on when their lair lit up with screeching wild men.

"Down, down," one ordered Reg and Annie at gunpoint.

They dropped to the ground. Annie gave a frightened whimper as her body hit the earth.

"Over and arms up," someone shouted.

Annie watched in wide-eyed terror as a man pressed the butt of his rifle into the side of Reg's shaking head.

"Do what they say," Reg said under his breath before they rolled over and had their faces shoved in the dirt.

They stared at the ground for a long time while the men argued in a language Reg didn't understand. One kneeled beside him and yanked his arms behind his back. He used a thin bandage to tie them together. It cut into his wrists.

"Up!" the man yelled. Reg rolled onto his side and drew his knees up to stand.

He staggered to get his balance before facing the barrels of four guns. Annie's hands weren't tied, but she was so scared she stumbled, and their captors yelled and waved their weapons again.

"Oh my God, they're going to kill us!" she cried.

"They're not," Reg muttered, though he wasn't sure.

"Shut up," yelled the leader.

The men took Reg's and Annie's backpacks and forced them to walk in the middle, single file, as they snaked their way through the dark scrubland. Reg tried to work out who these men were as he sidestepped tall grass and bushes with his hands behind his back. He was sure they were the same group that had passed them earlier in the truck, but what the hell did they want?

The vegetation thinned and the stony ground undulated as they traversed a narrow ledge, illuminated by the flashlights of the men at the back. Reg walked behind Annie, concentrating on keeping his balance as she groped the rocks and roots protruding from the steep bank. After a while, the drop to the right of the ledge deepened, and the man in front vaulted off down a rough embankment, beckoning them to follow. Reg had trouble getting down, so the man behind him untied his wrists and prodded him in the back with his gun.

They assembled at the bottom, fifty feet from the remnants of an abandoned building, a gray, crumbling shell daubed with mud and graffiti. It looked damaged rather than decayed, not particularly old. Reg was sure these men had been here before as they trailed their torch over weed-infested concrete foundations strewn with broken bottles and rusty cans.

Reg and Annie were ushered into the burnt-out remains of a room. They were pushed onto one of the soiled mattresses that lined the battered walls. One man held a flame to a rusty gas lamp in the middle of the floor, lighting up the interior. It was a large bleak space, squalid and dank. Something bad had happened here, something really bad. Blankets, old pots and pans, and faded cigarette packets proved that others had passed this way. Annie hoped they'd been homeless locals; Reg knew the pockmarked walls indicated something more sinister.

He felt Annie shaking beside him and grasped her hand, stroking the palm with his thumb as he studied the guards. Two of the four spoke in English. The leader appeared to be called Zuma. His men had darker skin; their colored shirts and droopy shorts made them look even darker. Two looked much younger than Zuma and the other man. They were boys, really, thought Reg, and likely to be more unpredictable than the other two.

They were strutting around the room brandishing guns like kids with toys. Reg thought the guns looked like the Kalashnikov AK-47s he'd seen in movies about Vietnam.

Zuma tipped the contents of Reg's and Annie's backpacks into the middle of the floor. Clothes, shoes, and toothpaste toppled out, followed by the koala. Reg thought how incongruous Oscar looked in this godforsaken place. One of the boy soldiers grabbed the koala, held it close to his face, and babbled gibberish to it. Reg felt trapped in some bizarre cabaret, until the ventriloquist grew bored with his dummy and hurled it across the room.

Zuma was thrilled to find the tin of coffee. Reg prayed the men didn't search him because the remainder of the money that Paddy had given him was in the pocket of his trousers. Zuma's accomplice took the passports from the front compartment of Reg's bag. One boy kept his gun pointed at Reg while Zuma and the others sat on the floor and pored over the documents. They squabbled as they tried to make sense of them.

"So what you doin' in Zambia if you're French?" Zuma asked Reg.

"Having a holiday, just having a holiday."

"So 'ow come you don't speak French, then?"

"Because I live in New Zealand. My dad speaks French, but I was born in New Zealand."

Zuma shrugged. He'd not found anything to contradict Reg's story.

"What were you doin' in the bush?" the other man asked.

"Couldn't get a lift to Kabwe, so we were gonna sleep there," said Reg.

"Where's the rest of your money?" asked Zuma.

"Gone, all gone."

Zuma looked at Reg for a few seconds, saying nothing, trying to weigh him up. Then Zuma yelled at the boy who was still goading Reg and Annie with his gun. The boy gave a disappointed sigh and chucked the weapon onto his mattress. The youngsters were ordered out, and Reg and Annie heard them clanging metal objects in another part of the building. Reg had grave fears about what might happen next. If this gang just wanted to rob them, why bring them here? He imagined Annie's bullet-ridden body slumped against his own. What a sad ending after all they'd gone through—blown away in some hovel in Zambia. He had to pull himself together.

He squeezed Annie's hand as Zuma and the other man had an intense exchange. Reg knew that he and Annie were being discussed when the two men kept nodding in their direction.

"What do you think they are saying?" Annie whispered.

"Don't know," said Reg, "but I think the other guy is called Tasiki."

"D'you think they're in the army?"

"Some kind of militia group, I reckon. Don't think they see us as any threat. Look, they don't even mind us talking. Just play it cool and we'll be okay."

"We eatin' yet?" Tasiki called down the passageway when the smell of cooking drifted through the dimly lit ruins.

Reg was feeling a little easier; their captors seemed calmer now. Tasiki smiled when a boy brought a pot of something hot and placed it on the floor next to the lamp. The other boy kneeled to pour steaming brown liquid into dented tin bowls.

"Come," Tasiki called to Reg and Annie.

"Thanks, fellows," Reg said, uncurling his stiff limbs. "Starving."

Zuma translated "starving," and the boy soldiers laughed.

Annie was still scared. She couldn't forget that Tasiki had held a gun to Reg's head a few hours earlier. The two captives sat crossed-legged on the floor and waited to see how to eat without cutlery. A boy opened a crumpled paper bag and took out a burnt loaf of bread. He handed it to Tasiki, who broke it into hunks and passed them around.

The room fell silent, save for the hissing lamp and the slurping of the men as they ate. The liquid had a strange salty taste, but Reg and Annie were glad to fill their stomachs. After the boys took the bowls away, Zuma pulled grubby packets from the pocket of his khaki trousers and rolled a big joint. He lit it and sucked the pungent smoke into his lungs.

"Dagga?" Zuma passed the smoke to Reg and chuckled as he watched Reg inhale.

Reg relaxed. These blokes weren't going to harm them—you don't share a smoke with someone and then blow their brains out. It was all a mix-up; they'd probably let them go in the morning.

When it was Annie's turn to smoke the joint she declined; she was feeling a bit queasy after eating the strange liquid and was now wondering what was in it. Nobody was pointing guns anymore, and their captors were scattered on the mattresses. The two boys were asleep before Zuma turned off the gas lamp. Annie was exhausted. She discreetly collected her koala from the corner of the room and curled up beside Reg, her head on Oscar.

"We can give you a ride tomorrow," Tasiki's deep voice called across the gloom.

"Thanks," Reg replied, hoping to God that the guy didn't change his mind by the morning.

"How far you going?"

"Want to get to Cape Town, then on to Sri Lanka."

"We're headin' to Livingstone in a couple of days," said Tasiki. "We can take you as far as there."

"Brilliant," said Reg. He was starting to warm to Tasiki.

"Who are you guys running from?" Reg asked Tasiki.

"The most dangerous enemies of all, those from within. And you, who are you running from?"

Reg was taken aback. "What makes you think I'm running?"

"A man gets a look," said Tasiki. He lowered his voice. "Like a hunted animal."

Reg lay in the darkness and considered his situation, Tasiki's words playing on his mind. They'd come a hell of a long way, he and Annie, but they couldn't keep running forever. They had to get to Cape Town and look for an opportunity to make some decent money in Sri Lanka, as Paddy had suggested. Two or three days hitching rides from Livingstone should get them through Botswana into South Africa. He was sure they'd have enough money for the Blue Train from Kimberley to Cape Town. That was where he planned to set up a new deal. But it had to be something mega-lucrative this time, enough for them to start a new life back in Australia.

Everything would fall into place when they got to Sri Lanka. As Paddy had said, Sri Lanka was where the action was.

CHAPTER 39

COLOMBO, SRI LANKA, DECEMBER 1, 1984

Reg finished shaving at the bathroom mirror of his penthouse suite at the Meridien Hotel.

Annie's head emerged from their king-size bed. "What time's your flight?"

"Around nine," Reg called back.

He whistled as he entered the gushing shower and lifted his head to take the full force of the flow. He could get used to this, he thought, as he lathered his hair. Life was definitely looking up. Everything had gone according to plan since he'd started his latest enterprise, conducting business between Colombo, Trivandrum in India, and Amsterdam.

Now he had to convince Annie that he should continue until they'd made enough money to get out. They wouldn't get this kind of reward for anything else, but last night she'd made it clear that she wasn't happy about his new operation. Truth was, she'd had enough of their insecure, nomadic existence and wanted to get back to Australia. He wanted that too, to see his mum and dad again, Adelaide, and all his old mates.

They'd been everywhere, lived the life of kings and vagabonds on four continents. If they could just get back to good old Oz, he wouldn't need to get on another plane for a very long time. The important thing now was to stop Annie from worrying and convince her that the kind of money they were making here was their only ticket home.

Annie propped herself on two pillows when Reg appeared from the bathroom. She watched him pull the black T-shirt over his muscled torso; he still had the build of a javelin thrower. Perhaps he would start training and competing again when they got home.

"How many more times, Reggie?" she asked.

"A couple."

"Including this one?"

"Whatever it takes. You've got to stop fretting, Annie; you're making me nervous. I can't afford to be nervous. Nervous looks guilty."

"Sorry, but how do you think I feel?" Annie became impatient. "You think I'm not nervous every time you go? Sitting here in this damn room wondering if I'll ever see you again. We never planned it this way."

"I never planned it any damn way. I'm trying to get us out of this, okay? If you've got a better idea, feel free to let me know."

"You always promised it would only be hash," Annie wailed. "Not the hard stuff that fucks up kids' lives. You want to be a part of that? Just stop and look at yourself for a second. Look what we've become."

"We've been through all this," sighed Reg. "The reality is that if we don't do it, someone else will. You really think Reg's and Annie's moral principles are going to make a shit of difference? They've got fucking *thousands* of guys lining up to take our place. Look—I'm not particularly thrilled about this either, but what do you want me to do? Say I'd rather run something else: gold, cash, stolen stuff? Maybe next time I'll ask if anyone's got a menu," Reg snorted. "We're trapped. We're victims here as well."

"That's bloody pathetic! No way are we victims." Annie's face flushed with anger. "Nobody put us in this position. We did it all by ourselves!" She burst into tears.

"Annie, Annie." Reg stopped dressing and threw himself on the bed.

"I'm so sorry, darling. Sorry about this whole bloody mess." He pulled her head onto his chest and stroked her hair. "Sorry I started it, but I'm going to get us out, back to Adelaide, with Niko and the others. You don't think I haven't wished I could turn the clock back?" Reg's voice cracked. "I didn't think about much else in jail. Except you." He lifted her face and looked tenderly into her eyes. "Only two more, I promise, baby. We'll have enough for tickets and getting settled. Two more, then we're heading home."

Annie sniffed and reached for a tissue from the bedside table. "Two including today?" She wiped her eyes and blew her nose.

"Including today," Reg reassured her. "Oh Christ, look at the time!" He jumped off the bed.

He quickly combed his hair and squeezed the bulky boom-box into his shoulder bag.

"Gotta go, darling," He went to the bed and kissed her. "See you in a couple of days, green-eyed girl. We'll do dinner at that Sawsal restaurant place, you can have that chicken dish you like . . . Don't forget to keep the door locked." He hurried out.

Annie sat in silence. She wished they hadn't argued. Why had she hit him with everything just before he had to go? Why not last night, when they would have had time to make up?

She sighed as she slipped on a silk kaftan, enjoying the luxurious feel of it against her skin. She padded barefoot across the tiles to make coffee. Reggie was right. Everything would work out. There was nothing to worry about.

She turned on the radio and hummed to a local folk song as she looked in the closet for something to wear. Their old clothing and backpacks were long gone, replaced with new clothes and expensive luggage. She glanced at the safe where Reg stored one of their latest methods of saving—gold Krugerrands. The kettle switched off. Strands of sandy red hair fell in front of her eyes as she poured it. She tucked them behind her ear and watched the patterns of steaming water melt the little brown granules in the cup. Calm again.

✈ ✈ ✈

Reg tipped the taxi driver, and then straightened his leather shoulder bag and picked up his overnight case. He strode confidently into the departures terminal of Colombo International Airport and joined the throng of travelers swarming around the check-in counters.

"Ledoux." Reg slid his passport and ticket across the counter to an exotic brunette.

"Thank you, Mr. Ledoux. Just hand luggage today?" she beamed.

"Yep, traveling light," he smiled.

"Your boarding pass, sir. Gate thirteen."

The Amsterdam flight always left from gate thirteen, a five-minute walk from the check-in counter. Reg cruised it with a confident stroll. It didn't matter that Annie questioned everything. He liked having a woman with opinions. Of course she was right, and he'd meant what he said, just a couple more.

Just a couple more, he thought again as he stood behind an Arab in a headdress at the passport control desk.

The official returned the man's documents and stretched out his hand to hurry Reg along. He cocked his head as he studied the picture of Patrick Ledoux. Then he stamped the passport and waved Reg through. Easy, thought Reg. God, he was looking forward to a beer and sandwich on the plane . . .

The next line at security control was different. Reg stood behind a tall German man in a tartan cap, complaining loudly about the delay. The line of passengers shuffled toward the barrier. Reg got a better view of the proceedings. Five more people to be processed, and then it would be his turn. He watched. Then he leaned to observe more carefully as the cause of the delay became apparent. One, then two, then three people were ordered to unpack their hand luggage onto the counter.

"Bomb scare," the man in the cap told him.

"Right," Reg muttered.

His mind spun. The blood drained from his face, and he felt queasy. He took several deep breaths and tried to compose himself. The man in the cap stepped up to the counter. Reg's turn next. Was every piece of luggage being scrutinized or was it random? The echoey woman's voice on the loudspeaker was drowned by a new static that invaded his head.

The man in the cap in front of Reg was told to unpack his hand luggage. Oh God, there was definitely nothing random about it. They were searching everyone! Reg watched the official flip the pages of a book, and he was swamped with panic. The leather bag felt like a dead weight on his shoulder. If only he could change his mind about Amsterdam and walk casually out of the airport. Get back to Annie. He swallowed and turned to look at the line behind. Two uniformed guards hovered along the line. They had guns in their holsters; one glanced in his direction.

He felt his heart thumping. "Steady, calm," he breathed.

Then he was at the counter. The thin bald customs official gestured to Reg to open his bag.

"You pack this yourself?" the official asked as his female colleague finished inspecting her nails and moved closer.

"Sure did." Reg tried to sound casual. Then he had to cough before he could speak again. "Yes, I did."

He ignored the bag on his shoulder and cooperatively unpacked the underclothes and toiletries in his small overnight case. The official unzipped the toilet bag and turned the twist of the stick deodorant. Reg stood motionless, thinking that all nightmares eventually end. He noticed a mole on the man's shiny skull as he fiddled with the tube, and heard his amused snigger as he tried to rewind it.

"That's okay," said Reg. "I can do that."

He fumbled with the deodorant and quickly replaced the toothpaste and razor. It felt like a reprieve when the woman behind him dumped her bag beside his. Surely they'd tell him to get going now. He piled his belongings haphazardly back into his case. The zip made an urgent squeak. That's it now. Free to go. Walk away. *Slowly.*

"Just a minute," the official called after him. He pointed. "That one."

It was a shock. Reg turned in slow motion. Everything slowed. He gave a little laugh; of course, silly me, I've forgotten about the shoulder bag . . . He shakily lifted the strap over his head and placed the bag on the counter. His heart clicked into a faster gear. The official seemed agitated now, impatient. His female colleague signaled to the rotund woman next to Reg that she would have to wait. Heat radiated up Reg's body and became trapped at the back of his neck. The female officer whispered something in Sinhalese in the bald official's ear as he undid the buckle of Reg's bag.

"Everything out," he snapped.

Reg glanced at his watch as if he was worried about missing his plane, and then wished he hadn't done so. He removed the boombox as if it was his least concern. It didn't leave much else; only a plastic file of notes and receipts, a pair of running shoes, and his wallet. The rotund woman gave a sigh of impatience. Why the hell couldn't she do something dramatic like faint and take the heat off him? The officer unzipped the plastic folder, ran his hand inside. Reg tried to steady his breathing. He followed the man's methodical eyes as they darted from one item to another. Then they pounced on the boombox.

The official pushed and prodded the sealed panels at the back of the machine. Reg's heart thumped as he realized the man wasn't going to give up. The female officer looked intrigued, moving closer and running her manicured fingers across the veneer. She whispered again, studying Reg's face. Whatever she said prompted the official to action, and he lifted the boombox into the air and shook it violently.

Then he raised his arm and called to the guards.

This is it—I'm done for.

Within seconds a guard had the boombox in his possession. He ordered Reg to repack his luggage and accompany him to a room for questioning. Reg fumbled as he put the shoes and plastic file back into his bag. The impatient woman behind him wasn't in a hurry now. She stared, along with a dozen other passengers equally captivated by the spectacle. Reg was cold. He smoothed the hair across his damp forehead. His hands felt clammy. It was the first time he had ever experienced a cold sweat.

The guard escorted him down a long corridor to an interview room. It was sparsely furnished with a table, two chairs, and a row of cupboards. A large clock dominated the wall. He sat alone, staring at it for what seemed like ages, wishing he could wind the hands back. A couple of hours would do it, take him back to Annie. What would happen to her now? His senses were overpowered by erratic, jumbled thoughts. Should he pretend to be someone else? No point in that—he already was someone else. Raising identity issues wasn't such a bad idea, might divert their attention from the boombox. Should he pretend it was somebody else's boombox? What was the point? They were probably already pulling it apart next door.

The guard returned, businesslike as he placed a mug of coffee and a file of papers on the table and sat opposite Reg. A younger officer wheeled a trolley into the room. It contained Reg's shoulder bag, overnight bag, and the dreaded boombox.

"My name's Officer De Silva," announced the seated guard. "Did you know a bomb was found in one of these not long ago?" He sounded quite reasonable as he lifted the boombox from the trolley.

"I didn't," Reg replied. He wished he did.

De Silva beckoned to the younger officer. The man took a screwdriver from a container on the trolley and gauged the radio's outer casing. De Silva searched Reg's face for telltale signs while his colleague worked. Reg felt sick as the machine squeaked across the hard melamine surface. Soon the young officer had located the screws, unwound them, and disengaged the back panel of the machine. He glanced at his boss, and De Silva nodded, indicating he was ready to take over the proceedings. After the young man left the room, Reg heard every one of his own breaths, slow and quivering, as De Silva retrieved a large plastic packet from the interior of the boombox and placed it on the table.

De Silva removed his hat and smoothed his straight black hair over his big forehead. Reg stared at him, desperately worried about what was going to happen to Annie. Should he insist on having a solicitor present or would that just get this bloke's back up? The only sounds were the ticking clock and the clinking of De Silva's teeth against his pen as he tapped the end. Reg wished he would hurry up and ask him some questions. He didn't know what he was going to say, but it would help if De Silva got the ball rolling. At least Annie wasn't expecting him back until tomorrow—she'd have one more night thinking nothing was wrong.

De Silva looked over his shoulder and checked the time against his wristwatch. He scribbled the details from Reg's passport onto a form. The other guard came back with a set of scales. De Silva placed the packet from the boombox into one pan of the scales, and then selected a number of weights from a box.

He placed them in the corresponding pan, and it sunk to the tabletop with a bang. He replaced some weights with lighter ones until the pans teetered in balance. The two men conferred and fussed over the reading.

"One thousand one hundred and forty-nine grams," De Silva said loudly. "Mr. Ledoux, please come and confirm the weight."

Reg jumped up and peered at the numbers. "Yeah, sort of," he said. "But you blokes need to agree."

"Do you agree that you have one thousand, one hundred and forty-nine grams of heroin?" asked De Silva.

Reg made a mental note of the weight. How the hell were they so sure it was heroin?

"I don't agree with anything. I want a lawyer."

The two guards smirked at each other, and the young one mumbled in Sinhalese.

"You don't get a lawyer yet," De Silva snapped. "You cooperate and you get a lawyer at the detention center. Now stand up!"

The other guard ordered him into the center of the room, made him remove his jacket and shoes, and then frisked him. When Reg returned to his seat, De Silva was rifling through Reg's bags; he soon placed the plastic folder on the table. He pored over the receipts and scribbled on his form as he slurped his cold coffee.

"So you're staying at the Meridien?" he asked, waving the receipt for the bill Reg had just paid.

Why the hell did he have that on him? Now they had a clear path that could lead back to Annie.

"Mr. Ledoux," De Silva rasped. "This can take as long as you want. We're going to be taking you back to room fifty-one at the hotel and searching it, so you might as well start talking."

The younger guard had left the room. Reg leaned forward, rested his forearms on his knees, and stared at the pattern in the tiled floor. He'd lost everything now, even Annie. Everything was gone, all their plans. He had to get Annie off the hook. She couldn't face another prison stint—this one would probably be a lot longer. De Silva would have seen her name on the receipt.

Reg said, "I'm willing to cooperate, Mr. De Silva, but I find it difficult to talk when I'm worried about my girlfriend."

De Silva gave a little hunch of his shoulders and stroked his chin. "The one at the hotel?" He looked at the details on the receipt. "Miss Annette Chamberlain?"

"That's her," said Reg. "I'd like her left out of this if possible." He stared at the guard's big, square face. "Could you make sure she's okay for me?" He looked him in the eye.

De Silva glanced at the door and shifted on his seat.

"That depends." He leaned over the table and lowered his voice. "If there's anything else I can take care of."

"Gold Krugerrand," said Reg, "about eight, in the safe . . . But she knows nothing, she walks away."

"She walks away," whispered De Silva, "and never comes back."

Chapter 40

Two Months Later

Reg sat at an interview table in the Negombo Detention Centre on the outskirts of Colombo. An older table; the rough timber scrawled with messages. He looked at the names: Sinhalese, Chinese, Indian. Several English. All the other risk-takers who'd paid the price. "Davy Dunston Rocks, 1962," was decipherable in the right-hand corner. What was he doing when poor old Davy was banged up in Sri Lanka? Commonwealth Games in Perth, that's what. He was young and hopeful, and all he wanted to do was hurl that javelin into oblivion.

He thought he'd join Davy and his friends on the roll of honor, and found a patch of bare wood for his calling card. He inscribed a tiny stick figure in black pen of a man standing on a box. He drew the arm holding a spear in the throwing position and printed "Boxed again, 1984," along the top.

When he'd finished his inscription, Reg gave a long sigh, full of despair over how much the last three years had cost him. He'd lost everything, including his family and friends, and perhaps now, even Annie. Losing Annie would be worse than any prison sentence they could chuck at him. They'd had a good life with Niko and Ted and the others, and he'd do anything to have it back. Anything.

It had been that karma thing again. Annie could see it coming, she'd even warned him on the morning of the bust. He'd warned himself, but they needed the money to get them home. It had been the wrong time, wrong place, total bloody disaster, and the court of public opinion wouldn't disagree that he'd made some pretty bad calls. But then again, he reminded himself, other people didn't walk in his shoes. If he'd served his time in Oz he would have missed everything he'd shared with Annie: the crazy journeys, their magical little house in Goa, bittersweet memories of the love and madness they'd shared along the way.

And he knew that even if they'd got back into Australia with enough money to set themselves up somewhere and find jobs, they might never have been able to resume a life in Adelaide as Reg and Annie. They'd be forced to hide, somewhere like the Northern Territory, and sneak about under assumed names. Who wanted to pretend to be someone bloody else all his life?

Now he had to work the system, easier said than done when the system lacked any discernible rules. His immediate task was to find a lawyer to replace the con man Annie had apparently entrusted with twelve thousand rupees of their seriously depleted funds. Reg had received his first letter from her only a few days ago. Apart from relaying the ill-fated saga with the lawyer, it was an ambiguous, un-Annie type of communication, and he knew exactly why: she was shit-scared of telling him anything, anything at all that the cops could use against either of them. Especially her. De Silva could still go back on his word and spill the beans, have her arrested for conspiracy or any other damn offense he cared to concoct.

In addition to paying the lawyer a large deposit up front for his services, Annie had given him a letter and several items she thought Reg would need in prison. The letter and belongings were never delivered, and the bloody lawyer had disappeared. There was no point in dwelling on it because it only made him angry. Anger could paralyze the mind, stop him from seeing straight, and stunt his imagination. Imagination was creativity. A creative mind could generate good ideas, just what he needed to get himself out of there.

Besides, it was the wrong day to be angry. Annie was visiting him that very afternoon, and he'd thought of nothing else since the superintendent had informed him a few days ago. It would be the first time he'd seen her since the big bust. De Silva had said she had to disappear and that's exactly what she'd done, as soon as she'd instructed the lawyer. God knows where she went, and it was going to be nigh on impossible for them to talk with the bloody guards hanging around. That was why he would write her a letter, but he needed to take his time and compose it carefully.

He stared at the sheets of old-fashioned paper; thick as a blotting pad with faint gray lines. Then he thought about what he wanted to say. All the things he shouldn't say in case they upset her, and all the things he shouldn't say because he knew his letter would be vetted.

Dear Annette, he started. Too risky to call her Annie, even though the names were similar.

What can I tell you? There's no point in giving you all the details about what happened. Let's just say it wasn't good. Now I'm here and you're there and there's nothing we can do about it. I'm so sorry you've had to go through all this because of me. Believe me when I say it's not what I had in mind when we met. Be careful, I'm worried about your safety. I'd love to be telling you that I'll be out soon and we can continue with our plans. Truth is, I've no idea when I'll be out, maybe not for a long time.

Reg's eyes floated around the dingy walls. God, this was hard. He wanted to be truthful but still give her hope. What was the point? He was out of hope. He didn't like the truth, but one thing was inescapable: he wasn't going to be back in the real world any time soon. Worst-case scenario—ever! His future was one big, black mess, but he couldn't let Annie know that.

You must carry on with your life and know I'll be thinking about you every day. The time will pass, that's about the only thing we can be sure of in this crazy world. Then, if you'll still have me, we can do all the things we talked about. I've been trying to find out how I can get a lawyer who won't rip us off. If I could just talk to a legal expert who knows what he's talking about, I should have a better idea about how long I'm going to be here.

What if it was years, what was she supposed to do in the meantime? Was he expecting her to wait for him? How would she live, survive?

Use whatever money you need, I know there's not much left. So sorry it's come to this, but I'm sure it will get better.

We will always have Goa, and I'll always love you.

Patrick x

Reg didn't have an envelope, so he folded the page into four, tucked it under unused sheets, and waited patiently to be collected. It seemed like an eternity before the tall, angular superintendent poked his head into the room.

"Your lady friend is in my office," he said with a knowing look. "Is your writing finished?"

Reg handed him the letter and followed him down the corridor, hoping to God the superintendent hadn't been interrogating Annie with dangerous questions.

They reached the square hallway adjoining the superintendent's command room. "You can entertain your visitor here." He indicated a bench facing the door of his office.

Reg didn't hear him because his eyes were focused on Annie. She looked pale, standing in the doorway in bell-bottom jeans and an oversized sweatshirt, clasping the strap of a big embroidered shoulder bag he'd never seen before. Her beautiful hair was hidden, tucked up inside a peaked cap. She thanked the superintendent, and then gave Reg her bravest smile and hurried to embrace him.

"You got my letter?" she asked, her green eyes pensive as they huddled on the bench. "About the lawyer and everything?"

"God, Annie," Reg sighed, leaned forward and rubbed his temples with his fingers.

"Can't get much worse, can it? Where did you go, after the lawyer business?"

"Keep your voice down." Annie's voice was tinged with desperation. "People are helping me but it's bad out there—I feel like I'm being followed all the time." She tightened her grip on his hand and implored him with her eyes. "I miss you, so much, but if I'm grabbed we're done for."

"I know, I know. But I've gotta have a lawyer," Reg almost whispered.

"That's why I came back," said Annie, as Reg traced comforting little circles over the back of her hand.

He followed the direction of her nervous eyes into the chief guard's office.

The superintendent had purposely left his door open. He was making a show of reading Reg's letter, coughing periodically so his presence was felt. Then he stood and shuffled papers on his desk, humming with an irritating cheerfulness. He rarely permitted prisoner's meetings outside his office, and considering what Ledoux was in for, the fellow was lucky to be allowed a visitor at all.

Reg and Annie's twenty-minute guarded conversation dangled in hushed tones, punctuated with despairing moments of silence. They took turns focusing on various aspects of Reg's arrest that might point to his innocence, clutching at anything that might alleviate the hopelessness of their situation.

They were suddenly disturbed when a door to their right was thrown open and a khaki-clad officer strode to the superintendent's door and spoke to him in Sinhalese. The superintendent jumped up, informed Reg that he had been called away and that he would return shortly. His guard remained at the door, arms folded as his dark eyes followed the foreign prisoner's every move. Reg had just said, "I need a decent lawyer, Annie—one with teeth," when another guard, a big burly man, burst into the hallway. There quickly followed a bedraggled prisoner: a thin, pathetic fellow frog-marched from the rear by five more guards.

Now the hallway was full of angry shouting men. The prisoner cowered beneath their tirade, protesting and pleading, screaming and shielding his face as his accusers drew their batons and rained dreadful blows on his back and chest. The man's agony was sickening: the thud of the guards' bludgeoning weapons as they yelled and kicked his shins; the brutality of the pack.

"God, no!" Annie whimpered, her heart racing. She threw an arm around Reg and buried her face in his shoulder to make the ugliness disappear. He gently released himself and stood.

"You wanna kill the poor bugger?" he demanded loudly, just as the superintendent entered the fray.

The commotion ceased; in the silence, all they could hear

was a low moaning sound from the breathless prisoner who was doubled with pain, kneeling against a wall. The superintendent fired instructions in his native tongue, drawing his men's attention to Reg and Annie's presence. The guards stepped aside, rearranging their uniforms and glancing furtively at the two Westerners who had just witnessed their display of savagery.

The superintendent almost looked embarrassed. Ledoux was of no consequence, but he would have preferred that the woman had not observed his methods for controlling wayward prisoners. The guards dissipated. Two of them hooked their arms under those of the battered man and dragged him through the door. The superintendent marched into his office and collected Reg's letter from his desk.

"All in order," he handed it to Reg with a condescending smile. "Time's up now."

Annie was visibly shaken as she stood to say good-bye. Her face looked red and hot, and her eyes welled with tears. Reg wished he could land his best punch squarely under the superintendent's jaw. Then he would grab Annie's hand and race her out of the building, laying out every guard along the way until he was free.

"For you," he said instead, tucking his letter safely into her bag. "I hate you going like this," he told her softly, aware that the superintendent was watching them.

Annie retrieved her sunglasses from the bag and quickly put them on. Reg could detect the sadness in her eyes behind the tinted shades.

She clenched her teeth and struggled to keep her mouth from quivering. "I'll be in touch, when I've worked things out," she said awkwardly.

Reg squeezed Annie's hands. "Wait for me," he mouthed as he released them.

She turned and walked down the passageway, looking back with one last sorrowful wave of farewell before she disappeared around a corner.

✈ ✈ ✈

Annie was let through the second checkpoint and hurried out of the main gates onto the street. She turned left and strode a few blocks, her face expressionless beneath her big, dark glasses and beneath the round peak of her cap, her square shoulder bag bouncing on her hip. Then she couldn't resist it any longer.

She leaned against a wall and retrieved Reg's letter from her bag. Her head moved gently from side to side as she read, oblivious to the bustling pedestrians and streaming traffic. A fly settled on the top corner of the page. She swatted it away, then carefully she refolded the letter and slid it back into the bag. A tear trickled down her cheek, and she pulled her glasses forward, just enough to wipe her eyes.

She hailed a cab. Brakes screeched as the vehicle swerved curbside. Annie leaned in the window to talk to the driver, and a wispy strand of hair escaped from the back of her cap. It glistened, a beautiful sandy red, fluttering in the breeze across the back of her shirt. She climbed into the rear of the car and vanished behind the tinted glass as the cab whisked her away.

PART FOUR

LATE 1980S

CHAPTER 41

SRI LANKA, 1987

The superintendent of Mahara Prison had given up trying to hear what Ledoux and his visitor were talking about and had fallen asleep in a bad mood. He was woken later by one of his men bringing him a mug of tea. He glanced at his watch and slurped his drink impatiently. Then he rose, threw open the door behind him, and told Denton his time was up.

"Heard anything about my parents—are they still alive?" Reg asked the journalist as they walked back into the corridor.

"I'm sure they are, I think your dad was interviewed by my old paper, *Express,* a couple of weeks ago," Denton said. He noticed Reg smile fondly and wipe the corner of his eye.

"Better go, mate, 'else I won't get fed," said Reg. "Might see you tomorrow, then?"

"What are you expecting?" Denton's voice turned serious.

"Dunno, but whatever happens I'll sort it out. Always do," Reg sounded hopeful.

"Good luck, mate, and thanks for all this," Denton gestured toward his briefcase.

They shook hands, and Reg waited until the superintendent was out of earshot. "I knew someone would eventually catch up with me," he lowered his voice and leaned closer to Denton. "Glad it was you," he whispered.

The soles of his sandals slapped the floor as he sauntered off to join the guards.

"Forgot to ask," Denton called after him. "Whatever happened to Annie?"

If he got a reply, it was drowned by the shrill voice of the superintendent, waiting at the end of the passageway.

Denton was escorted back to the main gate and walked into the dark, wet night in a daze. He sat in the back of a taxi, his mind buzzing with everything Reg had told him. He was on a high because he'd got his story, and thrilled that his detective work had paid off. He was also confounded by Reg's optimism in the face of everything he'd been through. Denton thought anyone else would be worn down by the years in jail and nervous as hell about what would happen in court the next day.

He was too hyped up to wait until he got to the hotel to speak to his editor, so Denton told the driver to stop at a phone booth. He had to yell over the noise from the speeding traffic, and the rain pounding the glass.

"It's him!" he shouted when Davies picked up the phone.

"Christ, d'you know what the bloody time is? Great, but is he talking?"

"He's talking all right," Denton yelled. "He didn't stop, and you wouldn't believe the guards. They love him. I've got it all. Got the lot, and I'm telling you. It's one hell of a story!"

✈ ✈ ✈

Denton worked late into the night in his hotel room. He sprawled on his disheveled bed with his tape recorder, surrounded by notes, his mind full of everything he'd witnessed at the prison that day. The moment he'd set eyes on the tall blond man in the white kaftan he knew it was Reg Spiers, ex-athlete extraordinaire, fugitive. The infamous Adelaide man who'd slipped off the radar back in 1981.

It had taken Spiers over two years to get his case heard. Denton intended to watch the proceedings in the Negombo courthouse the next day, and then telephone his office to report the verdict. Then he'd hop on a plane, spend the flight writing a killer article on the scoop of his life, and make the front page of the Saturday edition of the *Adelaide Inquirer*.

His elation was tinged with guilt: here he was reveling in his good fortune. Not just reveling, enjoying the drama-laden adrenaline rush of it all, while Spiers faced the possibility of the ultimate punishment. He knew Reg was guilty; the man had admitted it when they were alone. But murderers back home didn't have to go through what he'd endured already, and there was probably worse to come.

"They can string you up for what I'm charged with," Reg had said, grimly.

Who would have thought this good-natured Aussie larrikin would end up in such a bloody awful mess. Denton had known him for too long to be dispassionate about his plight. In spite of all Reg's wrongdoings—and God knew there were plenty—Denton really did like the guy.

Denton was exhausted; drained by the long flight followed by his session at the jail. He'd already listened to stacks of tapes he'd made at the prison. He poured a brandy from the minibar and dimmed the sidelight. He sipped his drink and lay back on the bed, staring at the ceiling. He would listen to the last half hour of Reg's story again.

✈ ✈ ✈

The tape crackled, and then picked up Denton's voice:

"So Reg, how's it been here?"

"Hey, how long you got, buddy? Let's say that Bombay was a walk in the park compared to this stint. I remember my first day in Negombo, and some bloke, I think he was from Sweden or somewhere, came up to me and asked me why I was so happy. So I told him that if it looks like you're gonna be in a place like this for a long time then you might as well make the most of it. Negombo was the first place they shoved me, and I'm telling you, I saw some bad things. Really bad."

"Like?"

"I saw men with a total indifference to their condition, and I'm talking mental and physical. Mind you, half the blokes at Negombo were mentally unstable. Some things have left me with images not easily forgotten. I thought, I've gotta get out of here, 'else I'm

*gonna end up as mad as everyone else in this hellhole.
So I tried to wangle my way into a job in the hospital. That's what you do if you want to escape. Hospi-
tals, kitchens, and laundries, all notorious in prisons
for having the easiest exit routes. I had to be ill, so
I feigned a bad back. The hospital was a big bloody
joke. You'd be more likely to die in the hospital than if
you tried to look after yourself."*

"How come?"

*"For a start, the so-called medical attendants do
nothing. I reckon they're just normal prison officers in
white coats. Old men are brought in and left rotting
for days. It doesn't matter how sick you are, some of
them had heart complaints and I just watched them
die. Day after day, week after week, and nobody cared
about it. There's a real shortage of any medical supplies. If anything is delivered, it's stolen by the guards,
and they sell it on the streets."*

"So who's watching the guards?"

*"Nobody, nobody gives a shit. The problems arise
because the guards are so poor. Mate, they're on a pittance. So what they do is, they bribe their senior officers for duties where they can nick stuff, like in the
kitchen. You've got some of them feeding their families with food stolen from the prisoners, and if they
don't have families, they just sell it."*

"Seen much violence?"

*"More than my fair share, mate, much more. There
are loads of gangs—I mean a lot—and they're all so
bloody volatile. I've seen cracked skulls, broken arms
and legs, busted internal organs, and a bucket-load
of death. If the guards catch a member of a criminal gang, they beat him for the names of the other
members. The members will forgive the squealer, but
only if he's almost beaten beyond recognition. If he's
squealed but he's not been beaten, you can guarantee
he'll be murdered within days of getting out. There's*

a criminal investigation department here, on the fourth floor, and it's the most dreaded place in the whole building."

"Why?"

"Because the bastards torture everyone, that's why. There's men walking around with mangled hands and scarred feet. They're living proof of what goes on. If you end up on the wrong end of a guard that's been drinking, then God help you, because nobody else will."

"You haven't been beaten or tortured, though?"

"No, but I got into a bad situation once. Only once, and then I learned how to avoid it. One guy was all over me; I'm talking real aggression here. I took him on and argued every point, just stood my ground. The other prisoners told me that if I hadn't been a foreigner, I'd probably have been killed."

"So where did you go after Negombo? Why did you leave Negombo, by the way?"

"Because I tried to escape and got bloody caught. I tried to go out with the laundry. Some of the laundry is done at the prison and some of it gets sent out in bins. I was hiding in a bin under a pile of sheets. Some of the prisoners kept quiet, but one bloke squealed his head off and that was that. Then they decided I was high risk. You know, that I might try to escape again, so they sent me to New Magazine Prison, a more secure place in Colombo."

"What was that like?"

"Heaps of foreign prisoners there: Nigerian, Indonesian, Indian, Argentinian, American, Austrian, Chinese. Man, the place was rife with heroin—a joke, isn't it, when you think about it?—and cocaine, grass, alcohol. Bloody awful conditions, but I was put in the white-foreigners section and I was grateful for that. I couldn't believe what they were telling me when I got there. Some of them have been here for years and *they still haven't had a trial. It's bloody inhumane. I remember once I was sent to see one of the guards about something, and he was on duty in another part of the prison I'd never seen. It was a gruesome place in the bowels of the building. Mate, it depressed me, because there were kids down there, close to one hundred, all different ages. Some of them were with their parents, because there was nobody to look after them on the outside. Then there were the ones who'd been convicted. Forget juvenile court, these kids get shoved in here. I asked the guard about one boy who was on his own. He wouldn't have been older than about fourteen; he looked so sad and I felt sorry for him. The guard told me he'd been found guilty of nicking bikes in Colombo. He'd nicked six bikes, and they could prove it. When the bastard judge sentenced him, he didn't give him one jail term for all the bikes, he gave him one term for each bike. New Magazine and Negombo were total corruption, indifference to the conditions that the majority of prisoners had to live in. I consider myself lucky because I was in the foreigners section, and that was still pretty bad. I've seen wards with a hundred and twenty men or more, and two toilets. I weighed ninety-five kilos when they first threw me in here. After one year, I was down to eighty."*

"Because of the food?"

"Yeah the food, and I probably wasn't looking after myself best I could. I missed Annie. Depression, I suppose. Then one day I looked at my body and thought, shit, I can't believe this is me. What if I've got years ahead of me here and I keep going downhill? Had a wake-up call; thought I'd better pull myself together."

"So what did you do about it?"

"Started making friends. That gets you more food for a start. And exercising; and of course, I know how to do that. Before long I'd persuaded the guards to let me off the ward for an hour a day. I wasn't exercising

alone because other blokes wanted to join me. I was taking a group for lessons, acting as a sort of sports instructor. Then some of the locals wanted to join in, and then I ended up teaching them English. They ended up with better English than my Sinhalese. I noticed that when I kept good manners, it sort of rubbed off on other people. Some of the Sinhalese prisoners started saying please and thank you in English. Boredom is the worst thing. You have to look for ways to beat it, like singing."

"You, singing?"

"I started by singing for the guards. Anything, Sinatra, Springsteen, pop stuff, they loved it all. One time I got together a group of over three hundred prisoners; we made instruments from anything we could find and we put on a performance."

"How come you left New Magazine?"

"Everything was good there for a while and then these crazy rumors started circulating that I was part of some European mafia group that was going to raid the prison and rescue me. Suddenly I'm shoved in a security and punishment place. P Ward it was called. Completely cut off from everyone else, and I'm there with just two Tamils and two Sinhalese. I spent seven months there and it was bloody horrible. Then I had one month back in the foreigners section before I was sent here."

"So how's it been here?"

"I couldn't believe it when I got here. Have you noticed there aren't any other white blokes? I'm the only one, the only white bloke in over fifteen hundred prisoners, and it's an Aussie. I was nervous because just before I left the other place, the Sinhalese told me Mahara was for the toughest habitual criminals in Sri Lanka. I thought I was in for a rough ride, but there were some prisoners I recognized from the other places, so that helped. Initially I got put in D Cell because

they'd heard I'd tried to break out of the other place.
It was worse than any other place I'd seen. So bad the
authorities have condemned it, but they still haven't
pulled it down. If you wanna know where hell on earth
is, it is D Cell at Mahara. The cell is a prison all on its
own, a prison within a prison. The building is a long,
dark passage with five cells and a flat concrete roof.
That fucking roof heated up like an oven, so by eve-
ning it was unbearable. Christ, I'd never been in such
a bad place, and I was stuck there for three months.
Loads of us had scabies but the others seemed to be
used to it. I wasn't, so I made a fuss because there'd
been no doctor available since I'd arrived. So I went on
a hunger strike. Bit of a joke really, going on a hunger
strike when you're already hungry. The food we were
given was vile, inadequate to keep you alive. After two
days they sent me to the chief jailer, the superinten-
dent bloke. He tried to tell me my skin looked okay."

"How bad was it?"

"Man, it was bad. I got penicillin cream and was
told to lie in the sun. So that's what I did, for half an
hour a day on our "let-outs." I would take off my sa-
rong and sunbathe naked. Caused quite a stir I did
because they're not used to nudity. I ended up with
a big audience. Things got a whole lot better then,
because I was like the prison mascot, a bit of a nov-
elty, I suppose. Then I couldn't stop myself from be-
ing outrageous, probably because of the boredom. I
started trying to organize things, like cricket. First
game I bowled the first five batsmen out and they're
thinking I'm Dennis Lillee in disguise or something.
If I walked to the other end of the prison I'd have to
talk to loads of people. Then they were asking me
to sing, so I belted out a Sinatra song with a really
deep voice and they loved it. Then I learnt one of their
songs word-perfect in Sinhalese, "Mage Kirilli." Then
I'd be asked to sing it all the time. Like on Buddha's
birthday. I was asked to sing it after a cricket match

once. I'd organized two teams and all the prisoners were allowed out of their cells to watch the game in this huge compound—like an arena. My team won, and after the last ball they carried me around on their shoulders with everyone clapping. Then they asked me to sing their song and the guards went wild for it. Everyone did. After that everyone started calling me "Sudda"—it means "white man." That's one of the good times I remember."

"There must have been others."

"Yeah, like one time when the whistle went for the prisoners to use the filthy outdoor baths, and I sprint over to the tank and I've got my clothes off before anyone else has even arrived. I dive straight in. Everyone goes wild, the other prisoners are falling about laughing and the guards can't control them. I find that my lack of inhibition is a bit of a weapon. If I've needed something doing, I would just breeze down the corridor, totally naked, starkers, and the guards would get into a panic. The other prisoners find it hilarious and I usually end up getting attention for whatever I need. I don't just use it for myself; I often get extra stuff for the others as well. Then there was the French-consul-bloke episode. Don't forget I'm Patrick Ledoux in here. So they send a bloke from the French consul to interview me. When someone says he's arrived, I hide, thinking I'm totally stuffed. Anyway, they find me, and I'm confronted with this French diplomat in front of the jailers. So I uttered a couple of mon dieus for the benefit of everyone around, and told the French bloke that it was a regulation of the prison that we had to speak in English. Just as well, because I don't speak a word of French. He looked totally bemused and decided not to push it, and off he went. Never heard from him again."

"I reckon he thought he'd do you a favor and wouldn't push it! God, there must have been some bad times as well?"

"*Yeah, more at the beginning. Days that were so long and lonely I thought I'd go mad. You think a lot about what you've left behind, what you've lost. The thing that keeps you going is hope, and, you know, I've always had more than my fair share of that! I remember one time when I'd been locked up for ages and not allowed out of the cell. I can see it now because it was so surreal. I could see the guard's table through the bars because my cell was at the end of the block. The table would've only been ten feet away. It was real quiet in the ward. I could hear prisoners sleeping, breathing, and stuff. The guard had left and I could hear him talking down the corridor. I heard something on his table, then I saw what it was: this huge, bloody silver rat on the table the guard used to make his tea. The rat had knocked over a packet of powdered milk and had its head in it. Then it's jumped off the table and it's walking past my cell with milk powder all over its snout. It's a massive bloody thing and it's stopped to look at me, full on, eye contact and everything. And I'd swear, by the look on its face, it's thinking, 'I might be a rat, but guess what buddy? My life's a whole lot better than yours because I'm not stuck in that fucking cell.'*"

"*Hopefully not for too much longer," laughed Denton. "But have you got yourself a decent lawyer?*"

"*I've been to the courthouse a few times already with one, for submissions and stuff. I always enjoyed it because it got me out of here, in the back of a little blue bus, waving to the villagers along the way. The one I've got tomorrow is just some court-appointed bloke. Don't know what he'll be like because I've only seen him once.*"

"*Tape's almost finished, so I'm turning off. Thanks mate. Phew! Unbelievable stuff! You wouldn't be . . .*"

✈ ✈ ✈

Denton yawned as he rewound the tape. He synchronized his watch with the bedside clock, 1:37 a.m. He needed some rest if he was going to make Reg's big day in court. He used the bathroom, got rid of the paraphernalia on his bed, and straightened the pillows. He couldn't stop thinking about a big, silver rat with powdered milk on its snout. It followed him down the grim, dark corridors of Mahara Prison, into a restless, dream-ridden sleep.

CHAPTER 42

Reg arrived in the courtroom escorted by two guards. His hands were cuffed in front. Denton thought him much more subdued than the previous day. The thick-rimmed spectacles gave him a serious look as he walked down the central aisle of the big courtroom. The hum of spectators ceased, and a sea of dark faces turned to the man they'd come to see fight for his life. Denton was surprised at such a big turnout. A ceiling fan lapped the warm air, rustling Reg's white kaftan. His guards seated him into the wooden dock behind the long bar, then sat on either side.

Denton was seated two rows behind the dock. He wrote notes in shorthand for his story. His article would start with a description of the setting: "An austere old courtroom lined with dark wooden benches, as solemn as the faces that would decide this man's fate." Then he pondered on the bizarre chain of events that had brought Reg to this life-and-death inquisition on the other side of the world. What were his chances of ever getting home?

A flustered little man in wig and gown walked around the front of the dock. He stooped to talk to Reg, taking a handkerchief from his breast pocket and wiping his forehead. Denton remembered Reg saying he'd met with his lawyer only once.

"We've already discussed this," he heard Reg's frustrated voice. The lawyer sighed and straightened his glasses. He turned and sat at the bar and spread out his papers.

The registrar bustled into court in his robes and took his seat below the judicial bench. A neat woman with her hair in a bun followed, heels clicking as she crossed the podium. She assumed her position near the registrar at the Palantype machine on which she would record the proceedings. The apparatus buzzed as she wound the paper into position. The prosecuting counsel entered and took his seat at the bar. He waved to Reg's counsel and sat. When he had unpacked his briefcase, he nodded to the registrar, who got up, mounted the bench, and disappeared through the judge's door.

A minute later, three loud raps rung out on the door. The court usher cried, "Silence in court."

Everyone stopped talking. All eyes were on the doorway. The judge entered wearing red robes, a white cravat, and a wig. He walked with authority to his high, carved chair at the center of the bench. He was followed by two men in ordinary suits who stood at smaller chairs on either side of him. They stood in a row and then solemnly bowed to the bar. They all sat. The registrar gravely intoned, "Case number 349 of 1987, Regina versus Patrick Albert Claude Ledoux."

The prosecutor stood up. "I appear for the Crown, my lord."

Reg's counsel rose. "I appear for the accused, my lord, pro deo."

The sallow-faced elderly judge nodded, his downturned mouth stern.

The registrar read the indictment:

"Patrick Albert Claude Ledoux," he announced in perfect English. "You are charged with contravening the Dangerous Drugs Act in that upon or about December the first, 1984, and at or near Colombo you did wrongfully and unlawfully have in your possession 1.149 kilograms of diacetylmorphine hydrochloride, commonly known as heroin, and thus did commit the crime of contravening section 16(1) of the Dangerous Drugs Act of 1941. Do you understand the charge?"

"What I understand is that it's a load of rubbish," said Reg loudly.

"I said, do you understand the charge?"

"Yes."

"And how plead you, guilty or not guilty?"

"Not guilty," Reg called out. "Definitely not guilty, your honor," he added.

The prosecuting counsel stood. He was a thin, middle-aged man with an arrogant demeanor.

"May it please my lord and gentlemen, I will now briefly outline this case before calling my first witness."

"Yes, Mr. Ranatunga." The judge flicked his hand impatiently.

Ranatunga summarized how Reg had been apprehended at Colombo Airport on December the first in 1984. He ended with, "I call Mr. Amil De Silva, my lord."

Here we go, thought Reg. "Here comes that bloody shark."

"Amil De Silva!" the registrar called.

De Silva emerged from the gallery and entered the well of the court. The tall, uniformed officer took the witness stand and smoothed his black hair across his big, square forehead.

The registrar administered the oath. De Silva agreed to tell the truth, the whole truth, and nothing but the truth.

The whole truth, you corrupt little shit, thought Reg, thinking back to the bribe he gave to De Silva to let Annie stay free.

"Mr. De Silva," Ranatunga said, "you are a police officer stationed at Colombo Airport?"

"I am, my lord. Narcotics division."

"Do you know the accused?"

"I do." He indicated Reg. "I arrested him."

"Tell us the circumstances."

De Silva produced a notebook. "May I refer to my notes?"

"Were they made at the time or shortly thereafter?"

"Yes, my lord."

"Very well," said the judge.

De Silva found the page he needed and read aloud.

"On the first day of December 1984, I observed the accused while he was queuing at one of the passport control desks. He appeared agitated. The duty customs officer was alerted when the accused failed to submit his shoulder bag for inspection. It contained a large cassette recorder. The back panel appeared to have been tampered with and glued into position. The officer called for my assistance. A short time later, my junior officer and I removed the back panel and found a large slab of substance wrapped in plastic."

The prosecutor pointed at the exhibit table. "Is this the said cassette recorder?"

The court usher carried the recorder to the witness stand.

Reg had a good look at it to make sure it was his machine. It was.

"It is," De Silva said.

"I put that into evidence as Exhibit One, my lord. And is this the slab you removed from the cassette player?"

"It is."

"I enter this as Exhibit Two, my lord. What did you do next, Mr. De Silva?"

"I arrested the accused and took him to the cells."

Made sure there was something in it for yourself first, though, didn't you? You greedy bastard, thought Reg.

De Silva coughed into his clenched fist before continuing.

"After that, I weighed the slab in the presence of the accused, and my officer and I took Exhibits One and Two to Dr. Lee at the Forensic Science Laboratory in Colombo for analysis. The doctor informed me of his findings, and while Dr. Lee compiled his report, I formally charged the accused with possession of heroin."

"Did you warn him that anything he said would be taken down and used in evidence?" asked the prosecutor.

"I did."

"Was he of sound and sober senses?"

"He was."

"Did he freely and voluntarily elect to make a reply?"

"He did."

"Did you record it in type and read it back to him?"

"I did."

"Did he adhere to it and sign it?"

"He did."

The prosecutor said, "I tender this statement in evidence, my lord."

The Palantype machine rattled to keep up with the proceedings.

"Any challenge, Mr. Fernando?" the judge inquired.

Reg sighed, about bloody time. He prayed that Fernando would blitz the opposition so he could be on his way.

Fernando stood up. "No, my lord."

"Hey!" Reg called out. "What d'you mean, no? I've got plenty of challenging."

"Yes, Mr. Ledoux," the judge said wearily. "That's what we are going to do." He turned to the witness. "Read it, please."

De Silva read Reg's signed statement aloud.

I deny the charge. Utter rubbish. I was going to spend a few days in Amsterdam sightseeing. A chap at the airport asked me if I would do him a favor and deliver the cassette player to his friend in Amsterdam. I had no idea it wasn't a normal cassette player. Signed, P Ledoux.

"That's right," Reg said with a look of triumph. "No bloody idea!"

"Please watch your language, Mr. Ledoux," the judge said.

"Sorry, sir, but I didn't have any idea."

"Thank you," the prosecutor said to De Silva, and sat.

The judge asked, "Any questions, Mr. Fernando?"

"No cross-examination, my lord," Fernando said.

"What? I've got some questions for this witness, my lord!" cried Reg.

The judge said, "Your client seems a trifle unhappy, Mr. Fernando." He looked at Reg. "Very well, proceed."

Reg squared himself and addressed De Silva. "You reckon I looked nervous at the airport, huh?"

"Yes," said De Silva. "Nervous and agitated."

"Why? How did I? What was I doing?"

De Silva hesitated. "You . . . you sort of shuffled a lot. Kind of . . . frowning. Eyes . . . sort of darting, nervously."

"Demonstrate it for us, please."

De Silva looked to the judge for support.

The judge scowled. "Mr. Ledoux, the witness has verbally described how you looked—he is not a professional actor who can effectively mimic your behavior," he said.

Reg pleaded, "But I'm terrified of flying, sir!"

"I think you were nervous about that cassette player," said De Silva.

Reg turned to him. "Oh, you're a psychiatrist too, are you? Don't people often look nervous at the airport about flying?"

"I don't know why they're nervous."

"Oh, but you know why I was nervous, huh? Do you stop and search them all?"

"No," De Silva said. "Only when I am suspicious."

"So why were you suspicious about my nervousness?"

The prosecutor smirked.

The judge scowled again and said, "Mr. Ledoux, it doesn't matter why Mr. De Silva was suspicious of your apparent nervousness—he has simply testified to the fact that you appeared nervous and so he became suspicious. Whether he was right or wrong about interpreting your nervousness does not matter. What matters is that he investigated the cassette player and found the drugs inside. Get to your next question, please."

Reg snorted and marshaled his thoughts. He would have loved to question the little shit about how he took a bribe and let Annie go—shatter his career—but it would also have incriminated Annie.

"Did you take my fingerprints?" Reg asked.

"Yes."

"And, did you test the plastic the slab of heroin was wrapped in to see if my fingerprints were on it?"

"Yes."

"And, were they?"

"No," De Silva admitted.

"No!" Reg echoed triumphantly. "But they were on the cassette player, of course! Because I was carrying the bloody thing! And your fingerprints must be on the machine and the packet of drugs, mustn't they?"

De Silva looked suspicious. "Why?"

"Why? Because you handled them, didn't you?"

"Oh. Yes."

"But mine weren't!"

The judge said, "Mr. Ledoux, are you suggesting that Mr. De Silva planted the drugs in the cassette player?"

"Yes, my lord!" said Reg.

Whispers drifted from the audience.

"I am suggesting," Reg continued, "that I had no idea drugs were in the player and because Mr. De Silva was suspicious, he planted the drugs so he could justify arresting me!"

The judge smiled. "That's a serious allegation—so you're suggesting Mr. De Silva is corrupt?"

"Yes, or he's a fool. Or both. Why not? He's saying I'm a crook!"

The judge smiled again. "Very well." He turned to the witness, "What do you say to that? Are you a crook, a fool, or both?"

De Silva smirked. "No, my lord."

The judge said to Reg, "But didn't you see Mr. De Silva discover the drugs in the cassette player whilst at the airport?"

"Yes, but I had no idea what they were."

"I see. So you suggest that Mr. De Silva exchanged the package for drugs at the forensic laboratory—or Dr. Lee did?"

"Yes, sir, or something fishy like that."

The judge turned to De Silva. "What's your answer? Did you do 'something fishy like that,' as the accused puts it?"

"No, my lord."

"Jesus Christ," said Reg in a stage whisper everybody heard.

"Next question?" asked the judge, patiently amused.

Reg turned to De Silva again.

"Okay. Do you remember all the events of this stupid case clearly?"

"Yes," De Silva said emphatically.

"Yes? You sure? Everything? Airport, your office, forensic lab?"

"I certainly do."

"Then why," Reg demanded, "did you need to refer to your notebook?"

De Silva smiled. "Standard police practice, Mr. Ledoux."

"Standard? You mean you cops are so dumb and forgetful you always have to refer to your notebooks to refresh your memory about who did what to whom and where on what day?"

"No . . ."

"Then why did you have to refer to your notebook?"

De Silva said, "Because I arrest many people in my job."

"Oh? So you forget the details?"

"Sometimes I need to refresh my memory."

"And in my case you needed to do that?"

"No."

"Then why did you do it? Because you forgot? You contradict yourself, so you are unreliable, aren't you?"

"No, I am reliable."

"How many people have you arrested in the last two years?"

"Many."

"Yes—so you get muddled up and mix up the facts!"

The judge said, "Mr. Ledoux, if you are suggesting that the witness is confusing your case with another one, please be specific and put it to him what he is mistaken about."

"He knows, sir . . . he knows," said Reg as he plonked onto his seat.

The judge grunted. "Very well. Any reexamination Mr. Ranatunga?"

"No, my lord," the prosecutor said. "I call Dr. Lee."

Dr. Lee was a stocky Chinese man with spectacles. He took the oath and told the court that he was a pathologist, in charge of the Police Forensic Science Laboratory in Colombo. On the first of December 1984, at the request of Mr. De Silva, he scientifically examined all of Exhibit Two and found it to consist of 99 percent pure diacetylmorphine hydrochloride, commonly called heroin. He had prepared a report that was handed in as Exhibit Three. Yes, he had personally weighed the heroin—in Mr. De Silva's presence. He produced the chemical balance that he had used, which was entered as Exhibit Four.

"Any cross-examination, Mr. Fernando?" the judge asked.

"No, my Lord, there is no dispute that Exhibit Two is heroin."

"Mr. Ledoux?"

Reg could not think of anything. "No, sir—I mean, my lord."

"By that you accept that Exhibit Two is heroin?"

"Okay, but I didn't know it was in that cassette player."

The prosecutor stood up. "I close the case for the crown, my lord."

The judge looked at the clock on the courtroom wall and stood.

"We'll take a tea adjournment and resume for the defense in fifteen minutes."

✈ ✈ ✈

Fernando wiped his brow with a handkerchief and stood in front of the dock. He looked irritated.

"Do you want to give evidence on oath in the witness stand?" he asked Reg. "Or do you prefer to make an unsworn statement from here in the dock? If you make an unsworn statement you cannot be cross-examined by the prosecutor, but an unsworn statement carries less weight with the court because you are not tested by cross-examination. Evidence on oath does carry more weight because you will be cross-examined." He smirked. "I advise you to make an unsworn statement."

"Why's that?" Reg demanded.

"Because your story is very weak, Mr. Ledoux, and you have been annoying the judge with your stupid questions."

"Stupid! Then why the hell didn't you cross-examine that bastard De Silva—that's your fucking job, isn't it?"

"Because there was nothing I could say. You were caught red-handed."

"But I didn't know the bloody cassette thing was full of heroin. You obviously don't believe me?"

"It doesn't matter what I believe or disbelieve—it only matters what the judge and assessors believe, and I can tell you, they don't believe you. So I advise you to not waste any more time and to make a short unsworn statement where you can't be asked any embarrassing questions."

"They can embarrass me all they like! You're talking like I'm as good as hanged already! Listen Fernando, I'm not going down without a bloody fight—I'll give my evidence, on oath!"

The court resumed.

"Yes, Mr. Fernando?" the judge said.

"I call the accused, my lord," the little barrister said unhappily.

Reg left the dock and mounted the witness stand. He felt sick in his guts, and his knees were trembling. He took the oath to tell the truth, the whole truth, and nothing but the truth.

If only he could.

"Where do you live, Mr. Ledoux?" asked Fernando.

"Nowhere at the moment because I'm touring the world, but I'm seeing a bit more of it than I intended." He added, "Right now I'm an unwilling guest of the Sri Lankan government, in Mahara Prison."

A ripple of laughter swept the gallery. Denton smiled.

Fernando pointed at the cassette player on the exhibit table. "On the first of December 1984, you were arrested at Colombo Airport, attempting to board a flight to Amsterdam, carrying Exhibit One. Is this your cassette player?"

"No—it belongs to someone from Gaborone, Botswana. He asked me to take it and give it to a Mr. van Heerden in Amsterdam. He offered me a thousand rupees for my trouble, so I agreed, as a favor. He seemed a nice chap."

"Who was this nice chap?"

"Don't know his name, seemed a decent fellow, well-dressed, and so on. So I agreed—wanted the money, you see, I was a bit low at the time and a thousand rupees would buy a good dinner."

"And how were you going to contact Mr. van Heerden in Amsterdam to give him the cassette player?"

"This chap said he would send a telegram to Mr. van Heerden telling him to meet my plane. He would have a sign with his name on it."

Mr. Fernando pointed at the heroin. "Did you know Exhibit Two was inside the cassette player?"

"No! No idea. If I'd known that I would have refused, of course! The first I saw of the heroin was at Colombo Airport when Mr. De Silva discovered it and arrested me."

"Thank you," Mr. Fernando said and sat down.

"Yes, Mr. Ranatunga?" the judge said dryly.

Ranatunga stood up assertively. He bunched the lapels of his gown in both hands.

"So did this, nice chap—whom you had never seen before— did he tell you why he wanted you to carry the cassette player for him?"

Reg thought fast. "Yes. He said it was expensive to post because it was quite heavy. And it was fragile, might get damaged."

"Oh, I see . . . expensive and fragile . . . But why didn't you mention this before?"

"Nobody asked me, sir."

"Did you tell your counsel this detail?"

"Can't remember."

"Ah . . . Maybe you need a notebook like Mr. De Silva?" Ranatunga's voice was scathing. "But why can't you remember? Doesn't it strike you as an important detail? Surely any passenger would wonder why a stranger asks him to deliver a cassette player to another stranger across the world."

Reg swallowed. "I remember now—I did tell my lawyer," he said.

"Oh, now you remember! I wonder why your lawyer didn't mention this while he was examining you."

Reg said, "I don't know. You better ask him."

"He's not in the witness box—you are!"

Reg looked to Fernando for a lifeline. The little lawyer had his brow propped in his hand and slowly shook his head.

Reg appealed to the judge. "The prosecutor is being sarcastic, sir—is he allowed to do that?"

The judge looked amused. "Yes, Mr. Ledoux," he assured Reg. "Provided that his questions are relevant—and they are. Very."

Denton groaned inwardly. Ranatunga looked smug. "So answer this question, please—were you not suspicious when this stranger asked you to carry this cassette player to Amsterdam, suspicious that it contained something illegal, fishy?"

Reg thought it was time to retreat. "Yes, I did start to worry a bit, but it was too late, the man had already gone into the crowd. But I never dreamed it contained heroin."

"Oh! Now you remember again! And what did you worry that it might contain?"

"Money, sir, I thought he might be smuggling money out of the country. You know, against the exchange control regulations."

"Ah! Money. So you must have thought it must be a great deal of money—because why would anybody use a big cassette player to smuggle a small amount for which he could easily use the bank or the post office?"

Reg swallowed. "Yes, I thought it must be quite a lot of money."

"So would anybody with half a brain! But I wonder why somebody would entrust a complete stranger to smuggle out money that the stranger could so easily steal? Did you consider that?"

Reg feigned indignation. "Consider stealing it? No, I'm not a thief!"

"Ah—just a smuggler, an honest smuggler. No, I meant, did you consider what a risk that nice chap was taking, because a cassette player can be easily opened at the back to change the batteries. Did you consider opening the machine to see what you might be smuggling?"

"No, sir."

"Why on earth not? As you were worried?"

Reg said, "Because the back of the cassette player was sealed with some kind of strong glue, sir."

"Ah! So you did try to open it! But you've just said you did not consider opening the cassette player. Now you say you tried but failed because it was strongly glued!" Ranatunga smirked and shook his head wearily. "Thank you. That will be all."

He sat down.

Reg returned to the dock, feeling exhausted, shaky.

The judge said, "Any more defense witnesses, Mr. Fernando?"

"No, my lord." The little man sighed wearily.

The judge turned to each assessor and whispered. Both nodded in turn. Then the judge turned to Ranatunga.

"There's no need to hear your submissions, Mr. Ranatunga." He turned to Reg's lawyer: "Yes, Mr. Fernando? What are your final submissions?"

Mr. Fernando stood up. He began unhappily, "the accused's evidence is believable, my lord and gentlemen . . ."

"Do you," the judge interrupted, "commend him to this court as an impressive, credible witness? His story is credible only if we assume he is a complete fool."

"Yes, he is a fool, my lord. Therefore he should be believed, and he should be acquitted." He sat down before he got more disagreement.

What? Denton thought. Is that the best you can do?

Reg liked the idea of playing the fool card. It wasn't without merit—but why hadn't his lawyer dealt it earlier and why the hell was he sitting down when he could be making more of it?

The judge sighed, eyebrows raised.

"Court will adjourn to consider its verdict."

✈ ✈ ✈

Fifteen minutes later, there were raps on the door. The usher shouted, "Silence in court," and the judge and assessors took their seats.

Christ! Denton thought, how quick was that? This looks bad.

"Will the accused please stand," said the judge.

Reg got to his feet shakily. He stared. The judge began.

"The accused in this case is charged with contravening Section 16 (1) (a) of the Dangerous Drugs Act. The facts are simple . . ."

He proceeded to sum up the evidence.

"The accused in his defense said that he had no idea that the cassette player contained heroin," the judge stated. "He claimed that he was approached at Colombo Airport by a complete stranger who, out of the blue, offered him one thousand rupees to carry the cassette player to Amsterdam and deliver it to a Mr. van Heerden. Another stranger."

Reg took a deep breath and listened intently. He thought the judge's summary of the defense's version of events thus far didn't sound totally implausible.

The judge continued.

"The accused at first denied having any suspicions about this unusual request, saying he undertook the mission because the first stranger was a nice, decently dressed man—and he needed the one thousand rupees on offer. However, under cross-examination, he finally admitted he did 'worry a bit.' He thought it might contain money being smuggled out of Botswana in contravention of their exchange control laws. He said he wanted to cancel the deal and give the cassette player back to the stranger, but alas, this nice stranger had disappeared. Why he thought a stranger would entrust him with a large sum of money that could be easily stolen he could not explain. At first he denied trying to check the amount of money inside the cassette player. Under cross-examination he finally admitted he did try to open the back of it, but found it was glued stuck. He said this detail only confirmed his suspicion that the cassette player might contain money and not anything more sinister."

Reg hung his head. Why the hell had he mentioned trying to open the bloody thing? All he'd done was dig an even bigger hole for himself.

"We do not believe the accused," the judge spoke up and addressed the courtroom. "His story is highly improbable, indeed borders on the ridiculous. He made an unimpressive witness: agitated, frequently contradicting himself. He could be believed only if it was assumed that he was a fool. It is clear from his cross-examination of Mr. De Silva that he is not that, though Mr. Fernando submitted that he was."

The judge raised his voice again. "Accordingly, we find the accused guilty."

Reg's ears were ringing, his heart pounding.

"Do you have anything to say before sentence is passed?" the judge asked him.

Reg swallowed. "I'm innocent!" he rasped. "I told the truth!" he stared.

The judge nodded. "Anything else?"

"I am innocent, sir."

The judge sighed.

"The sentence I am about to pass is mandatory under the Dangerous Drugs Act—I have no discretion." He paused and picked up a black cloth the size of a handkerchief. He placed it on his head, on top of his wig.

A number of spectators gasped. Denton stopped writing and stared at Reg in disbelief. He knew what was coming.

"The sentence of this court is that you be taken to a place of execution and there be hanged by the neck until you are dead."

He added, "And may the Lord have mercy upon your soul." But Reg didn't hear him. The words "execution," "hanged," and "dead" were ringing in his ears.

Another murmur erupted from the gallery. Denton closed his eyes. Reg stared, aghast, heart pounding.

"I want to appeal . . . " he blurted.

The judge nodded. "Yes, there is an automatic right of appeal in death sentence cases."

"I want it soon, my lord."

"Your lawyer will see to all that. He'll apply to the registrar for a date and get you a full transcript of all the evidence we've heard today."

Reg pleaded desperately. "My lord, I've been in prison waiting for a trial for almost two and a half years already—and there's blokes back there who only want to appeal something like a ten-year sentence. Some of them have done half of that already, waiting, and they've not even got a date for their appeal. My lawyer's useless! Couldn't save a fish from drowning! Would you want your life in his hands? I'm doing my own case next time. If I could have a date, please, your honor?"

A stunned silence had descended on the court. The judge considered his options. Foreign journalists were present, and he didn't want the Sri Lankan judicial process criticized by the international press. He glanced at the indignant little defense lawyer and thought the prisoner had a fair point about being disadvantaged. He nodded to the registrar. The man leafed hurriedly through a ledger. Then he got up and whispered to the judge.

The judge looked at Reg. "The registrar informs me that there is a free day in the appeals court calendar six months from now, Mr. Ledoux. Your representative will make the necessary submissions. The transcript of today's proceedings will be delivered to you forthwith."

"Many thanks, my lord!" said Reg gratefully.

The usher shouted, "Silence in court!" The judge and assessors stood, bowed, and filed solemnly out of the courtroom.

Conversations erupted in the gallery as the spectators prepared to leave the courtroom. Fernando pushed his papers into his briefcase and scurried up the aisle to the exit. Denton heard crying from the other side of the room. Reg walked toward him with his hands cuffed in front, escorted by his guards.

"See you back in Oz," he called to Denton with a hopeful smile. "Did we thrash them in the cricket?"

Denton fell into step alongside the nearest guard. "I'll get a copy of the transcript and see if I can get any advice," he told Reg.

"Thanks, mate," said Reg.

A sad Denton walked out into the afternoon sunshine. He'd get the next flight to Australia.

A crowd milled outside the entrance. He passed two men sitting on a bench. One of them seemed to be consoling a friend who was weeping. Denton stopped to talk to them.

"Do you mind telling me why you came today?" he asked the slim Sri Lankan in a neat white shirt and sarong.

The man looked up.

"We're friends of Sudda, we came to be with him in court."

"You mean Mr. Ledoux?"

"Yes, sir."

"But how do you know him, Sudda?"

"I was in prison at Mahara. So was Abdul," said the man. He indicated his gray-haired friend. "I am Anand and this is Abdul. Are you a friend of Sudda too, sir?"

Denton hesitated for a moment. "Yes . . . yes, I'm a friend of Sudda."

"He's a good man, Sudda, he has many friends in Mahara," said Anand.

Abdul wiped his red eyes with a crumpled handkerchief. "He has done many good things for all of us," he said. "They mustn't kill Sudda."

"Let's hope they won't. What sorts of things has he done?" asked Denton.

"He helped me get my legal papers into order, and he helped me write my statement. He helped many prisoners. He taught us English. Before Sudda came to Mahara, I could speak only a few words, but Sudda took classes every day, and before many months we are all speaking better English. He got better conditions for the prisoners. He was always getting extra food from the guards and sharing it with us."

Abdul added, "And if there was a weak person, a prisoner who was scared and having bad things done to him, Sudda would protect him. He looked after the downtrodden prisoners, and that is why everyone loved Sudda."

"There won't ever be another Sudda at Mahara," Anand shook his head sadly.

"I shouldn't think that there will," said Denton. There would probably never be another Reg Spiers either, he thought as he stood to leave.

That evening he boarded the plane for Melbourne, his collection of tapes in his briefcase. His mind was jumbled with details of Reg's story, the forthcoming appeal, and his conversation with Abdul and Anand. He would do as he'd promised and get some legal advice. As his plane took off, he wondered what Reg was feeling at that very moment. Was the poor bastard already on death row?

He was. Reg had been transferred to Welikada, a maximum-security prison in Colombo. The building was contained by an eight-meter concrete wall, patrolled by officers armed with automatic rifles; men who had undergone specialist training to guard prisoners condemned to death. Reg had taken up residence in the condemned cells as prisoner number forty-five of around sixty men. He had his own cell, housed down a long, dark tunnel, with a door at the end that led to the gallows.

He'd been given a thin mat, two shirts, and two sheets that he was told should double as clothing. The communal toilet was for urinating, defecating, and washing. Loneliness wasn't a problem because the prisoners had plenty of little friends for company: rats, bedbugs, lice, mosquitoes, flies, ants, and the biggest cockroaches he'd ever seen. Reg thought the place was a masterpiece of squalor and that he had truly reached the end of the line.

Buddhist monks chanted, praying to their master to purify the souls of the condemned. The melancholy incantations drifted into Reg's small, grimy cell. He lay back on his threadbare mat, head in hands as he followed a cockroach's journey across the treacherous stony terrain of the ceiling. Reg thought of his own journey: his airfreighting stunt back in '64, all the crazy twists and turns his life had taken since he got out of the box. And then he thought about Annie, and she seemed farther away than ever.

He was plagued by images of the gallows. Would that be his epilogue, his lifeless body dangling from a rope? No. It would be his body that would decide when it was time for him to die. Not a man. Not yet. Not like this. He had to pull himself together. If he wanted freedom, he had to be one hell of a lot smarter. He desperately tried to focus on every aspect of his case and how he was going to win his appeal.

CHAPTER 43

SIX MONTHS LATER

Three judges sat cloaked in black gowns that looked ominously funereal against their white cravats and solemn wigs. Reg searched for a glimmer of compassion in the three pairs of old, dark eyes. The man on the left was suffering from a head cold that left him sniffing into a large white handkerchief. The crooked features of the middle judge were disconcerting. His elbows rested on the bench with his hands clasped in front of his face, his spindly fingers continuously lacing and unlacing. Reg vested some hope in the round-faced, jolly-looking man on the right; he thought his chubby-cheeked demeanor almost promising.

"Could you repeat that, Mr. Ledoux," the judge-president strummed his fingers on the back of his other hand.

"I said I want to recall Mr. De Silva, my lord. And I want the scales that I requested in my written application. Please your honor, lord . . ."

The judge sighed.

"Mr. Ledoux, an appeal is not another trial where you can recall witnesses at will. An appeal is argued on the record, where everything everybody said is written down—you can argue about that." He sighed again. "However, if new evidence has come to light since the trial, something important and relevant, the appeals court may allow witnesses to be recalled for further questioning. Now, why do you want to question Mr. De Silva again? What new evidence can he give? And why didn't you mention this in your grounds of appeal?"

Reg said, "I didn't want Mr. De Silva to be warned, to give him time to cook up his answers."

A ripple of amusement ran through the journalists in the gallery.

"Oh," the judge said. "Cook up? So you're going to prove Mr. De Silva lied to the trial court, are you?"

Reg took a tense breath. I sure hope so, he thought. "Yes, my lord."

"Well, well, well," the judge mused. "Any objection, Mr. Ranatunga?"

Ranatunga stood. "It should have been specified in the grounds of appeal, my lord."

"Not necessarily," the judge said grudgingly. "It would seem that, 'Against the weight of evidence' covers allegations of 'cooking up evidence,' or perjury. And Mr. Ledoux is representing himself; in his wisdom, he has dispensed with the services of Mr. Fernando or any other lawyer. Very well," he turned to Reg, "you may recall Mr. De Silva. Where is he?"

Reg pointed. "Sitting over there, my lord."

De Silva stood up, taken aback, bemused. He walked to the witness stand. His face brimmed with a smug confidence. The registrar administered the oath.

"Yes, Mr. Ledoux," the judge said. "What questions?"

Reg cleared his throat. This was do or die—freedom or dangle from a rope.

He pointed at the exhibit table. "That grubby plastic bag of so-called heroin—where did you keep it from the moment you arrested me until my trial in the Supreme Court?"

De Silva frowned. "Locked in the Police Exhibit Room. Until I took it to Dr. Lee."

"And when did you take it to Dr. Lee?"

"Later that day."

"So it was in the Exhibit Room. And did you weigh it again before you took it to Dr. Lee?"

"No. I could tell by its weight it was about a kilo. Dr. Lee and I confirmed that in his lab."

"And, are you sure the slab weighed exactly 1.149 kilograms?"

"Yes."

"And, are you sure that the slab of so-called heroin in that plastic bag is the very same one you found in the cassette player at Colombo Airport?"

"Yes, I am."

"Same plastic and everything?"

De Silva shuffled his feet. "It looks the same."

"Oh, one plastic bag looks the same as another, does it? And who keeps the key to the Police Exhibit Room?"

"The desk sergeant."

"Oh! So any police officer that has a new exhibit to place in the Exhibit Room goes to the desk sergeant and asks for the key. Correct?"

De Silva fidgeted. He saw what was coming.

"Yes," he said grudgingly.

Reg said, "So any police officer who went into the Exhibit Room could have opened your bag? And . . . interfered with your heroin?"

"No!" De Silva snapped.

"Why not? The police officer would be alone in the room, wouldn't he?"

"The police are not criminals!" De Silva said vehemently.

"Oh," Reg said. "No corruption in the police force . . . ever . . . despite what we read in the newspapers."

"No!" an annoyed De Silva insisted loudly.

"Mr. Ledoux!" said the judge-president as he tapped his fingertips against each other. "What's printed in newspapers is not evidence a court can listen to, nor take judicial notice of. Kindly get on with your cross-examination with admissible questions."

"Sorry, my lord," Reg smiled nervously up at the bench.

The judge on the left blew his nose. The round-faced judge on the right smirked.

Reg marshaled his thoughts. God, this was brilliant. He was starting to feel like a proper lawyer!

Don't get ahead of yourself, or you'll stuff it up like you did the last time.

This was it: Annie or the executioner.

He strolled around the side of the evidence table. Confidently, like the lawyers he'd watched on television crime dramas.

"So you're telling this court that this," Reg pointed to the tatty gray rectangular packet on the table, "is the same slab you allegedly found in my cassette player on the first of December 1984?"

"I am!" De Silva was emphatic.

"So," Reg said, "please assist me to weigh it again."

De Silva looked astonished. The jolly judge could not hide his excitement. Silence hung over the courtroom. Reg prayed silently . . . Please God . . .

De Silva looked to the judge-president for guidance. The judge leaned to his right to confer with his nose-blowing colleague, and then nodded at the clerk to fetch the scales. He turned to De Silva and trailed his spindly index finger to the exhibit table. De Silva looked flustered as he descended from the witness stand.

The clerk lifted an old, brass, double-pan set of scales onto the exhibit table. Beads of sweat peppered De Silva's forehead. Reg forced a smile at him, his heart pounding. Then he placed the ragged package in one pan of the scales. The pan descended to the table with a small bang. Reg reached for the box of weights.

"You said the heroin weighed 1.149 kilograms?" he asked De Silva.

"Yes."

Reg stared at the box of weights. They ranged from four hundred, two hundred, one hundred, and fifty grams. He straightened the neckline of his kaftan and cleared his throat.

"Please continue with your demonstration, Mr. Ledoux," the judge-president called, over his twisted hands.

Reg selected a two-hundred-gram weight and held it up to the judges.

"Two hundred grams, my lords," he called.

Three intrigued old faces peered down at him.

He placed the weight in the corresponding pan. The scale did not move. He took another two-hundred-gram weight and demonstrated again. "This makes four hundred grams, my lords," he placed it in the pan with the first weight. It did not move the scales. "Now this makes six hundred grams, my lords," he held his third weight in the air. He placed it in the pan with the other two. The scales sat motionless.

Reg swallowed, ears ringing. It had to be the fourth. His hand shook as he selected another two-hundred-gram weight.

"This will make eight hundred grams, my lords," his voice croaked as he displayed it to the judges.

He placed the weight alongside the other three. The pan of weights descended to the tabletop with another small bang. A gasp rose from the sea of faces in the gallery. Reg dropped his head and sighed.

Thank you, God.

He raised his face to the judges and smiled. "Whatever the heroin weighs, my lords, we can be sure it is less than eight hundred grams."

The judges' faces were agape; De Silva's, a mask of astonishment.

All eyes were on Reg as he replaced one of the two-hundred-gram weights with a one-hundred-gram one. The scales reversed. He exchanged the hundred-gram weight with a small fifty-gram weight. The scales teetered in balance. He straightened and turned to De Silva.

"Mr. De Silva," Reg tried not to gloat. "Please verify the weight of the evidence."

De Silva leaned over the scales and stared in disbelief. He counted the weights, and then recounted them. Ranatunga bustled to the table and peered, equally astounded. Then he returned to the bar and slumped into his seat, deflated.

"Well?" Reg demanded.

"About six hundred and fifty grams." De Silva's tone was condescending.

"Louder, please, so everybody can hear."

"Six hundred and fifty grams," De Silva said resentfully.

Excited whispers stirred from the gallery. Reg beamed triumphantly as the clerk ordered silence.

"So," Reg said. "Did you pinch some of the heroin while it was stored in the Exhibit Room?"

"No!"

"Then either you are lying to this court," continued Reg, "or the heroin on these scales, the heroin that you produced in evidence against me in the Supreme Court, is not what you say you found in the cassette player at Colombo Airport in 1984!"

"No." De Silva began to protest, but the judge-president interrupted and snapped at the prosecutor. "What have you got to say, Mr. Ranatunga?"

Ranatunga stood up and said, "Whether it weighs six hundred and fifty grams or one kilo, it is still the heroin that was in the appellant's possession at Colombo Airport."

The judge-president scowled. "How can we be sure of that beyond reasonable doubt? How can we be sure that the heroin that is on the scales is the very same substance that was found in the cassette player?" he barked. "The chain of evidence has been well and truly broken!"

He stood up. "Court will adjourn for five minutes."

Reg sat back in the dock. Handcuffed again, eyes closed, enduring a long, long five minutes. The spectators fidgeted nervously. Had he done enough?

Then came the three raps on the door. The usher cried, "Silence in court," and the three judges entered in a swirl of red cloaks. The expectant crowd hushed.

The judge-president settled into his ornate, high chair at the center of the bench. The other two judges sat on either side of him.

The judge-president glared at De Silva and announced:

"The appellant in this case was convicted in the Supreme Court six months ago of being in possession of over a kilogram of heroin, and he received the mandatory death sentence. Today he shattered the chain of evidence required to prove that what was found in his possession at Colombo Airport was the same exhibited to the Supreme Court and to this court, nor therefore that what was testified as being heroin was the very same substance that was found in the cassette player at Colombo Airport. Accordingly, the crown has failed to prove that what was found in the cassette player at Colombo Airport is indeed, heroin."

He glanced sternly at De Silva again, then Ranatunga.

"Accordingly, the appeal is upheld, and the appellant is discharged."

The spectators at the back of the court erupted into applause, which soon engulfed the whole courtroom. Reg heard the din of his supporters, but his mind was numb. An officer helped him to his feet, and he walked a heady gauntlet of backslappers and well-wishers, escorted by two guards.

"Good on you, Reggie," a twangy voice called from the steps outside.

Reg turned and waved to Denton, who'd sat through the last hour's proceedings with other Australian journalists.

"Anything you wanna say to the folks back home?"

"Just tell my family and friends I'll see them soon," Reg grinned, blinking back tears.

Members of the Australian and Sri Lankan press followed Reg's party, vying for photographs as he climbed happily into the back of a prison van.

"Hey Reggie," someone yelled. "Where is Annie Hayes? She left Australia with you, didn't she?"

Reg didn't answer. He laughed and cried into his hands, hardly noticing the short journey back through Colombo to Welikada Prison. His mind was befuddled with exhilaration as he tried to compose joyful plans of what he would do next. He was taken to the prison administration area, where he waited for his meager belongings. He was still in a daze when the officer handed him the small bag he had with him when he was arrested at Colombo Airport. He was surprised to find the rectangular leather tag still intact, bearing the name Patrick Albert Claude Ledoux in ornate, curled writing. Reg gazed at it, picturing Annie sitting at a table in their hotel room, carefully inscribing the words.

He found a pair of jeans to wear, but everything else was musty and creased, so he didn't change out of his kaftan. He quickly signed his release documents, and the official told him he would be escorted to a back exit because the main front entrance was clogged with members of the press. A couple of guards whom he had known back in his Mahara days chaperoned him down a network of passageways to a door at the back of the jail.

"Bye, Sudda," one said when he'd opened the last outer door. He shook Reg's hand. "We will miss you!"

Reg stepped into the narrow side street. He heard the familiar clang of the heavy metal door as it shut behind him. This time he was on the right side of it. He strode off with his bag swinging by his side and didn't look back.

His senses sharpened. The sound of his own footsteps left him vulnerable along the quiet, unfamiliar street. Late afternoon clouds were gathering. He thought he saw the shadowy figure of a woman hovering behind a window. A cat scampered across the bumpy lane ahead. He could see the end of the walkway, glistening with sunlit movement. It beckoned him.

He would let the crowd swallow him up. Get the hell out of Colombo and lie low. Annie was waiting for him somewhere. Somewhere she was waiting, and he'd find her. They would make up for all this madness. Do normal things, have kids together. Oh God, he wanted all that now as he jogged the last twenty meters of the lane.

"Reginald James Spiers?"

A burly uniformed police officer confronted him, blocking his path. Reg was quickly surrounded by half a dozen gun-wielding officers. He was boxed in.

"That's me, fellas," he said. Patrick Ledoux had outlived his credibility. "What took you so long?"

"I'm Superintendent David Carswell of the Australian Federal Police." The officer flashed his emu-and-kangaroo badge. "Reginald Spiers, I have a warrant for your arrest."

Reg's blue eyes clouded. But hell, this was only a setback . . . He'd find her. He would.

Chapter 44

Adelaide, 1990

"Excuse me officer," John McSorley called through the window of the station wagon. "Could you help me? Long shot, I know, but I'm looking for an old friend. He's inside . . . Reg Spiers?"

"Reggie?" The policeman's face lit up. "Everyone knows Reggie! He's in Mobilong now. Was at Yatala when they brought him back. But Murray Bridge you want."

John thanked the officer, weaved back onto the road, and headed for Murray Bridge. He hadn't seen Reg since the day he closed the lid of the box back in Twickenham almost thirty years before. A hell of a lot had happened to his old friend in the intervening years. Was he going to find the same Reggie? Perhaps being locked away for so long had broken his spirit.

"Left here." Julie had been following a map.

"Is this the prison?" eight-year-old Marcus asked when they drove into the car park.

"Certainly is," John said. "It's where naughty boys end up."

"Is this where the box man lives?"

"It is at the moment," said John, and Julie stifled a laugh.

As they walked through the prison entrance, a man leaned over the counter, sharing a joke with the duty officer. He turned to them and fixed his blue eyes on John. His expression changed from puzzlement to surprise, then joy.

"Don't bloody believe it!" He strode to John, arms stretched wide. "Johnny Mac! It's my old friend Johnny Mac!" They bear-hugged.

Julie shot the officer an apologetic smile because his orderly reception area had erupted with excited chatter.

"Reg, Julie my wife, and young Marcus!" said John.

"Hi, Julie," Reg smiled. "And no trouble working out who this little fellow is, a dead ringer for his dad I'd say." He turned to the officer. "John is the bloke I told you about, the box maker."

"So you're the one who kick-started his life of crime," the officer said jovially. "You blokes go and have your reunion in the officers' lounge, tell them Burt says it's okay."

Reg led John and his family down the corridor.

"Burt says it's okay," he said to the guards when they entered a big dayroom scattered with easy chairs and a couple of tables. "Any chance of a cup of tea for my visitors?"

The two officers rose. "Can do Reggie, but I'll have you cleaning my shoes next week," one smirked.

"So Johnny Mac's a family man. Well, what d'you know." Reg grinned and plonked himself next to John.

One of the guards brought a tray of tea and a glass of orange soda.

"Gotta be a good boy if you don't want to end up in here." He winked at Marcus.

Marcus thought "in here" seemed okay. It was just like a big house, with drinks and stories. His eyes widened as the box man started to talk about a strange flight from London to Perth.

"We'll take a walk, leave you guys to chat," said Julie.

"God, it's good to see you, Mac," said Reg, when they were alone. "I would have written, but you know. Things got difficult . . . in Sri Lanka."

"Yeah, someone sent me a newspaper clipping from the day of your sentence. Looked bad for you, Reg . . . really bad."

"You've no idea." A shadow of regret crossed Reg's face. "But listen," he rallied, "compared to Mahara, this is a walk in the park. I got ten years when they brought me back, and they reckon I'll end up doing less than four."

"You don't look any different from the day you climbed into that bloody box, Reggie."

"And that was a while ago, buddy," Reg said. "A torrent of

water under the bridge since then! So how did you find me?"

"First bloke I asked. Don't think you're going to be able to abscond any time soon. You're too well-known!"

"Think I might be done with that for a while." Reg looked thoughtful.

"Bloody glad to hear it, you mad, crazy bastard," said John. "But forget 'for a while.'"

"Life's only for a while, Mac."

"Right," said John. He sat straight and looked directly into Reg's eyes. "But remember what you told me before I closed that box?"

"God, Mac, that was a hell of a long time ago . . ."

"Okay, well, I said it wasn't too late to change your mind . . . and you said . . . you said that every person's life should have one reckless moment . . ."

"That's right."

"One moment, you said, and yours was supposed to be the box. One moment, not a quarter-century!"

"But I live for those moments, Mac, those moments are what it's all about."

"Well, you're gonna have to wean yourself off them, if you want any kind of normal life."

"That's the point," Reg shook his head. "I don't want a normal life."

"What's wrong with normal?"

"Nothing," said Reg. "I envy people who are happy with normality, people like you, old buddy—a teacher, a family, and all that."

"People who do 'normal' aren't happy all the time, Reg. You don't think I never had days when I didn't feel like a bit of freedom?" said John. "In fact, I'll own up to something right now."

Reg looked intrigued. "Yeah?"

"You took a part of me with you in that box."

"What part of you?"

"Just a tiny little part," said John. "The part of people like me who occasionally wish, not in an everyday way, but somewhere in the recesses of their consciousness, that just for once, they could do something that doesn't feel so bloody safe."

Reg studied his friend's face as though he was looking at it for the first time.

"I'd never thought of it like that," said Reg. "Bit like that song, what is it? Take a walk on the wild side." He smiled. "And I've certainly done that. We're all destined, Mac, I reckon risk-taking is in my DNA."

"But if you weighed things up a bit, looked at the alternatives on offer, 'normal' wouldn't seem so bad."

Reg leaned back in his chair and folded his arms. "Like I told that writer Denton when I was in Sri Lanka. After the life I've lived, you don't honestly expect me to take an office job?"

"There are other ways to make a living," laughed John, "besides drug-running and office work, that is. Hey, bet you could still make that spear fly!"

"Plenty of time for training in here. Might even take it up again when I get out, who knows?"

"How about the others?" John asked. "What about Niko, the guy you left with?"

"Niko's good. Gave himself up shortly after I was shoved in the slammer in Bombay. On my first day here, some prisoners sought me out and told me they'd already heard about me from Niko when he was in here. He's out now."

"And Ted?"

"Picking up the pieces." Reg's mouth tightened. "He's been paroled, but Cheryl worries a bit. She comes to see me. I feel bad for him, really bad."

"I understand that," said John. "Suppose it's taken a while for you to realize not everyone's as indestructible as you." He patted Reg on the back, and detected a hint of sadness in his blue eyes.

There was something else on John's mind.

"Hope you don't mind me asking," he said quietly. "What about Annie? What happened to her?"

Reg's eyes clouded. "Nobody knows," he said. "We were more than just lovers, Mac, she was the love of my life." He swallowed, and sadness fell over the room. "We were best friends, too . . . I think about her every day."

"Hasn't anyone heard anything?"

"Nobody," Reg shook his head, "apart from this local journalist mate of mine, Denton. He has a newspaper friend in London who told him that some guy walked into his office with a story—reckoned Annie had shared a flat with him and a load of other people in Amsterdam."

"Why was she in Amsterdam?"

"Money, money we were owed."

"And?"

"That's about it, really. According to this mystery bloke, Annie went out to post a letter one morning and never returned. Left everything, walked out with just the clothes on her back."

"She must have taken something."

"No . . . Just one thing they couldn't find after she'd left. Her koala. You know, one of those soft toys. She'd had it since she was a kid, traipsed it half way round the world."

"God, how weird," John said. "I'm sorry Reggie. That's tough, but don't give up. She's bound to show up eventually."

✈ ✈ ✈

John and Reg went to look for Julie and Marcus and found them chatting with the duty officer at the end of the corridor.

John was still thinking about Annie when he walked out into the car park with Reg. A light rain had fallen, and a huge rainbow arched across the sky. Afternoon sunshine patterned the glistening cars. John looked back at the entrance, expecting to see the guards watching Reg's every move. Nobody was there.

He caught sight of Reg in his side mirror as he maneuvered his car toward the exit.

"If you need another box, I'm your man," he yelled out of the window.

"Only if it comes with spaghetti bolognese!" Reg laughed back.

John honked a double beep of his horn. Marcus turned so he could see the box man through the rear window. Reg waved with his widest smile, and watched the boy's face until it disappeared through the main gate.

"It would be easy to escape from prison, wouldn't it, Daddy?"

AFTERWORD

Those who shared Reg's adventures and misadventures have since traveled a wide variety of paths.

John McSorley retired from athletics in 1971 and became a high school sports teacher. His friend Tom died in a motor accident some years later. John's colleague, sports writer James Coote, was killed when a plane he was piloting crashed in the French Alps.

Reg and his wife, Marion, remained happily married for several years after his boxed journey in 1964, and they became the proud parents of a second daughter. They eventually grew apart, however, and went their separate ways.

Members of Reg's Adelaide drug syndicate received prison sentences of between six and fourteen years, but served less time. They went on to have fulfilling careers, and settled quietly into family life. Ted was released six months before Reg was extradited back to South Australia, and became a successful businessman. The close friendship of the group has endured, and several members still live in and around Adelaide.

The customs officer from Colombo Airport was later dismissed on the grounds of corruption.

Reg's notoriety lived on in the Sri Lankan jails long after he left. A fellow inmate later wrote to him:

> Reg, while watching T.V. last week I heard your song "Mage Kirilli—So Ya Yan—Nay Ma." Everybody was talking about you, saying "Sudda's song" and how well you sing it. Reg, to be very honest, a day doesn't pass without your name being mentioned. A song, a word, a deed, some food, a joke, anything, and your name comes up in our conversation. This morning I read a letter written by you to the Sri Lanka Prison

*Department, which was published in the prison paper
January issue. I will post the issue to you next time. It
has the words "Bohoma Sthuthi," the first Singhalese
words you learnt. Many people are touched by your
message and I too am.*

Reg served more than three years in Yatala, Mobilong, and
Cadell prisons in Adelaide. He continued to make inquiries
about Annie, and letters from the time reveal he had grave fears
for her safety.

Annie finally presented herself to the Australian embassy in
Bonn, Germany, in 1994. She was extradited to Australia, where
she was given only a six-month prison term, the judge heeding a
psychologist's report that her crimes were the result of "infatua-
tion, bordering on obsession," for Reg.

By the time Annie returned from the wilderness she hadn't
seen Reg for almost nine years, although they had exchanged letters while Reg was in jail in Sri Lanka. After serving her short prison sentence, Annie visited Reg in Adelaide, and they renewed a
close friendship. After so long apart, however, they decided that
the love they had shared should remain a sweet memory.

The years since Reg was released from jail have been kind to
him. Although he is now in his seventies, he has lost none of the
joie de vivre of his youth, and he lives happily in South Australia
with his partner. If you should happen upon a beautiful Adelaide
beach early one morning, you might spot Reg and his two faithful dogs strolling along the sand.

AN AUSTRALIAN/BRITISH AND AMERICAN GLOSSARY

Australian/British	American
advert	ad (in a newspaper)
biscuits	cookies
bacon rasher	slice of bacon
boot	trunk
car park	parking lot
called	named
cottoned on	caught on
couldn't half	could really
chips/crisps	chips
dab hand at	good at
unit/flat	apartment
flog	sell
ogle/gawp	gape or gawk
graft	work
in Porter Street	*on* Porter Street
home straight	home stretch
jumped-up	stuck-up
undies/knickers	panties
lift	elevator
lodge	submit (e.g., forms)
lounge	living room
lurk	trick
overhead locker	overhead compartment
the penny's dropped	now I get it
pick up a pace	hurry, or pick up *the* pace

queue	line up
railway wagons	railway (or railroad) cars
rubbish bin	garbage bin
skint	broke
skylarking	joking around
smoko	cigarette/smoke break
solicitor	lawyer
splash out on	splurge
sporting	athletic
stuffed	messed up or injured
tail	trail or follow
toilets	restrooms
track pants	sweat pants
track top	track jacket
tucker/grub	food
twigged	suddenly realized
ute	pickup truck
wharfie	stevedore

ABOUT THE AUTHORS

A native of Adelaide, South Australia, **Julie McSorley** has worked as a freelance illustrator for various Fleet Street publications, studied at the University of London, and taught art in schools. She returned to Australia in the late 1980s and lectured on university art education programs. She has a PhD in educational art criticism. A children's book she illustrated for Angus & Robertson was short-listed in the book of the year awards by the Children's Book Council of Australia. She currently lives in Spain with her husband, John McSorley, and divides her time between writing and painting.

Marcus McSorley lives on the same street in London where his father built the infamous box in 1964. He studied acting at QUT University in Brisbane, Australia, and then returned to England with his partner, Lucia. Growing up, he was as comfortable visiting the theatre as he was playing rugby or cricket. As an actor he has built a diverse list of theatre, television, and film credits, and played opposite the Portuguese Golden Globe and MTV award winner Aurea in her music video *The Only Thing That I Wanted*. One of his abiding childhood memories is of badgering his dad to tell the "box story." Ironically, Marcus has maintained his interest in freight and now has a stake in an international shipping company.